The image of the First World War is one of stagnation and slaughter: of cratered trenches and of exhausted men charging hopelessly into the mechanical scythe of the machine guns. The Western Front has become the symbol of that static, wholesale warfare of attrition that reduced gentle farmland to deadly moonscape, where ten thousand lives might be spent to win a hundred yards of desolate mud. It is all too often forgotten that the Western Front was also the scene of the Allies' final victory—a victory won in open warfare against the Kaiser's army on the battlefield, and not, as often alleged, the work of traitors among the German people.

For the weary Allies—and especially for the British—1918 was a triumph of arms. Lloyd George, no friend either of Marshal Haig or of the Western Front in general, called the last hundred days of the war to end all wars "the greatest chapter in Britain's military history." And yet this period is almost forgotten, obscured by a dangerous myth of be-

(continued on back flap)

TO WIN A WAR

JOHN TERRAINE
TO WIN A WAR

1918, THE YEAR OF VICTORY

1981

DOUBLEDAY & COMPANY, INC., GARDEN CITY, NEW YORK

First published in Great Britain in 1978
by Sidgwick and Jackson Limited

Library of Congress Cataloging in Publication Data

Terraine, John.
  To win a war.

  Bibliography: p. 237
  Includes index.
  1. European War, 1914–18—Campaigns—France.
2. France—History—German occupation, 1914–18.
I. Title.
D544.T43   1981   940.4'35
ISBN: 0-385-15316-3
Library of Congress Catalog Card Number 79–7119

To those who won the forgotten victory
and for Cathy

ACKNOWLEDGEMENTS

The publishers wish to thank the following for permission to publish extracts from copyright material in their possession: Allen & Unwin Ltd. for *A Fatalist at War* by R. Binding (1929). Ernest Benn Ltd. for *Breaking the Hindenburg Line* by Major R. E. Priestley (1919) and *Foch: Le Vainqueur de la Guerre* by Raymond Recouly (1920). Cassell Ltd. for *Into Battle* by Sir John Glubb (1978 edition), *Out of My Life* by Field-Marshal Hindenburg (1920) and *The Last Four Months* by Sir Frederick Maurice (1919). Curtis Brown Ltd. for *Haig* by Duff Cooper (Faber, 1936). J. M. Dent & Sons for *Armistice 1918* by Brigadier C. N. Barclay (1968). Lord Esher for *The Journals and Letters of Reginald, Viscount Esher* (Nicholson & Watson, 1938). Eyre & Spottiswoode for *The Private Letters of Douglas Haig* edited by Robert Blake (1952), *The Aftermath* by Winston Churchill (1929) and *As From Kemmel Hill* by Arthur Behrend (1963). Elaine Greene Ltd. for *Dare Call it Treason* by Richard Watt (1964). Hamish Hamilton Ltd. for *The Course of German History* by A. J. P. Taylor (1945). The Hamlyn Group for *The Tank Corps* by C. & A. Williams-Ellis (1919), *The War Memoirs of David Lloyd-George* by David Lloyd-George (1936), *The World Crisis* by Winston Churchill and *Great Contemporaries* by Winston Churchill (1942 edition). Heinemann Ltd. for *The Memoirs of Raymond Poincaré* translated by Sir George Arthur (1929), and *Winston S. Churchill* by Martin Gilbert (1977). David Higham Associates Ltd. for *Mutiny 1917* by John Williams (Heinemann, 1962), *The Swordbearers* by Correlli Barnett (Eyre & Spottiswoode, 1963) and *The Conduct of War* by Maj.-Gen. J. F. C. Fuller (1961 edition). Hodder & Stoughton Ltd. for *My Experiences in the Great War* by John J. Pershing (1931). Hutchinson & Co. for *My War Memories* by General Ludendorff (1919) and *The Australian Victories in France in 1918* by Lt.-Gen. Sir John Monash (1936). Macmillan, London and Basingstoke, for *Brest-Litovsk: The*

Forgotten Peace by Sir John Wheeler-Bennett (1963), *The Anvil of War* by F. S. Oliver (1963) and *Hindenburg* by Sir John Wheeler-Bennett (1936). McCaw Stevenson & Orr Ltd. for *The History of the 36th (Ulster) Division* by Cyril Falls (1922). The Medici Press for *The Eighth Division at War 1914–18* by J. H. Boraston & E. O. Bax (1926) and *The War History of the First Battalion Queen's Westminster Rifles 1914–18* by Major J. Q. Henriques (1923). The Librairie Arthème Fayard for *Lettres de la Guerre* by General Mangin (1950). The Librairie Plon for *Au Service de la France* by Raymond Poincaré. Charles Scribner's Sons for *Fix Bayonets!* by John W. Thomasson Jnr. (1926). Secker & Warburg Ltd. for *The First World War* by Richard Thoumin (1963). *The Times* for various extracts reproduced from *The Times* of 1918. Anthony Sheil Associates Ltd. for *The Fifth Army* by General Sir Hubert Gough (Hodder & Stoughton, 1931), and *The Home Fronts* by John Williams (Constable & Co.). A. P. Watt Ltd. for *The Story of the Fourth Army* by Archibald Montgomery (Hodder & Stoughton, 1920) and *Field Marshal Sir Henry Wilson* by Maj.-Gen. Sir C. E. Callwell (Hodder & Stoughton, 1927) and Weidenfeld & Nicolson for *The Last of the Ebb* by Sidney Rogerson (1937).

CONTENTS

LIST OF PLATES

Brest-Litovsk, 3 March 1918 (Ullstein Bilderdienst)
Grand Hotel Britannique, Spa (Ullstein Bilderdienst)
Kaiser Wilhelm II with Hindenburg and Ludendorff (National Archives)
Prince Max of Baden (Ullstein Bilderdienst)
General Wilhelm Gröner (Ullstein Bilderdienst)
German infantry moving up for the March Offensive (Bildarchiv Preussischer Kulturbesitz)
French infantry arriving on the Somme, March 1918 (Roger Viollet)
British troops at the Battle of the Lys (Imperial War Museum)
German troops on the Chemin des Dames Ridge (Bildarchiv Preussischer Kulturbesitz)
M. Georges Clemenceau and Field-Marshal Sir Douglas Haig (Imperial War Museum)
Lloyd George (Imperial War Museum)
President Woodrow Wilson (Roger Viollet)
Marshal Foch with General Maxime Weygand (Roger Viollet)
General John J. Pershing and Lieutenant-General Sir Arthur Currie (Imperial War Museum)
American troops at St. Valery-sur-Somme (Imperial War Museum)
French tanks at the Second Battle of the Marne (Ullstein Bilderdienst)
General Charles Mangin (Roger Viollet)
American troops capturing Cantigny (Ullstein Bilderdienst)
French prisoners on the Aisne (U. S. War Dept., General Staff: Photo, Robert Hunt Library)
German prisoners taken in the Battle of Amiens (Imperial War Museum)
George V at Fourth Army Headquarters, Flixecourt (Imperial War Museum)

Patrols entering Cambrai, 9 October (Bildarchiv Preussischer Kultur-besitz)

Mark V tanks crossing the Hindenburg Line, 29 September (Imperial War Museum)

Horses pulling an 18-pounder across a dry canal (Imperial War Museum)

Sketch of Le Cateau, from *The Story of the Fourth Army*

French infantryman (Roger Viollet)

Dead German soldier with his caisson (Roger Viollet)

Revolution in Berlin, 9 November (Imperial War Museum)

British entering Lille (Imperial War Museum)

Canadians entering Mons (Imperial War Museum)

The Sambre-et-Oise Canal, from *The Story of the Fourth Army*

Lieutenant-General Sir Julian Byng (Imperial War Museum)

Major-General Sir Andrew Russell with staff officers (Imperial War Museum)

New Zealanders at kit inspection (Roger Viollet)

German prisoners in a clearing depot at Abbeville (Imperial War Museum)

Armistice group leaving the railway carriage at Compiègne (Popperfoto)

Interior of the Armistice railway carriage (Conway Picture Library)

Sir William Orpen's *Armistice Night: Amiens* from *An Onlooker in France, 1917–1919*

Picture research by Annie Horton

INTRODUCTION

The final campaign of 1918—the last victorious "Hundred Days"—is virtually an unknown story. The great catastrophes of the First World War have lingered in men's minds for six decades: the savage Battles of the Frontiers at the very opening, the slaughters of 1915, Verdun, the Somme, the worst parts (usually only the worst parts) of "Passchendaele," the great German attacks of 1918. Strangely, when the tide turned, the interest seemed to die away. Yet during these last months, starting on 18 July with the Second—the *unknown*—Battle of the Marne, and continuing through the Battle of Amiens, 8 August, Germany's "black day," and 29 September, the breaking of the Hindenburg Line, right to the very end, great feats of arms were performed and great victories won as deserving of commemoration as Austerlitz or Waterloo.

Why have they been so ignored? It is easy to see why the Germans should have preferred to draw a veil over this period, even if there had been no subsequent political reasons for doing so. For France the cost of this victory was so terrible that the flavour was marred—though the fact of it being won under a French generalissimo was a salve to pain and wounded pride. For complex causes, America also preferred to forget this time. In Britain there were several reasons, none of them very appealing.

Above all, there was the Prime Minister's dislike and contempt for the Commander-in-Chief. Field-Marshal Sir Douglas Haig and the British Expeditionary Force were the chief architects of Allied victory during the "Hundred Days." Prompted by his Cabinet colleagues (and Marshal Foch), Lloyd George at the time described their deeds as "the greatest chapter in our military history." Later, however, he made it his business to take away all credit from Haig, and in so doing robbed the Army of its just renown. In this he was fortified by his equal dislike of the theatre of war where the victory was won. Lloyd George hated the Western Front; that the war should be won there, largely by the man he so despised, made nonsense of his own cherished strategies and threw an unpleasant light on many of his policies. So he tried to pretend that it had not happened—and was supported in this by all those who, for reasons of their own, emotional or doctrinaire, saw the Western Front and its generals as villains of history. Such an attitude, of course, chimed well with postwar disenchantment and pacifism, while journalism is always happier with disaster.

So it came about that the greatest succession of victories in the British Army's whole history—victories won against the main body of the main enemy in a continental war, for the *only* time in British history—have been allowed to fade in forgetfulness and ignorance. This was not only dismal from the point of view of the men who suffered and died to win those victories, it was tragic for future history. By robbing Haig and his army of their laurels, the lessons they had so painfully learned were wasted, and this augured ill for the conduct of the next war.

It also made it more certain that there would be a next war. By November 1918 the German Army was at its last gasp, saved from immediate surrender in the field only by the Allies' logistical difficulties. Yet the ink was scarcely dry upon the armistice agreement than the legend began to circulate that the German Army had not really been beaten at all, that it had been "stabbed in the back" by communists and Jews at home. When the Nazis appeared on the scene they traded powerfully upon this legend. To allow British victories to be forgotten was to allow German defeat to be minimized—and to allow that was to ensure an attempt to reverse the "unfair" outcome. It was not enough for the Allies to occupy Cologne, Coblenz and Mainz; when the German Army returned to Berlin in 1918 it did so with oak-leaves on its helmets and under triumphal arches. This accolade should have been reserved for the Allies themselves, and indeed, so it was—but not until 1945.

Successive British governments bear a heavy load of responsibility for what followed the armistice. They gave their name to a peace dictated to a beaten enemy on the assumption of victory, but allowed the victory which was the sanction of that peace to be forgotten, and the sinews that should have upheld the victory to wither away. In short, by disparaging the soldiers' capacity to win a war, the politicians made certain that they would lose a peace.

This book will, I hope, do something to straighten the record of 1918, the year of victory, and give honour where it is due.

John Terraine

". . . the conclusion is inescapable that Germany and her allies were in fact defeated in the field. . . ."

Lloyd George: *War Memoirs*

TO WIN A WAR

I

"ONLY WAR. NOTHING BUT WAR!"

"No more pacifist campaigns, no treachery, no semi-treachery—only war. Nothing but war! . . . The country shall know that it is being defended." (Georges Clemenceau, 20 November 1917)

Another new year; it would be the fifth to bear the brand of war. Already, by 1 January 1918, some of the most important facts of the twentieth century were a matter of record. It was a fact that the Russian Empire was no more; Soviet Russia, the world's first communist state, was also a fact—not very robust or permanent-looking, but a fact. Not yet so apparent, but equally a fact, was the exhaustion by war of the great European powers which had, during the last four centuries, pushed their influence or their rule across the globe. Russia's fate was a portent for them all. And yet another fact was the advent of a new world power, the United States of America, wearing an unfamiliar warlike costume, taking up a rôle that was going to become familiar, whether Americans liked it or not.

This war was still a fresh thing in the American mind; it had not acquired (and never would, except at second hand) the staleness and shabbiness of its look in Europe. Although the United States had been a belligerent for eight months, few Americans had yet seen action, except as volunteers in foreign armies or air forces.[1] The contrast between America's minuscule loss in battle and her very substantial commercial gain did not escape notice on either side of the Atlantic. A fire-eating frame of mind in America fed on the impatience born of inactivity; it was incomprehensible and somehow shameful to the American public that it should take this lusty young democracy so long to show its strength. Americans inside and outside the armed forces were in a bellicose mood, fanned (as everywhere) by propaganda.[2] It was the more ironical, therefore, that the first major political gesture of

1918 should have been a statement about peace, and that it should
have come from the President of the United States.

This is not the place for a detailed consideration of the Fourteen
Points for Peace proclaimed to Congress by President Woodrow Wilson on 8 January.[3] Only three considerations need concern us now.
First, the principles invoked—open covenants of peace, freedom of
navigation upon the seas, removal of economic barriers, an "association
of nations," etc., etc.—reflect the idealism with which a democracy
seeks to clothe its actions when thrust into the distasteful condition of
war. Neither American democracy nor British democracy suffered the
inconvenience of invasion during the First World War. Neither, therefore, could find satisfaction in merely fighting *against* a state of affairs;
they had to fight *for* something, and President Wilson's appeal seemed,
in broad terms, to supply what they needed. His reference to an "association of nations" nicely echoed that of the British Prime Minister,
Mr. Lloyd George, addressing a Trade Union Conference only three
days earlier, when he spoke of establishing "by some international organisation an alternative to war as a means of settling international dis-
putes." America and Britain seemed to stand close together on this
issue.

In other respects—and this is our second consideration—they were
less close. The unfortunate truth was that President Wilson had omit-
ted to consult his allies in the matter of war aims, just as he later omit-
ted to consult Congress in the matter of peace-making. What made this
omission the more curious, however, was that an organ of inter-Allied
consultation—the Supreme War Council—had only recently[4] been set
up; when at last the Fourteen Points came under the scrutiny of this
body their attractiveness quickly began to fade. This confusion about
making peace reflected the Allied method of making war.

The third consideration follows with heavy-footed certainty: the
Germans, who were not in the least attracted by the Fourteen Points in
January 1918, having their own very different ideas about peace,
could well, if they happened to change their minds, profit by this
confusion among the Allies. And this, indeed, they tried to do—but
with no profit (as it turned out) either to themselves, or to anyone else
at the time, or to future generations. That was the price of confusion.

The President's peace initiative failed, so after all it was America's
war potential that was going to matter. And America's war potential in
January 1918, to those who knew, looked very disappointing, a situation full of contradictions. America's entry into the war the previous
April had produced understandable euphoria among her allies, match-
ing her own enthusiasm. Already she was an important source of munitions, both for France and Britain, and her productive capacity seemed
to be as limitless as her manpower. It did not take long for the slogan

"Wait for America" to be coined, and to work its magic among the growing number of Europeans who observed with horror the decimation of their own manhood in the great battles of the Western Front. There was a disagreeable shock in store for them.

France and Britain had lost no time in sending missions to America to discuss the innumerable matters arising out of America's entry, and on 14 June the military representative in the British mission, Major-General Tom Bridges, gave the War Cabinet his official "Forecast of the Arrival of American Land Forces in France," based on discussions with the American Government and with General John Joseph Pershing, Commander-in-Chief-designate of the Expeditionary Force:

> . . .
> 4. *Time*. The first division—20–25,000 men—should be in France by end July (America says end June[5]). The second by end of August, and after this a division per month may be calculated upon, making six divisions, or 120–150,000 men, by the end of 1917.
>   During next year favourable circumstances may allow of further speeding up, but it is safer to calculate on the same rate of progress, and to count on twelve divisions coming over in 1918.
> 5. *Totals*. The above will bring the total up to 500,000 men—i.e. 18 divisions, 360,000 men; services, 140,000 men.
> 6. *Reinforcements*. There will be no lack of reinforcements by the end of this year, as 980,000 men will then be available, of whom none have less than four months' service.
>   . . .
> 12. *Conclusions*. To sum up, leaving all matters of sea-transport out of the question, it seems probable that America can have an army of 120–150,000 men in France by 1st January 1918, and 500,000 men by the end of 1918. That these figures for 1918 may, under favourable circumstances, be improved upon.[6]

It was scarcely to be wondered at that one Cabinet minister "described it as the most depressing statement that the Cabinet had received for a long time. . . . The Cabinet were expecting a million, and were proportionately depressed."[7]

It seemed so extraordinary. America, after all, had not exactly been dormant until April 1917. A vigorous campaign for national "preparedness" had been waged since October 1914; Allied orders had expanded the American munitions industry and given it experience; an attempt had been made both to rationalize the military system and to build up the Navy in 1916; above all, war with Mexico in that year had resulted in there being some 200,000 men under arms in the United States when war with Germany followed. To cap everything, thanks to the Mexican preliminary, an Army Bill bringing in immediate conscription had been passed without difficulty only three weeks after America's entry into the war (in Britain this took nearly two years).

There seemed to be no reason, then, to doubt that American intervention would become very effective very soon. Not knowing what the War Cabinet had been told (and no doubt the French Government was similarly informed), both Europeans and Americans became more and more puzzled as the months of 1917 ticked by—months of heavy fighting in Champagne, at Verdun, at Ypres and at Cambrai—with the American Army always a conspicuous absentee from the battlefield. The Germans, on the other hand, became over-complacent and unwisely disdainful of America; the *Frankfurter Zeitung,* for example, surveying the new year's prospects, spoke of the next six months as "the eminently important period during which the hopes which the Western Powers set upon America's masses cannot in any circumstances be fulfilled." Colonel Repington, *The Times* military correspondent, dined at Claridge's on 4 January with "a well-known man" who told him many things. They discussed manpower, the failings of the War Cabinet, and of the newly created Supreme War Council at Versailles, and the need for an Allied general reserve. The "well-known man" said: "America was coming on very slowly. The 4th Division was only now arriving in France, where the numbers were not over 140,000. Most Americans believed that they had over half a million men in France, and would be very disgusted when they learnt the truth. The U. S. Parliamentary Committees [*sic*] were beginning to examine things, and all the faults would come out."

And so it was; bit by bit the true state of America was revealed. "Preparedness" was seen to be partly a sham: "Preparedness laid the whole groundwork of ideas and conditioned the attitudes which were to make possible the American intervention. . . . Only one thing it did not do. It did not prepare the nation or its military structure for that intervention—which was so soon to come."[8] "Preparedness," in other words, was an abstraction, unrelated to the true nature of the war intended. In 1916 it was planned to increase the U. S. Navy by sixteen battleships and battle-cruisers—in the event *none* was built, but instead about 300 destroyers to fight the U-boat war; the Army, for all its 200,000 men, did not have one formed division. Nor was there any organizational framework (such as existed in Britain in 1914) on which an army—as opposed to a mass of armed men—could be quickly built; for brigades, divisions and army corps there was an almost total lack of commanders and staff officers which was to dog the American effort from beginning to end.

There were equally serious deficiences in other respects. The "well-known man" continued to Repington:

> The Americans were not using their merchant ships sufficiently, and were leaving too many at their normal commercial work. Also, the American decision not to use our plant in America for turning out our rifles, 8-inch and 9.2-inch guns, etc., had proved disastrous, and America had not yet turned out a single heavy gun as she had neither the tools nor the workmen. She had been bluffed by M. Thomas into accepting French guns and so had not accepted our field guns and had also chosen the French calibre of 9.5-inch instead of our 9.2-inch, and so all new plant for it had to be made in America and was not yet ready.[9]

Lloyd George suggests another reason for the slowness of American production:

> "Europe" and "effete" were inseparable words in all popular American rhetoric at that date. . . . So when we thought America might like to profit by the lessons we had learned in the trials of actual warfare, the American industrialists were inclined to regard our lectures as an invitation to them, who were masters of all the manufacturing arts, to take a post-graduate course at a dame's school. Hence they would have none of our aeroplanes nor of our cannon. They assumed on traditional principles the inferiority of these and they decided to have patterns of their own, which would demonstrate to antiquated European craftsmen what could be done by a nation which had demonstrated its supremacy in machinery.

The result, unthinkable in April 1917, and still unforeseeable in its dismal totality in January 1918, was that:

> When the Armistice was signed on November 11th, half the aeroplanes used by the American Army were of French and British make. . . . The light and medium artillery used up to the end of the War by the American Army was supplied by the French. The heaviest artillery was furnished by the British. No field guns of American pattern or manufacture fired a shot in the War. The same applies to tanks. Here one would have thought that the nation who were the greatest manufacturers of automobiles in the world could have turned out tanks with the greatest facility and in the largest numbers, but not a single tank of American manufacture ever rolled into action in the War.[10]

It was fortunate that all this was hidden in the future; there was enough to depress the leaders of the Entente at the beginning of 1918

without prophecies of this sort. They had come through a bad year—
indeed, a turning point of the century and of world history—with all
the unpleasantness that so often accompanies decisive occasions.
France, in particular, was in a delicate condition which more bad news
might have made fatal. In 1917 both the Army and the nation had
passed through a crisis of morale foreshadowing the collapse which
came twenty-three years later. The failure of General Nivelle's vaunted
offensive in April, which was supposed to end the war in forty-eight
hours, lay at the root of the trouble. In fact, the French Army
achieved much in this offensive, but the non-fulfilment of Nivelle's
promise, turning it into yet one more battle of attrition, so dejected the
Army that no less than 110 units, belonging to fifty-four divisions on
the Western Front, were affected in some degree or other (sometimes
very seriously) by mutiny.

From his somewhat mysterious semi-official vantage-point in Paris,
Lord Esher, long before the grim truths from the front had filtered
through, warned the Secretary of State for War, Lord Derby, of "the
growing reluctance of the French soldier to go over the parapet. . . .
we have arrived," he said, "at a psychological moment when discour-
agement may lead to any sort of acquiescence in any sort of peace
rather than continue the war. . . . France is very, very tired."[11] The
full truth of Nivelle's fiasco came slowly but the sense of things not
being well was soon conveyed. The French, naturally, looked to their
new ally for encouragement: "The French are suffering from the
American miasma. They see visions of myriads of men, stacks of
money, and supplies abundant."[12] But there was no disguising the
harshness of the immediate truth, when it appeared in the form of tens
of thousands of embittered, wounded and demoralized leave-men, revolutionary scenes behind the front, disaffected soldiers marching on
Paris. No distant prospects of help from America could mitigate present portents such as these. On 24 May Lord Esher wrote to the Chief
of Imperial General Staff, Sir William Robertson:

> In every quarter, in town and country, you find symptoms of fatigue, of
> war-weariness, of discontent. The bright animation with which the peo-
> ple looked forward to the "great offensive" of 1917 has died out of their
> faces, and those who have large knowledge and insight into the secret
> heart of France tell you that the unconscious purpose of the nation is
> moving away from absolute to qualified victory. It is just as well to en-
> visage the truth, if truth it be.[13]

Just over a month later Esher warned Derby: "Revolution is never very
deep under the surface in France. The crust is very thin just now."[14]

There were moments in 1917 when a new French revolution did, indeed, seem imminent. The *"union sacrée"* of 1914 seemed to be in shreds, with Socialist deputies like Pierre Laval demanding French participation in the international Socialist Conference in Stockholm as the only road to peace. More significant than Laval was Joseph Caillaux, the most important figure in the important Radical-Socialist Party, prewar apostle of Franco-German détente, now standing in the wings awaiting a call to head a government of peace by negotiation—or, as his enemies would have said, peace at any price. Caillaux's career had been in a state of suspension ever since that day in March 1914 when his wife had pulled a pistol from her handbag and shot the editor of *Le Figaro* six times at point-blank range.[15] This hasty deed cost her husband his post (Finance Minister), but because of his great influence in the Radical-Socialist Party he was still allowed to nominate its representative in the government; his nominee for the post of Minister of the Interior was Louis Malvy. Even in peacetime, because of his power to appoint the prefects of departments, the Minister of the Interior enjoyed great authority in the Third Republic. In wartime, with the increased importance of internal security, the post held still more weight; governments might come and go, but Louis Malvy would remain at the Ministry of the Interior until 31 August 1917.[16] All that time he continued to be the devoted friend and protector of Caillaux, whose position was becoming more and more clearly identified with pacifism and downright defeatism.

Such attitudes brought in their train some strange associates for a Minister of the Interior. There was, for example, Miguel Almereyda (an assumed name, the second part of which is an anagram for "'y a la merde"—"it's all shit"), founder and editor of a militant left-wing weekly, *Le Bonnet Rouge*. Almereyda was a supporter of Caillaux, who rewarded him so handsomely with subsidies that his weekly became a daily; he was also one of the 2,501 names in the secret list (Carnet B) of those whom the *Sûreté Générale* considered socially dangerous (Laval was another). Some of these people, of course, were spies; the overwhelming majority, however, were socialists, anarchists and syndicalists, representatives of the extreme and often violent fringe of the French Left which had been responsible for numerous bomb outrages in the 1890s[17] and for the venomous quality of some industrial agitation in the years just before the war. When war came, many expected all the people named in Carnet B to be rounded up—but Malvy was a Radical-Socialist, the party whose motto was "no enemies on the Left." He ordered that only the spies should be arrested; all the rest were allowed to go their ways, including Almereyda.

By 1917 Almereyda had reached a position of great influence in the pacifist-defeatist areas of the Left. He had an entrée to the Ministry of the Interior which enabled him to cover and protect all manner of shady persons on the borders of actual espionage; until March he continued to enjoy secret subsidies from the Ministry to *Le Bonnet Rouge;* and when Malvy's subsidy was cut off (because of Almereyda's too blatantly anti-war propaganda) he found funds from another source ample enough to support both the newspaper and his own recently acquired addiction to heroin. This source was Germany. Through his business manager, Emile Duval, Almereyda received large sums from a former banker named Marx, stationed in Switzerland, who became the paymaster of Germany's subversive agents in France. Already another French newspaper, *Le Journal* (the third largest, with a circulation of 1,100,000), had fallen into German ownership through the machinations of an adventurer going under the title of Bolo Pasha. Not only the Ministry of the Interior but also the Senate and the Chamber of Deputies were compromised by these nefarious activities, and the threads of friendship or political association linked almost everyone concerned to Joseph Caillaux.

It was against this background of corruption in high places that the news of Nivelle's failure was presented to the French people. The pacifist agitation redoubled. One of the most urgent (and reasonable) demands of the army mutineers was for leave, too long withheld, and this was lavishly granted by Nivelle's successor,[18] General Pétain. The anti-war elements seized their chance:

Daily the packed leave-trains were rolling into Paris. . . . Along the platforms of the Gare de l'Est and Gare du Nord swarmed the crowds of tired, pack-burdened *poilus* from the front and men about to entrain on their way back. In the seething mass of uniform the few Military Police dotted about did not notice the unobtrusive drab-suited civilians pushing leaflets into the hands of passing soldiers. "Comrades!" these said, "yours is the strength. Do not forget it!" Or: "Down with the war! Death to those responsible! Comrades, it is time to act. Let it be seen that you are men, not beasts!" . . .

And while the stealthy men with the leaflets were busy on the concourses and platforms, at the barriers painted harpies were waiting to lure woman-starved *poilus*—many of them strangers to Paris—to rooms near by, where they thrust more tracts on them and used their wiles on them to desert. Close at hand, illicit clothing agencies were rigging out the deserters with "civvies." And in their reach-me-down mufti, soldiers were slinking out onto the Paris streets to swell the army of deserters that before the year was out was to reach the record total of 27,000.[19]

On 5 June Lord Esher, with his habitual penetration, wrote to Lloyd George of "the longing for peace that comes like some mephitic perfume from Russia. It is affecting the nerves of soldiers and civilians. France is feeling overburdened just now by the weight of war. . . ." "Overburdened" was about it: there was a continuing coal shortage (a severe affliction during the hard winter of 1916–17) affecting industry; there was a manpower shortage, also affecting industry but above all agriculture;[20] the cost of living was about 80 per cent higher than before the war; soon there would be bread rationing. The sight of profiteers doing themselves well inflamed the unfortunate in and out of uniform. By the end of June there were 170 strikes or stoppages in war factories, a figure which rose to 689, involving 293,000 workers, by the end of the year.[21] What particularly worried officials and army officers observing the various demonstrations in the streets was the increasing tendency of soldiers to join the demonstrators, and, under the tender ministration of Malvy and his Director of the Sûreté, Leymarie, the reluctance of the police to do anything about it. Soldiers—and women; careful observers noted that it was on these two sections of French society that the burden lay heaviest. An informed British officer, travelling behind the front, reported to Sir William Robertson: "The countrywomen of France—the real mainstay of the country—are tired. They dread more heavy losses, they are frightened of greater taxation, they can no longer work their little farms and their little businesses. . . . In short, France is beginning to die away."[22]

In fact, however, though things were bad, they were not that bad; well concealed by a dark cloud of scandal and sensation, a silver lining was at hand. On 5 July Duval of Le Bonnet Rouge was arrested, having been caught returning from Switzerland with a cheque for 150,000 francs signed by Herr Marx. Leymarie had let him go, had even returned the cheque to him, but Duval was denounced in a secret session of the Chamber, the whole story came out, and with his arrest began a process, painful but beneficial, which can only be likened to the lancing of a boil. A week after Duval's arrest Le Bonnet Rouge was suppressed. On 6 August Almereyda was arrested, and in less than a fortnight there was a new sensation when he was found strangled in his cell by a bootlace—suicide through drug deprivation? suicide through fear? murder, because he knew too much? No one knows; but by virtue of these very speculations his death was another unsteadying factor for French opinion.

The lancing continued, nevertheless: on 24 August Leymarie was relieved of his duties; on the 31st Malvy, destroyed by a Ciceronian denunciation in the Senate on 22 July delivered by Georges Clemenceau,[23] at last resigned. Bolo Pasha was arrested on 28 September, Leymarie on 9 November, and on 22 November a committee of the Chamber of Deputies was formed to investigate "crimes committed by M. Malvy in the exercise of his functions." After only six days' consideration (on 28 November) the committee recommended that Malvy be brought to trial before the Senate, sitting as a High Court. The "crimes" in question were, of course, treason.

Outwardly, all this seemed like a series of hammer-blows upon the weakened morale of France; in fact, however, the worst was over, and the benefits were now beginning to flow. The short-lived government of Paul Painlevé,[24] racked by unedifying accusations and counter-accusations, seemingly surrounded by a horde of spies[25] and traitors, collapsed on 13 November. The next day President Poincaré sent for Clemenceau; it cannot have been an easy thing to do. Not only was there a personal enmity between them—and Clemenceau's idea of enmity was liable to be emphasized by sword or pistol on a duelling ground; there was also the grave doubt felt by one strong character who recognizes the authoritarian tendencies of another. "The more I think of the matter," Poincaré had once confessed, "the more I say to myself: 'So long as victory is possible, he is capable of upsetting everything!' A day will perhaps come when I shall add: 'Now that everything seems to be lost, he alone is capable of saving everything.' "[26] The day had come; on 16 November Clemenceau formed his ministry.

He was seventy-six years old, and he was called "The Tiger." He was unquestionably the most formidable man in France. Indeed, he was more; according to Winston Churchill, "As much as any single human being, miraculously magnified, can ever be a nation, he was France."[27] He was called a Radical Republican, and in the early stages of his career the radicalism was obvious enough; his political lineage seemed to trace back convincingly to the Jacobins. But as the years passed he found the new-style, twentieth-century Jacobins, the socialists, anarchists and communists and their assorted running mates, less and less to his liking. A confirmed destructor of governments and reputations (hence his nickname) he had steadily refused to head a government himself; but when at last he did so, in 1906, although depending on left-wing support, he suppressed strikes and industrial agitation with notable savagery. Yet he remained a Republican, passionate and undiminished, through all crises and all scandals; as Churchill said: "The existence of the Republic hung for years by a thread. In Clemenceau, at least, the thread had one unsleeping guardian."[28]

It was as more than the guardian, it was as champion of the Republic, that Clemenceau returned to power in November 1917. He lost no time in nailing his colours to the mast; on 20 November he went to the Chamber of Deputies to ask for their confidence, and he said:

> We have accepted the government in order to conduct the war with redoubled energy. . . . We shall carry out this programme. . . . There will be no consideration of persons or partisan passions—No more pacifist campaigns, no treachery, no semi-treachery—only war. Nothing but war! Our armies are not going to be caught between two fires. Justice shall be established. The country shall know that it is being defended![29]

As he barked out these staccato phrases, says Churchill, who was watching,

> He looked like a wild animal pacing to and fro behind bars, growling and glaring; and all around him was an assembly which would have done anything to avoid having him there, but, having put him there, felt they must obey. . . . France had resolved to unbar the cage and let her tiger loose upon all foes, beyond the trenches or in her midst. Language, eloquence, arguments were not needed to express the situation. With snarls and growls, the ferocious, aged, dauntless beast of prey went into action.[30]

And to some effect. Clemenceau's rule was as close to personal dictatorship as a democracy can get without losing its nature, but at the root of his power lay one vital consideration: he was there by consent, and when he lost this consent he would go. Meanwhile, "the moment the Tiger went into action, democracy temporarily died in France. And died unmourned."[31] By the end of the year no less than 1,700 people, suspected of anti-war activities, had been arrested; in January 1918 the list was extended to include the arch-defeatist of them all, Joseph Caillaux. So whatever the new year might bring, whatever shocks the enemy might produce in the field, there would be no enemy within the gates to help him with demoralizing words and deeds. The Tiger would see to that.

This revitalization of the French home front was virtually the only encouraging omen for the Allies as the year opened. The French Army, admittedly, had come through its worst period (May and June were the peak months of mutinous activity, though isolated incidents continued into September) and was still in the field, an impressive-looking force of 100 divisions. It had fought much harder in 1917 than British historians generally recognize: in May, reacting to Nivelle's advance,[32] the Germans made not less than thirty-nine counter-at-

tacks (probably many more) on the French along the Aisne, in June
not less than twenty-three and in July not less than thirty-six, including
a major effort on a front of ten miles along the Chemin des Dames. All
this (and vigorous French responses) coincided with the worst of the
mutiny. Even after the British had launched their Flanders offensive
(31 July) the month of August saw not less than thirty-one German
attacks or counter-attacks on the French—though as the British offensive reached its climax in September and October these tailed away to
thirteen and fourteen respectively.

All this throws important light on the nature of the French mutinies: evidently, against the German enemy, the French Army remained steadfast. The mutinies were not against the war; they were not
a rejection of the necessity of fighting Germany. They were a passionate protest against stupidity, incompetence and indifference, against
bad food, sour wine, miserable pay, inadequate leave, dreadful discom-
fort, shirkers and profiteers, against fire-eating generals who threw
away lives in futile "stunts" for the sake of *"la gloire."* There was
plenty to protest about. But under the careful "nursing" of the new
Commander-in-Chief, General Pétain, the soldiers agreed to give up
mutiny and instead resume their ancient privilege of everlasting grum-
bling—were not Napoleon's Old Guard veterans known as *"les gro-
gnards?"* They did more. Pétain knew his men, and they knew him.
They knew that he was a meticulous practitioner of the art of battle;
they knew that he was no dedicated apostle of the offensive; they knew
he would always be careful of their lives. So when he asked them to
carry out an attack at Verdun on 20 August they knew that this would
not be a folly; they observed the massive artillery support that the infantry would enjoy, the tanks, the industrious preparation of every detail of the operation. And they responded: they took and held all their
objectives and 10,000 prisoners besides. In October they repeated the
treatment at Malmaison on the Chemin des Dames: an advance of
three and a half miles, 11,157 prisoners, 180 guns.

All seemed to be well. The French Army, noted General Ludendorff,
the German First Quartermaster-General, "had quickly overcome its
depression." But had it? Pétain himself was by no means certain; caution had always been his watchword, and would remain so. Other close
observers at the beginning of 1918 also had their doubts. Captain Cyril
Falls, who was serving as a liaison officer with the French, posing the
question: "was the French Army's recovery complete?", says, "I
should answer that in the best formations and units it was, but on the
whole not."[33] He found it significant that in early 1918 staff officers
had still not resumed wearing their distinctive brassards, discarded

during the mutinies, when these made their wearers targets of abuse and assault. So the French Army was still, after all, an unknown quantity.

With other allies there was less uncertainty—and far less encouragement. The memory of the Caporetto disaster was all too fresh in Italy; if General Pétain's army was convalescent, General Armando Diaz, Italy's new Commander-in-Chief, looked upon his as requiring intensive care. Italian casualties in 1917 cannot be stated with precision, but must have been between 600,000 and 700,000—probably nearer the latter. The Eleventh Battle of the Isonzo, with its estimated loss of 165,000 men in twenty-six days (18 August–12 September), stands out as perhaps the most dreadful example of blind attrition in a war which has been blamed, sometimes unjustly, for that unlovely practice. When the Austrian-German blow (in which the future Field-Marshal Rommel greatly distinguished himself) fell at Caporetto on 24 October it found the Italian Army already tired and dejected. In a very short time its casualties amounted to well over 300,000—and more than 250,000 were prisoners. By mid-November the impetus of the attack had petered out, and the Italians were able to rally on the Piave with the help and moral support of eleven French and British divisions. But as far as 1918 was concerned, all their allies could realistically hope for was that they would not give way again—no repetition of Caporetto.

In Russia, of course, the situation was even worse. "The whole of Russia," pronounced General Max Hoffmann, the German Chief of Staff in the East, "is no more than a vast heap of maggots." That was early in the new year, by which time Russia's position was abject indeed. Faithful to its promises, the new Bolshevik Government[34] lost no time in suing for an armistice: firing ceased on the Eastern Front on 28 November, and by mid-December terms were agreed with the Germans and Austrians. Full-scale peace negotiations began at the German headquarters at Brest-Litovsk on 20 December, a scene loaded with ironies: "The whim of history willed that representatives of the most revolutionary régime ever known should sit at the same diplomatic table with the representatives of the most reactionary military caste among all ruling classes."[35] The negotiations would last ten weeks—ten weeks during which Leftist illusion after illusion was swept away, and the ancient truth grimly reasserted, that Might is Right. The Eastern Front had long been Germany's nightmare; its liquidation was her opportunity—her last opportunity—of seizing victory. For the Allies this was the culminating misfortune of a dreadful year, a frightening omen for the one to come.

There remained Britain: Germany's opportunity spelt for Britain a special peril. To appreciate this, it is necessary first to examine the German situation, which provides the true setting for the paradoxes and perplexities which surrounded British policy as 1918 came in.

Chapter I: Notes

1. (p. 1) It was reported in *The Times* as early as 29 August 1914 that no less than 60,000 Americans had crossed the frontier to volunteer in the Canadian Army. The Lafayette Escadrille, serving in the French Air Force, not only secured its own fame, but made an important contribution to the build-up of the U.S. Air Force in 1917.
2. (p. 1) Major-Gen. J. F. C. Fuller (*The Conduct of War, 1789–1961,* Eyre and Spottiswoode, 1961, p. 180) quotes an American source: "We hated with a common hate that was exhilarating. The writer of this review remembers attending a great meeting in New England, held under the auspices of a Christian Church—God save the mark! A speaker demanded that the Kaiser, when captured, be boiled in oil, and the entire audience stood on chairs to scream its hysterical approval. That was the kind of madness that had seized us."
3. (p. 2) See Appendix A.
4. (p. 2) The Supreme War Council, consisting of representatives of the governments of France, Britain and Italy, supported by "Permanent Military Representatives" and a secretariat, came into existence at Rapallo on 7 November 1917. United States participation in its proceedings began with its second session, at Versailles, on 1 December.
5. (p. 3) In fact the 1st Division (a somewhat "scratch" formation) began to disembark at Brest on 25 June.
6. (p. 3) Cabinet Papers: Appendix to War Cabinet 164, 15 June 1917 (CAB 23/3).
7. (p. 3) Col. Repington: *The First World War,* Constable, 1920, vol. i, pp. 581–82.
8. (p. 4) Walter Millis: *Arms and Men: A Study of American Military History,* Mentor Books, 1958, p. 198.
9. (p. 5) Repington, op. cit., vol. ii, p. 169. Albert Thomas was the French Minister of Munitions.
10. (p. 5) Lloyd George: *War Memoirs,* Odhams, 1936, ii, pp. 1830–33. The contrast between 1917–18 and 1941–42 is striking; it shows how much America, like other countries, learned from the mistakes made, understandably enough, the first time the conditions of twentieth-century war were encountered. It is sad, however, that so little was learned from the earlier misfortunes of the French and British.
11. (p. 6) Lord Esher: *Journals and Letters of Reginald Viscount Esher,* Nicholson and Watson, 1938, vol. iv, pp. 103–4; 17 April.
12. (p. 6) Ibid., p. 108; 23 April.
13. (p. 6) Ibid., pp. 117–18.
14. (p. 6) Ibid., p. 127, 26 June.
15. (p. 7) The unfortunate man, Gaston Calmette, later died, but a French jury acquitted Mme. Caillaux on 28 July after a sensational trial which diverted much French attention from the international crisis.
16. (p. 7) Such was the power of the Radical Socialists that when Alexandre Ribot tried to form a government without them on 9 June 1914 it lasted precisely three days.

17. (p. 7) Culminating in the assasination of the President of the Republic, Sadi Carnot, in June 1894.
18. (p. 8) General Henri Philippe Pétain succeeded Nivelle as Commander-in-Chief on 15 May.
19. (p. 8) John Williams: *Mutiny 1917*, Heinemann, 1962, pp. 97–98.
20. (p. 9) Between April 1917 and January 1918, 300,000 agricultural workers were withdrawn from the Army.
21. (p. 9) This figure has to be compared with none in 1914, ninety-eight in 1915 and 314 in 1916; on the other hand it should be noted that 688 strikes in Britain involved 860,000 workers—an indication of the different degrees of industrialization in the two countries.
22. (p. 9) Lieut.-Gen. Sir Henry Wilson to Robertson, quoted by Lloyd George, op. cit., ii, p. 1268.
23. (p. 10) Like Cicero's orations, this one had a name: "L'Antipatriotisme."
24. (p. 10) 12 September–13 November.
25. (p. 10) The famous woman spy, Mata Hari, was executed in the moat of Vincennes on 15 October.
26. (p. 10) Raymond Poincaré: *Au Service de la France;* Paris, Plon; vol. v., pp. 188–91.
27. (p. 10) Winston Churchill: *Great Contemporaries,* Macmillan, 1942 edition, p. 230.
28. (p. 10) Ibid., p. 232.
29. (p. 11) Richard Thoumin: *The First World War,* Secker and Warburg, 1963, p. 425, fn.
30. (p. 11) Churchill, op. cit., p. 239.
31. (p. 11) Richard M. Watt: *Dare Call it Treason,* Chatto and Windus, 1964, p. 237.
32. (p. 11) Nivelle attacked on a front of thirty-five miles; in some places he was completely unsuccessful, but on a base of sixteen miles his armies captured a salient four miles deep—some seventy square miles of ground. In the first ten days (16–25 April) they took 28,815 prisoners and 183 guns. Their losses were high—probably about 187,000—but in other circumstances such results would have been considered good. What did the damage was Nivelle's promise of a decisive breakthrough; the mutinies were the fruit of the hope which, too much deferred, maketh the heart sick.
33. (p. 12) Watt, op. cit., p. 10; Introduction by Captain Cyril Falls.
34. (p. 13) The Bolsheviks seized power on 7 November, by the Western calendar, 26 October according to the old Russian calendar.
35. (p. 13) Sir John Wheeler-Bennett: *Brest Litovsk: The Forgotten Peace, March 1918,* Macmillan, 1963, pp. 114–15.

"NEW YEAR'S WISHES!
NEW YEAR'S HOPES!"

". . . people talk now of Calais, Amiens, and Paris as they did in
the first months of the War, and at the same time they speak of
peace as a fact which will happen as surely as the beginning of
spring or the solstice. New Year's wishes! New Year's hopes! They
have an almost friendly appearance. But I don't believe any of it. We
shall never have peace with England and America so long as they do
not need to make it, and they do not need to yet." (Captain Rudolf
Binding: Diary, New Year's Eve 1917)

In a total war—the style of war of great industrial states committing
all their resources, material and human—if military operations reach
an equilibrium the hardest thing is to see "over the hill." In 1915,
1916 and 1917 a freak balance of technological power had been
struck; the populations of France, Italy, Russia and Britain were
cheated of decisive military successes in the field, but were sharply
aware of their own mounting misfortunes—cold hearths, bare larders,
fear and sorrow. They did not know that Germany's condition was in
many respects as bad, and in some respects worse.

The people of Germany emerged from the notorious "turnip winter"
of 1916–17[1] with a desperately lean and hungry look. "The rounded
contours of the German nation have become a legend of the past. We
are all gaunt and bony now," wrote Princess Blücher.[2] Here, certainly,
Germany was worse off than France; food was the obsessive topic, the
national preoccupation. Food shortages were the pretext for strikes
which, as the year went by, became more and more political in content. They began in the Ruhr, a straight demand for more food leading
to disturbances so serious that troops had to be called in; in April the
reduction of the (adulterated) bread ration brought 220,000 workers

out in Berlin, shortly followed by more in Leipzig. In June the Ruhr was out again, in July there were strikes in Düsseldorf and in Upper Silesia, the latter costing half a million tons of badly needed coal. In January 1918 food was again high on the agenda of strikers in key munitions factories in Berlin, Hamburg, Essen and Leipzig. Beginning in some cases with acts of sabotage, leading later to riot, these strikes soon affected 250,000 workers in Berlin alone and finally a total of over half a million. Strike meetings were broken up by the police, Berlin was declared to be in a state of siege, leaders were arrested, seven large concerns were placed under military control, and the High Command was forced to leave troops at home in Germany to preserve order.

The coal shortage, serious enough in France, was calamitous in Germany: non-essential industries suspended overtime and nightwork; shops, cafés, hotels and restaurants had to reduce fuel consumption to one-third; lights went out in Berlin apartment blocks at 9 P.M.; in Munich all public buildings, theatres and cinemas were closed. As the last winter of the war descended, wrote one German, "One of the most terrible of our many sufferings was having to sit in the dark. It became dark at four. . . . It was not light until eight o'clock. Even the children could not sleep all that time. . . . And when they had gone to bed we were left shivering with the chill which comes from semi-starvation and which no additional clothing seems to alleviate."[3]

Partly responsible for the coal shortage, and partly deriving from it, was the breakdown of the German railways in 1917. The German rail network was the largest in Europe; the continent's biggest railway station was Leipzig—opened in 1915. Planned strategically, the German railways were the foundation of the Schlieffen Plan in 1914; since then they had been the vital element in the conduct of Germany's war on two fronts and her repeated rescue operations in aid of her Austrian and Turkish allies. By 1917 the strain on this admirable system had become too great: track-servicing had gravely deteriorated (through moblization of regular workers), causing a severe restriction of speed and lower carrying capacity; rolling stock had also deteriorated through lack of maintenance, and for the same reason engines had lost efficiency—in some cases by as much as 40 per cent. Accidents increased; freight movement during the winter of 1916–17 fell to 25 per cent of normal. And this decline in a sector which had been the pride of the German economy continued through the year—a grim omen for 1918.

In truth, however, this decline, like the coal crisis, was only a symptom of a more profound sickness. As John Williams says: "After some thirty months of total war, the mighty German machine was beginning slowly but surely to run down. Such was the pressure on the nation's manpower and material resources that its highly complex life could no longer be maintained at an effective level."[4] That is the measure of the difference between Germany's position and that of her Western enemies, and at the core of it lay the Allied blockade, chiefly carried out by the Royal Navy, thus winning "a great maritime victory in the war."[5] The effect of the blockade was to force Germany "into an ever more rigid self-sufficiency, without hope of renewal of supplies from outside."[6] And the effect of that was "a great European nation living as a starving pauper, with all the moral hopelessness and collapse of will that goes with pauperism."[7]

As may be supposed, the social and political results of this economic collapse were most serious. We have already seen the industrial unrest that was produced, but the depression ran right through the nation. By the beginning of 1918 adult civilians were existing on 1,000 calories a day—less than half what is required for a healthy diet; even army rations had been reduced, though naturally not so much. When the great influenza pandemic arrived, however, it found German civilians and soldiers alike much weakened in their resistance. Meanwhile, in 1917, further signs of ills to come were the mutiny of part of the fleet at Wilhelmshaven[8] and the peace agitation which came to a crescendo in the Reichstag at the same time. The passing of the famous "Peace Resolution" by the majority parties (Centre, Progressives and Socialists) on 19 July was accompanied by the resignation of Chancellor von Bethmann-Hollweg and his replacement by a nonentity who was merely the mouthpiece of the High Command, consisting of Field-Marshal von Hindenburg, and his First Quartermaster-General, Ludendorff. Effectively, the High Command now ruled Germany, a function for which it was utterly unfitted. The result, naturally enough, was on the one hand an increasing alienation of the democratic forces in Germany (not great, but larger than often supposed) and on the other a further serious diminution of the Kaiser's already weakened authority. Already there was talk of his abdication. Increasingly the German people looked to Hindenburg as their hero and leader-figure. "Hindenburg," wrote the *Leipzig Nachrichten,* "has never yet deceived us; he will not deceive us now. We shall fight and conquer with him. Only let us trust in our Hindenburg. . . . Then our day must and will come, the day of Germany's splendour, the day of groaning and lamentation, and the gnashing of teeth and tearing of hair in London and Paris, in Rome and in Washington, in all the capitals of the accursed of God. Only our trust in our Hindenburg must be perfect."[9] Unfortunately, "our Hindenburg" was now seventy years old, and completely dominated by the livelier brain and strong but unstable personality of his First Quartermaster-General.

In all this darkness there was, for Germany, one strong beam of light: the Russian collapse. The urgent question was how to extract the utmost possible benefit from that happy event. When the Russians sued for an armistice in November 1917, Ludendorff doubtingly asked Major-General Max Hoffmann, the German Chief of Staff in the East: "Is it possible to negotiate with these people?"

Hoffmann replied: "Yes, it is possible. Your Excellency needs troops, and this is the easiest way to get them."

For the High Command, the Russian collapse meant an early prospect of heaven-sent reinforcement which might, with luck, clinch matters before the slowly mustering Americans could intervene. For the home front, it held out a promise of new food supplies from the "granary" of the Ukraine and by forcible requisition (thanks to Ludendorff these expectations remained largely unfulfilled), while psychologically it provided an uplift to counteract the prevalent war-weariness. An instructive exercise was carried out during January 1918 by the newspaper *Berlin Lokalanzeiger,* as peace negotiations proceeded at Brest-Litovsk. It put to its readers the question: "What do you expect from Brest-Litovsk?", and in one respect the published replies showed an impressive unanimity. Thus Professor von Wilamovitz, of the University of Berlin, a famous classical scholar and exemplar of what unfriendly critics called Germany's "pedantocracy":

> My expectations are of such a kind that my anxiety about the future of the Fatherland rudely disturbs my sleep at nights; this is the experience of many whose Fatherland is still Germany and not a Utopian Europe, or even a Utopian world. What the real men of this Germany demand is, above all, *a peace with Russia which will leave our hands entirely free against our other enemies. Any abandonment of this point of view I regard as a crime* [my italics]. The needs of our allies will be easily satisfied, but our needs must be satisfied also. . . . We are victors and conquerors.[10]

A Conservative leader, Herr von Heydebrand, was more succinct: "What I expect from Brest-Litovsk is a serviceable peace with Russia, *while we tie our helmets on all the tighter against our other enemies.*"[11]

Such were the New Year hopes of German patriots at home; even the discontented—workers, strikers, socialists—at least hoped that peace with Russia would lead to general peace. The Army reflected the nation; this is what Captain Rudolf Binding meant when he said that people were talking of Calais, Amiens, Paris and peace. The German

Army clutched at these hopes as its only salvation. It had borne the weight of the war, single-handed in the West, predominant in the East, since August 1914. Throughout it had been the "motor," the driving force of the war; now it was in palpable decline. "As our best men became casualties," wrote Ludendorff, "our infantry approximated more nearly in character to a militia, and discipline declined." Deserters were numerous—tens of thousands of them had fled to Holland. "They and the skrimshankers at the front, of whom there were thousands more, reduced the battle strength of the fighting troops . . . to a vital degree." The strategy of attrition, initiated by the Germans themselves at Verdun, adopted by the Allies on the Somme and all through the heavy fighting of 1917, was bearing fruit at last. Unfortunately, as we shall see, the Allied political leaders did not recognize this fact. Ludendorff was in no doubt:

> Against the weight of the enemy's material, the troops no longer displayed their old stubbornness; they thought with horror of fresh defensive battles and longed for a war of movement. . . . In the West the Army pined for the offensive, and after Russia's collapse expected it with the most intense relief. . . . The condition of our allies and our Army all called for an offensive that would bring about an early decision. This was only possible on the Western Front.[12]

Germany's allies, Austria-Hungary, Turkey and Bulgaria, were—still are—often referred to as her "props"; a whole strategic theory was founded on the idea of "knocking away the props." It was rubbish: Germany's allies were at the end of their tether—*she* propped them up. "We had to take into consideration," said Ludendorff, "that Austria-Hungary might actually arrive at the end of her military power. . . . Turkey was faithful to the alliance, but at the end of her strength. . . ." The Bulgarian Chief of Staff informed him that Bulgaria was "secure"—but active operations had practically ceased on the Bulgarian front. "That he could, of course, never ask for enough German stores and German troops was inherent in his office. With every word he expressed the hope of a German victory in the West." The conclusion was inescapable: "All that mattered was to get together enough troops for an attack in the West."

The time factor was vital:

> The American danger rendered it desirable to strike in the West as early as possible; the state of training of the Army for attack enabled us to contemplate doing so about the middle of March. . . . If all went smoothly at Brest-Litovsk, if our people there worked with real energy, we could expect to have our forces ready for a successful attack in the

West by the time mentioned. No delay could be justified. It will be obvious with what interest we watched the peace negotiations.

Ludendorff himself, by now, was displaying symptoms of paranoia—a "Napoleon complex" which led him into extraordinary dreams of annexations to the German Empire in Poland and the Baltic states, and grand partitions of Russia herself. These brought him into conflict with Hoffmann and the Foreign Minister, von Kühlmann (Germany's only politician of statesman quality), and led to an ugly scene with the Kaiser himself. He had the support of Hindenburg, however, and when the exasperated Kühlmann asked the Field-Marshal why he so particularly wanted these alien Eastern territories, Hindenburg replied: "I need them for the manoeuvring of my left wing in the next war." To which, of course, there was no conceivable answer, though there was a readily conceivable consequence: the peace negotiations broke down.

Relying on world opinion, and even more on the revolutionary instincts of "the masses" in Germany and Austria-Hungary, the Bolshevik delegates refused to sign the harsh terms offered them and left Brest-Litovsk. Trotsky, their leader, proclaimed the policy of "neither war nor peace,"[13] believing it to be a master-stroke. Many other members of his party thought so too; Lenin was not among them. And though the Austrians were appalled at the breakdown of negotiations, in Germany it was greeted with grim satisfaction, even, in some places, with bell-ringing. On 18 February the German armies were on the move again, and the Bolsheviks' self-congratulation died on their lips. In five days the Germans advanced 150 miles; opposition was negligible everywhere. Kiev and Odessa fell, the Ukraine, Livonia and Estonia were occupied; the Germans arrived within 120 miles of Petrograd. Then Russia surrendered. There was no further question of negotiations, only of cutting losses, saving what was left while there was still time. On 3 March the Treaty of Brest-Litovsk was signed.

The Bolsheviks had come to power on the slogan "Down with the war!" Now they redeemed their pledge to the Russian people—at a cost. By the terms of this treaty, "Russia lost 34% of her population, 32% of her agricultural land, 85% of her beet-sugar land, 54% of her industrial undertakings, and 89% of her coal mines."[14] This was a German peace. Exasperation at Bolshevik tactics and propaganda brought out the worst in the German character—its harshness and its hypocrisy. The newspaper *Norddeutsche Allgemeine Zeitung*, for example, wrote on the day after the signature: "The significance of the treaty with Russia lies in the fact that the German Government has worked only for a peace of understanding and conciliation." One way of putting it. The Bolshevik delegate G. I. Sokolnikov, on the other hand, called it "a peace which Russia, grinding its teeth, is forced to accept." Outside Russia and Germany the effects of the treaty were profound. "If it did nothing else," says Sir John Wheeler-Bennett, "the peace of Brest-Litovsk, as Kühlmann had feared and foreseen, showed clearly to the world what mercy the conquered enemies of Germany might expect. The effect in the Allied countries was a grim tightening of the belt and an increased determination to destroy the régime which could make such a peace." Brest-Litovsk, too often forgotten now, was, in fact, what the war was about.

Yet there was a payment, a tax levied on this seemingly entirely successful robbery, even as it was being committed. Ludendorff's grandiose and anachronistic dreams of calling ancient Germanic kingdoms and grand-duchies back into being required force to make them real. There was a German expeditionary force in Finland, another penetrating towards the oil-fields of Batoum and Baku, another at Odessa; the Ukraine was under occupation, as was Rumania.[15] Altogether, no less than a million German soldiers were retained in the East to support Ludendorff's fantasies, at a time when, on his own admission, everything was needed for the final stroke on the Western Front. This was the first of many blunders.

Nevertheless, the build-up of German strength in the West, watched with careful attention by the Allied Intelligence Services, was formidable. It had begun as far back as November 1917: at the beginning of that month there were some 150 German divisions on the Western Front; by the end of the year the figure had risen to 171. The Intelligence Section at British G.H.Q. accurately plotted further arrivals within a surprisingly short time of each completion:

6 February	174
21 February	179
25 February	180
3 March	182
10 March	184
11 March	185
18 March	187

By 21 March there were 192, 190 of which were identified by G.H.Q. Intelligence on 22 March. The number finally rose to a peak of 208.

Mass is important, but it is not everything in war. This vast array required intensive training for the task it had to perform. The divisions coming from the East were in many cases unfamiliar with Western Front conditions, where they were bound, no matter how successful, to face a technological opposition never remotely matched on the Russian front. The divisions already located in the West had to be brought up to strength after the heavy losses of 1917; they then had to be taught to eradicate the habits formed in three years of defensive fighting and to learn the new tactics of offensive warfare which had been evolved. The essence of the training laid down, says Ludendorff, was "to adopt loose formations and work out infantry group tactics clearly. We must not copy the enemy's mass tactics, which offer advantages only in the case of untrained troops." Penetration, envelopment and swift reinforcement of success were the ideas inculcated into all ranks—the concept propagandized in the name "Storm Troops." But the Storm Troops were only a part of the German Army of 1918; the quality of the whole mass, in view of serious losses of N.C.O.s, was too uneven for the universal application of the new elixirs. The Storm Troop system was not a trump card, as sometimes stated, but an expedient. None knew this better than the German High Command, which had to allot training and equipment priorities to "attack divisions" as opposed to "trench divisions." "General Headquarters," wrote Ludendorff, "regretted that the distinction . . . became established in the Army. We tried to eradicate it, without being able to alter the situation which gave rise to it." He was referring to the deterioration resulting from attrition, not least the Third Battle of Ypres—Passchendaele.

The German attack, when it came, was to prove, after all, a conventional attack. The patient, obedient, adept German soldiery, led by what remained of their peacetime-trained officers and N.C.O.s, proved able to do many things better than most of their opponents had yet been able to do; but they did little that their opponents had not attempted, and were in some cases soon to surpass. And the mainspring of their battle would be what it had been all through the war: artillery. By 1918, however, this meant artillery in a quantity never before dreamed of, and used with great sophistication. Out of their 13,832 pieces of artillery on the Western Front (a huge number, itself one of the determining factors of the nature of this war), the Germans assembled 6,473 on the sector of attack—a concentration beyond any previous comparison, and "orchestrated" at the key point by the outstanding artillerist of the war, Lieutenant-Colonel Bruchmüller.

"We had no tanks . . . our attacks succeeded without them," says Ludendorff. Tanks did not impress him. "Not until our infantry lost its discipline and fighting capacity did the employment of massed tanks, combined with artificial smoke, produce a fatal effect on the course of events." It is not precisely true that the Germans had no tanks at all for their forthcoming attack; in the event they used nine—four of their own A7Vs and five captured British Mark IVs.[16] But Ludendorff was in essence correct, since few would dispute his verdict that "tanks are

only effective in masses." This was also the official doctrine of the
Royal Tank Corps, warmly supported by the British Commander-in-
Chief, Field-Marshal Sir Douglas Haig. This doctrine did, however,
depend on the "masses" being available, which was only the case on
the British front on two days during the entire war. But the Germans
never at any time employed more than thirteen on a single occasion.
Ludendorff's doubts about the new arm reveal a defect of imagination,
but are less interesting in themselves than the broader situation which
they reflect. Not only did the Germans not produce tanks for their
great offensive; armoured cars were equally absent, and to the best of
my knowledge, so were motorized machine-guns (carried in motor-cy-
cle side-cars), which the British certainly possessed.

Nor was it only mechanical aids that were lacking; so also was the
traditional mobile arm—cavalry. The effectiveness of cavalry on the
Western Front after the opening combats of the war of movement in
1914 was always limited. Yet it was the only arm which retained any
true cross-country mobility—provided it could move at all, which
depended largely on the enemy's machine-guns. Armoured cars and
motor-cycles were essentially road-bound; the maximum speed of a
Mark IV tank (1917) was 3.7 m.p.h., of a Mark V (1918) 4.6 m.p.h.,
and of a Medium Mark A ("Whippet," 1918) 8.3 m.p.h.—but these
were all road speeds; over rough ground they rarely averaged better
than 1 or 1.5 m.p.h. Thus the mechanical element could hardly be
regarded as a weapon of pursuit, while, in certain conditions, cavalry
might be. But Germany's cavalry divisions were in the Ukraine and the
Baltic states, supporting grandiose and senseless dreams of power. And
so it came about that the German Great General Staff launched what it
envisaged as the decisive battle of the war, in an area which, Ludendorff admits, "seemed to lack any definite limit," with no mobile arm
for exploitation at all. It hardly seems credible, yet it was so. This attack would go as far as the German infantryman's legs would carry
him, no further. As Sir John Wheeler-Bennett has said, it was Ludendorff the politician who defeated Ludendorff the soldier.[17]

There was long discussion in the German High Command about the
locale of the great offensive. Another assault on the French at Verdun
was contemplated, but rejected. An attack on the British in Flanders
seemed the most promising possibility, but March was too early for operations in that low-lying region, and time pressed. So the final choice
fell "on the area between Arras and Péronne, towards the coast. If this
blow succeeded the strategic result might indeed be enormous, as we
should separate the bulk of the English Army from the French and
crowd it up with its back to the sea."[18] It was recognized by the German High Command that there were drawbacks to this proposal: the

"lack of any definite limit" mentioned by Ludendorff, and the wilderness of the 1916 Somme battlefields not far behind the British front, through which the momentum of the advance would have to be maintained. Preparations were therefore also set in hand for an attack in Flanders, aimed at the vital Channel Ports, which the British could not possibly afford to lose. If the first attack was successful, the Flanders blow would clinch the matter; if the first attack should, by any chance, fall short of its purpose, the second might yet fulfil Germany's hopes.

So the stage was set for the *"Kaiserschlacht"*—the "Emperor Battle" —which would be fought for the ultimate stakes. Three armies, the *Eighteenth, Second* and *Seventeenth,* would deliver the attack: seventy-one divisions, of which thirty-two would be in the first line of assault. They faced the fronts of the British Third and Fifth Armies, commanded respectively by Generals Sir Julian Byng and Sir Hubert Gough. It is time now to consider in what posture the British faced this overwhelming onslaught.

Chapter II: Notes

1. (p. 16) So-called because, due to the failure of the 1916 potato crop through early frosts, turnips and other roots became standard diet in Germany.
2. (p. 16) An Englishwoman, married to a German prince, who spent the war in her husband's country.
3. (p. 17) Quoted by John Williams: *The Home Fronts: Britain, France and Germany 1914–1918,* Constable, 1972, p. 240.
4. (p. 18) Ibid., p. 227.
5. (p. 18) Correlli Barnett: *The Swordbearers,* Eyre and Spottiswoode, 1963, p. 303.
6. (p. 18) Williams, op. cit., p. 229.
7. (p. 18) Barnett, op. cit.
8. (p. 18) On August 1 forty-nine stokers of the battleship *Prinzregent Luitpold* left the ship without permission in protest over cancellation of recreation periods. The next day some 600 crew members also left the ship and attended a meeting at which there were shouts of "Down with the war! We do not want to fight this war any longer!" The men marched back to the ship, which was placed under a state of siege, while the ringleaders were later arrested. This led, on 8 August, to a sympathetic demonstration by seamen of the battleship *Heligoland.*
9. (p. 18) Williams, op. cit., pp. 236–37.
10. (p. 19) Quoted in *The Times,* 18 January 1918.
11. (p. 19) Ibid.
12. (p. 20) All Ludendorff quotations from *My War Memories,* Hutchinson, 1919, vol. ii.
13. (p. 21) See Sir John Wheeler-Bennett: *Brest-Litovsk: The Forgotten Peace, March 1918,* Macmillan, 1963, p. 227: Trotsky's declaration at Brest-Litovsk, February 10: "The Governments of Germany and Austria-Hungary are determined to possess lands and peoples by might. Let them do so openly. We cannot approve violence. We are going out of the war, but we feel ourselves compelled to refuse to sign the peace treaty."
14. (p. 21) Ibid., p. 269.

15. (p. 22) A peace almost as draconian as Brest-Litovsk was imposed on defeated Rumania: the Treaty of Bucharest, signed on 7 May.
16. (p. 23) See Col. H. C. B. Rogers: *Tanks in Battle,* Seeley Service, 1965, pp. 64–65.
17. (p. 24) Wheeler-Bennett, op. cit., p. 237.
18. (p. 24) Ludendorff, op. cit.

III

"GO ON OR GO UNDER"

"My own conviction is this, the people must either go on or go under." (Lloyd George to trade union leaders, January 1918)

Germany's intentions were clearly formulated; her preparations were vast and meticulous, her progress towards her appointed goal firm and deliberate. The opposite was the case on the other side of the line, and much of the blame for this has to be laid at the door of the British Government. All through 1917 the Government (above all, the Prime Minister) had been conducting irregular warfare against its military advisers, Robertson and Haig. In November Lloyd George had won a considerable victory over the generals (as pleasing as if it had been over the Germans) with the setting up of an inter-Allied Supreme War Council to direct and co-ordinate strategy (see p. 2). To make doubly sure of reducing the power of the military he took the grave further step of withholding from the British Expeditionary Force the most vital of the sinews of war: manpower.

There is no doubt that by January 1918 some members of the British Government had become well-nigh hysterical about the casualties of a manpower war. This was not entirely surprising: British casualties by the end of 1917 totalled over 2 million, a figure far beyond all previous experience or imagining. The reaction, among those who were aware of it, to the war's continuing insatiable greed for men, was such that one might have supposed that every dead soldier in France wore khaki. That France, with her smaller population, had lost over a million more, was scarcely known, certainly not taken into account. As early as 1916, when he was Secretary of State for War, Lloyd George had coined the phrase "military Moloch"; by 1918 he had come to loathe this beast and despise Robertson and Haig and the General

Staff, whom he regarded as its mindless servants. With the memory of Passchendaele and the bitter disappointment of victory turned into defeat at Cambrai fresh in his mind, the prospects for a new year of similar battles seemed to him bleak indeed. "Every nation," he later wrote,

> was profligate of its man-power in the early stages of the war and conducted its war activities as if there were no limit to the number of young men of military age who were fit to be thrown into the furnace to feed the flames of war. The Allies, who had an enormous superiority in the number of fit young men available, nearly threw away their advantage by the reckless prodigality of their military leaders. . . . The idea of a war of attrition was the refuge of stupidity and it was stupidly operated, with the consequence that the overwhelming superiority in man-power which the Allies enjoyed at the beginning of the War had by the fourth year been melted down to the dimensions of a dubious equality.[1]

We shall shortly see how this frame of mind affected the crisis of the war which was about to occur. But it must be remembered that the attitudes crystallized and perpetuated in his *War Memoirs* fifteen years later were not always the attitudes which he displayed most prominently at the time. Lloyd George did indeed growl and grumble when the military leaders presented their strategy and their demands for men; but towards the country at large he adopted a different tone. To organized labour in particular he spoke winningly, in case nothing should be forthcoming at all. "The desire for peace," he tells us—and here he is unquestionably correct—

> was spreading amongst men and women who, although they were convinced of the righteousness of the War, felt that the time had come for putting an end to its horrors in the name of humanity, if it could be done on any terms that were honourable and safe. . . . Amongst the workmen there was an unrest that was disturbing and might at any moment become dangerous. The efforts we were making to comb out more men for the Army were meeting with resistance amongst the Trade Unions, whose loyalty and patriotism had throughout been above reproach. I attached great importance to their continued support in the prosecution of the War.[2]

A conference with trade union leaders on manpower was convened in January 1918; Lloyd George addressed it twice, first at the inaugural meeting on 5 January, when he delivered a carefully considered statement on war aims:

64

Scenes of destiny. *Above:* Brest-Litovsk, where the Germans imposed a conqueror's peace on Russia, 3 March 1918. 'Brest-Litovsk was what the war was about'. *Below:* Spa, in eastern Belgium, 'the last citadel of the German Empire'. The German High Command occupied the Grand Hotel Britannique; the beflagged building opposite was the headquarters of the Allied Armistice Commission

Men of destiny. *Above:* Kaiser Wilhelm II (centre), 'never in touch with reality, let alone in control of it'; on his right (pointing), Field-Marshal von Hindenburg, Germany's 'hero and leader-figure'; and on the Kaiser's left, General Erich Ludendorff, 'a man whose nerve and judgment were seriously impaired' in the last phase of the war. *Below left:* Prince Max of Baden, Imperial Chancellor, October–November 1918; 'the one prominent royalist liberal in the Empire'. *Below right:* General Wilhelm Gröner, First Quartermaster-General, October–November 1918: 'one of the great tragic figures of German military history'

The Emperor Battle. *Above:* '. . . the build-up of German strength in the West was formidable'; German infantry moving up for the March offensive. Fifty divisions were identified in action against the British on the first day alone. *Below:* '. . . a mutual agreement that each ally would come to the help of the other'; French infantry arriving in the British sector on the Somme, March 1918. The French suffered 77,000 casualties in sixteen days of 'ferocious and critical battle'

The Battle of the Lys, 9-29 April: a decisive feature was 'the astonishing powers of resistance displayed by the decimated British units'; their casualties were 76,300, but the Germans gained no strategic objective

The Battle of the Aisne, May-June 1918: German troops crossing 'the Chemins des Dames ridge of evil memory'. They inflicted a heavy defeat on the Allies, but once more gained no strategic objective

We are fighting for a just and lasting peace, and we believe that before permanent peace can be hoped for three conditions must be fulfilled.

First, the sanctity of treaties must be re-established; secondly, a territorial settlement must be secured based on the right of self-determination or the consent of the governed; and, lastly, we must seek by the creation of some international organisation to limit the burdens of armaments and diminish the probability of war. In these conditions the British Empire would welcome peace, to secure those conditions its peoples are prepared to make even greater sacrifices than those they have yet endured.[3]

Lloyd George had taken steps to ensure a solid political consensus behind him before he made his speech. It was well received by the trade union audience, and rapturously acclaimed by *The Times* next day: "There has been nothing in the long history of British politics comparable with the demonstration of national unity which the Prime Minister made in his war aims speech to the trade union delegates. . . . It was instantly recognised as the most important State document which has appeared since the outbreak of the war. . . ."[4] And the next day, 8 January, *The Times* was commenting, under the heading "The Allies and the Speech": "Rarely since the war began has British opinion been so unanimous as in its approbation of the Prime Minister's speech. Not a single discordant note has been heard in any responsible quarter."

Fortified by these reactions, Lloyd George once more addressed the trade union leaders on 18 January, and carried his argument somewhat further. "Do not," he urged them, "let us harbour any delusions. . . . You might as well stop fighting unless you are going to do it well. If you are not going to do it with all your might, it is real murder of gallant fellows who have been in the trenches for three years (Hear! Hear!). . . . If there are men who say that they will not go into the trenches, then the men in the trenches have a right to say, 'Neither will we remain here!' Supposing they did, would that bring the War to an end? Yes, it would. But what sort of an end?"[5]

The answer was obvious, as *The Times* had told its readers two days earlier:

The Germans are bluntly telling the Bolshevists at Brest-Litovsk that they propose to deal with them as victors deal with the vanquished. Unless the Western Allies are prepared to back up their declared purposes by fighting for them, we shall run the risk of ending in a similar situation. We have now had the plainest of warnings that to hold the fighting front large and prompt reinforcements are required, and every man of common sense in the land sees that they must be provided.[6]

Lloyd George stated his own conclusion to the trade unionists with crushing force:

> We must take the world as it is, and the story of democracy is this: no democracy has ever long survived the failure of its adherents to be ready to die for it. . . . If one profession, one trade, one section, or one class in a community claims to be immune from obligations which are imposed upon the rest, that is a fundamental travesty of the principles of democracy. . . . Democracy must mean that the people of all classes . . . must merge their privileges and their rights in the common stock. . . . My own conviction is this, the people must either go on or go under.[7]

It was a remarkable speech, an example of the great strength and rhetorical skill which Lloyd George could bring to the rallying of the nation in difficult times—the reason, in fact, why he received such support as Prime Minister. Hard facts, however, could be less encouraging than brave words. Whatever long-term effects Lloyd George's speech might have on trade unionists and others, the short-term prospects for the 1918 campaign were gloomy. Colonel Repington noted on 15 January:

> We are only to get 430,000 men from youths in essential trades, such as munitions—but these are for Army, Navy, and Aircraft; and the Army —though Geddes[8] concealed this fact—only gets 100,000 "A" men, as I expected. Moreover, as men twice severely wounded are to be kept at home, the net increase probably will vanish. Geddes stated that 1,600,000 enemies may reinforce the Western front! A nice reply! Is all the British world mad?

This was something that no rhetoric could alter, a reflection of government policies which, by 1918, had produced a very serious situation indeed.

To understand this we should first look at the broader picture: the new framework of Allied strategy which owed its existence to such a large extent to Lloyd George. It is very difficult to produce strong theoretical arguments against the setting up of the Supreme War Council: that the Allies needed a machinery for central control of the war is axiomatic; that such a machinery had previously been (formally, at any rate) lacking is an undoubted fact. Why, then, does it have to be stated that the Supreme War Council was a liability, not an asset, at this crisis of the war? The answer, sadly, lies in the manner of its creation. For Lloyd George the Council was not merely a step towards the desirable goal of Allied unity, it was also a step towards the even more desirable goal of reducing the authority of Robertson, Haig and the General Staff.

The Supreme War Council was set up by agreement between the British, French and Italian governments at a conference at Rapallo on 7 November 1917 (the Americans came in shortly afterwards). It was to consist of the Prime Ministers and a representative of the government of each of the great powers, together with a Permanent Military Representative. Its mission was "to watch over the general conduct of the War. It prepares recommendations for the decisions of the Governments and keeps itself informed of their execution and reports thereon to the respective Governments. . . ."[9] It would reside at Versailles. In other words, the Council would have both a co-ordinating and an initiating function, superior to that of the general staff of any single member state; it was, in theory, impeccable.

In practice, however, it was nothing of the kind, and it is the composition of the list of Permanent Military Representatives that illustrates the point. Lloyd George, from first to last, saw the Supreme Council as an alternative to the General Staff, with the power to override the General Staff; it was precisely for this purpose that he proposed it. The other Allies, however, saw it differently: the French named General Foch, their Chief of the General Staff, as their Military Representative, the Italians named General Cadorna, who could only be a mouthpiece of their General Staff. If the French persisted with Foch, Lloyd George would be obliged to nominate Robertson, which was exactly what he wanted to avoid; he protested hotly, but the most that he could do was to effect the substitution of General Weygand for Foch, and Weygand was no more than Foch's staff officer and spokesman. The British equivalent of Weygand was Major-General Sir Frederick Maurice, Director of Military Operations at the War Office under Robertson, and virtually his *alter ego*. But the officer Lloyd George actually selected was Sir Henry Wilson, a sharp critic of the General Staff and the Western strategy. Wilson's position, as his biographer, Sir Charles Callwell, remarks, "was going to be an exceptional one." So it was, and so was Britain's—a fact re-emphasized when the Americans unhesitatingly appointed their Chief of Staff, General Bliss, as their representative.

There was thus confusion from the first as to the very nature of the Supreme War Council, a confusion soon reflected in the strategic advice which it gave. Late in December, as the evidence mounted of an impending German attack in the West on a grand scale, the Versailles staff, at General Wilson's instigation, mounted a "war game" to fathom German intentions. This was one of Wilson's favourite occupations; he always insisted that the section of the staff responsible for the enemy's manoeuvres should turn their hats round back to front to heighten the illusion. Whether thanks to this precaution or not, the conclusions arrived at by the Supreme War Council as a result of the game were, firstly, that no decision was likely on the Western Front during 1918, so that the Allies would do best to concentrate their efforts against Turkey; secondly, that the British should extend their front in France by forty miles instead of the twenty-eight miles to which Haig had already reluctantly agreed.

This "war game" was repeated at intervals throughout January, for the benefit of awed visitors. When Lloyd George heard of it, he was "much interested," says Wilson. "He made several valuable suggestions, especially about the Boches not attacking in the West, but going for Odessa and the north of the Black Sea, and holding us off meanwhile." Robertson, on the other hand, when he was told, was "a good deal knocked about by all this." Haig remarked that "The whole position would be laughable but for the seriousness of it." Equally laughable, in a similar wry fashion (though once again impeccable on paper) was the Supreme War Council's proposal for creating an Allied General Reserve which would be interchangeable between the British, French and Italian fronts. Once more, the advantages were obvious, but the question was, where was such a force to come from? The Supreme Council's decision was to set up an Executive Committee to handle the reserve, under Foch as chairman—a decision, as Haig said, that "to some extent . . . makes Foch a 'Generalissimo.' "

But he was a Generalissimo with no troops, for Haig himself, lacking reinforcements for his extended front, flatly refused to part with any men, and Pétain, who was anxiously trying to build up a reserve of his own, took the same view. The most that either Commander-in-Chief would accept was that the British and French divisions which had been sent to Italy after the Caporetto disaster might be earmarked for the Reserve, or failing that an equivalent number of Italians. As to present emergencies, Haig and Pétain preferred to depend on mutual agreements for support. And with that unsatisfactory arrangement, since the Supreme War Council was unable to persuade the British Government to revise its manpower policies, all had to be as contented as possible.

So it all came back to manpower, a central issue throughout 1918 which the Supreme War Council's strange strategic prognoses merely helped to obscure. At the turn of the year the British manpower problem resolved itself into two issues: the number of men required for the Army in 1918 (long-term) and the distribution of the forces already in arms (immediate). To resolve the first question, a Cabinet Committee on Manpower was set up in December 1917; it consisted of Lord Curzon, Mr. G. N. Barnes (for Labour), Sir Edward Carson and General

Smuts, with the Prime Minister in the chair. The Official History remarks that not a single soldier was invited to sit on it—a significant omission.

The task of the Cabinet Committee was to determine priorities for the coming year, and its conclusion was that the Navy, the Air Force, ship-building, munitions, food production, timber-felling and the provision of cold-storage accommodation[10] should all have priority over the Army. "The Army had no special knowledge of these problems," wrote Lloyd George, "and could claim no more right than the Navy, the Ministry of Munitions, the Treasury, the Board of Trade, the Ministries of Labour and Agriculture, the Shipping, Coal or Food Controllers to a representative on the Committee." It is quite true, of course, that in a total war every part of the nation is involved in the struggle for survival, and a careful balance has to be struck between conflicting demands. Every one of the departments mentioned had a vital part to play—but there was this difference: none of them was designated as the immediate target of the vast preparations of the German High Command. Only the Army was in that position, and it could therefore anticipate substantially larger casualties than, say, agricultural workers or lumberjacks.

The Army authorities, on the basis of past experience and reasonable future expectations, had asked for 615,000 men; it was a daunting figure, but, considering that British casualties in 1917 had approached 900,000, if anything it was too few. Yet the Cabinet Committee decided to allot 50,000 of the Category "A" men available to the Navy, and only 100,000 to the Army, plus another 100,000 men of lower medical grades. The Committee, in its wisdom, took leave to doubt the figures on which the Army based its demands: "The British Army," said Lloyd George, "had of course been fighting hard on the offensive all through 1917; but as it was to stand on the defensive for the early part of 1918, the Committee considered that the military estimate was likely to prove unduly large." The belief that the defensive was less costly than the offensive was deeply entrenched; Lloyd George was quite certain of it; Winston Churchill made it a powerful argument against the concept of attrition; it persists strongly to this day. However, it does not bear the light of battlefield realities, and its influence in 1918 was wholly pernicious.

Unwilling to find the men to bring the British Expeditionary Force up to its proper established strength, the five political gentlemen of the Cabinet Committee decided that the B.E.F. must be "re-tailored" to fit their conclusions. This meant, quite simply, either reducing the number of divisions in the field (fifty-seven British and Dominion, plus two Portuguese) or reducing the establishment of divisions. Both France and Germany had already reduced the size of their divisions from 1914–15 standards, and this was made the excuse for adopting the latter course. It ignored the brute fact that the French and Germans had reduced establishments in order to create more divisions; the British did it to disguise a failure to meet manpower needs. Despite the formal opposition of the Army Council and the explicit protest of the Commander-in-Chief, the Cabinet Committee insisted that British divisions should be reduced from twelve to nine battalions, and brigades from four to three battalions, and on 10 January the War Office was compelled to order a reorganization on these lines. So, as German preparations for the greatest battle of the war remorselessly proceeded, the British Commander-in-Chief found himself forced to disband two out of his five cavalry divisions (another Cabinet Committee edict) and was given a list of 145 infantry battalions out of which he was permitted to select the four which might survive and the 141 which must go.

It need hardly be said that such reorganization meant disorganization to a fearful degree. This entire astonishing and demoralizing exercise took time—time during which the roads of France were filled with British units seeking new homes in strange divisions,[11] and during which an *esprit de corps* built up over years of common experience was thrown away, while all existing tactical principles and schemes had to be scrapped. Of the four British armies comprising the B.E.F. in 1918,[12] the First completed its reorganization by 19 February, the Fifth by 25 February, the Third by 27 February, and the Fourth (in Flanders) not until 4 March. As a final complication, it must be added that the governments of Australia, Canada and New Zealand declined to adopt similar measures, with the result that the ten Dominion divisions on the Western Front retained their twelve battalions each; this turned out to be most fortunate.

So we find the extraordinary spectacle of the British Army, facing the most formidable offensive of the war, actually disbanding units and thrown into confusion by the ensuing arrangements. Lloyd George, of course, by every device of pleading, sought to shuffle off responsibility for putting the country in such deadly danger. "In March 1918," he wrote,

> the total strength of the British Army, Regular and Territorial, raised in this country—excluding all Dominion, Colonial, Indian and native troops—was 3,889,990. This was the colossal giant which the War Cabinet are accused of having reduced to a skeleton army. *It was the highest total strength which the British Army ever reached. At no time in the whole course of the War were there so many men from this country in the ranks of the Army at home and overseas as at the date of the German offensive in March, 1918* [his italics].[13]

He adds, with similar emphasis, that at the same time the expeditionary forces in all theatres also reached their high-water mark for the war. He does everything that a man can do with figures, except explain those 141 battalions which vanished from the Order of Battle in France on the eve of the German attack.

It is quite true, of course, that there were a lot of men in uniform at the beginning of 1918. On 5 January the B.E.F. numbered 1,949,100; at home, in the United Kingdom, there were 1,560,862 officers and men. Both totals require a word of explanation. As regards the B.E.F., there is no question that the ration strength was higher by over 300,000 than it had been a year before. But 271,000 of this increase is accounted for by labour units (white and coloured[14]) and a further 37,000 by Transportation. The Royal Flying Corps, Royal Artillery, Machine Gun Corps and Tank Corps also showed increases. The infantry were decreased by 126,000, however—and as usual it was on the infantry that the brunt of loss would fall. The 1½ million men at home also need to be explained. A large number of them were in hospital or convalescing from wounds; others were in training formations; others again constituted the Home Forces under Field-Marshal Lord French, the nation's "second shield" (behind the Navy) against invasion. It is an interesting fact that invasion was still being talked of as a practical possibility in 1918; the general commanding the "Southern Army" told Repington that the Germans could land under cover of smoke-screens in Kent, and "30,000 Boches would be in Maidstone by the third day, and he had no confidence that he could stop them." Ireland, also, was still in a simmering condition after the 1916 Rising, and required a garrison of 90,000 men, 62,000 of them being infantry performing a gendarme role. Nevertheless, despite these deductions, there remained over 600,000 trained Category "A" men in the country; the Cabinet Committee considered 449,000 of them available for drafts—but preferred not to use them as such. In addition to this array at home it must also be recorded that there were just under 900,000 officers and men in the subsidiary theatres of war. Admittedly, a large proportion of these were Indian or colonial contingents, who would not have been considered as potential reinforcements for the Western Front; yet the harsh truth remains that when the storm broke it was found possible to bring 100,000 British soldiers from these theatres to France—and many more from home—when it was nearly too late.

False strategic advice from the Supreme War Council; a grave diminution of the most important fighting arm; organizational confusion on the eve of enemy attack—all this might be thought a sufficient burden for the B.E.F. to have borne in 1918. But there was more. Beginning in December and running through January, important changes took place by decree in the personnel of General Headquarters. Some of these were understandable and justified: Brigadier-General John Charteris, Head of Military Intelligence, had exercised a baneful influence on Haig during much of 1917 and was decidedly unpopular in the Army; his replacement by Major-General the Hon. Sir Herbert Lawrence, himself succeeded by Brigadier-General E. Cox on 24 January, was certainly a step forward. On the same date Lawrence, with the rank of lieutenant-general, moved up to take the place of Haig's Chief of Staff, Lieutenant-General Sir Lancelot Kiggell; this was also a good thing. Other changes were the Deputy Chief of Staff Major-General Sir Richard Butler (who went to command a corps), the Quartermaster-General, the Engineer-in-Chief, and Major-General Hugh Trenchard, commanding the Royal Flying Corps, who went to London to become Chief of Air Staff. There were justifications, some weighty, some less so, for all these moves, but it is hard to justify such a wholesale alteration of the Commander-in-Chief's immediate entourage at such a critical moment. Excellent officers though some of the newcomers were, Haig would have to get to know them, they would have to learn his ways. For a man notoriously inarticulate, and therefore dependent to an unusual degree on sensitive interpretation, the upheaval was particularly hard to bear.

Change at G.H.Q., however, was only a part—the lesser part—of the change in the military direction of the war. The position of the C.I.G.S., Sir William Robertson, had become increasingly intolerable throughout 1917. It was he who was in almost daily contact with the War Cabinet and the Prime Minister, he and his deputy, General Maurice, who were, in the words of Sir Edward Spears, "daily on the track of Mr. Lloyd George's strategic conceptions, and it must be admitted that two colder-nosed hounds never hunted out a wily Welsh fox."[15] Fighting stubbornly for the principle in which he devoutly believed, concentration of decisive force at the decisive point—which in his view, like Ludendorff's, could only be the Western Front—Robertson found himself in endless abrasive conflict with his political superior. In September 1917, unable to bear any longer the sensation of beating his head on a wall, Lloyd George took the amazing step of calling in what he called "a second opinion"—transferring a medical practice into a military situation, but ignoring the simple point that in a medical situation it is not the patient who calls in the second opinion but the doctor. If the doctor refuses to consult a second opinion when the patient thinks he should, then the patient must change his doctor. But Lloyd George did not see it that way, and so found himself in the interesting predicament of a patient with two doctors (indeed, three!), one recommending some very nasty medicine indeed, the other some nicer medicine, but not recommended by the rest of the profession. It is not a choice that patients should be called on to make!

The two "second opinions" which Lloyd George chose to consult were those of Field-Marshal Lord French, who had commanded the B.E.F. in 1914 until he was supplanted by Haig at the end of 1915, and Sir Henry Wilson, British Liaison Officer at G.Q.G. (Grand Quartier-Générale—French General Headquarters) until the advent of Pétain, and currently unemployed. French had been a palpable failure in command, and had never forgiven either Haig, who had taken his place, or Robertson who, he believed, had done much to bring that about. When he discussed his opinion of War Office and G.H.Q. strategy with Sir Maurice (later Lord) Hankey, Secretary to the War Cabinet, the latter perceptively commented: "There was envy, hatred, and malice in the old boy's heart as he spoke."[16] Envy, hatred and malice were not part of Wilson's make-up: an agile but shallow mind, a relish for intrigue, a plausible manner with politicians—those were the characteristics that caused him to be "universally distrusted throughout the Army . . . our only military blackleg."[17] Such were the men whose opinions Lloyd George valued above those of his responsible advisers; small wonder that Robertson told Haig, "I am sick of this d——d life."[18]

In the event, it proved that neither French nor Wilson had much to offer except suggestions for a "Superior Direction" of the war, a prompting out of which was born the Supreme War Council. For Robertson this was a fatal moment; if his position had been difficult before, it now became intolerable. As Wilson and Lloyd George saw it (but not, as we have seen, any of the other governments concerned), the Permanent Military Representative at Versailles now took precedence over the C.I.G.S. A head-on clash became inevitable, and was not long in arriving. Wilson's view, which he did not hesitate to air freely, was confided to his diary on 31 December: "Really we must change in 1918 our puerile, useless, costly strategy of 1916 and 1917."[19] As Robertson and Haig were the champions of that strategy, they were scarcely likely to agree, and on 14 January Haig put the matter in a nutshell in a letter to Robertson: "The Government now have two advisers! Will they accept the advice of the Versailles gentlemen (who have no responsibility) or will they take my advice?"[20] The question was soon resolved.

The Third Session of the Supreme War Council opened at Versailles on 30 January and continued until 2 February. It was a stormy occasion, with a sharp dispute between Lloyd George and General Foch on the always sensitive subject of manpower, and another sharp dispute between Lloyd George and Clemenceau on the recommendation of the

Permanent Military Representatives that the Allies should concentrate their efforts against Turkey in 1918. Clemenceau, to Lloyd George's disgust, insisted that the Western Front was vital, and its security the overriding factor. Not only that, but he invited Robertson to comment on the Versailles proposal. The latter promptly pronounced that the annihilation of Turkey was not a practical plan, and that to attempt it would be very dangerous and detrimental to the prospects of winning the war. Haig's opinion was not invited, and he did not offer it, but he noted: "I saw L.G. was much annoyed with Robertson but he said nothing at the time. Later he told R. that, having given his advice in London, it was not necessary for him to have repeated it here."[21]

This public clash between the Prime Minister and the C.I.G.S. proved to be the last straw. By 7 February it was clear to those close to the inner circles of power that Lloyd George was now determined to part with Robertson. And rightly: he should, in fact, have dismissed Robertson long before—not because the latter's views were wrong; on the contrary, they were shortly to be spectacularly proved right—but because it is madness for the political and military heads of the state to try to work in harness when they are really pulling in opposite directions. As Hankey said to Esher, "the incompatibility of temper between the two men and the ever-recurring quarrels depreciate L.G.'s vitality and governing power."[22] And, of course, the same was true in reverse; Repington remarked to Maurice "that after the war it would be found that 50% of the time and energy of soldiers had been expended in fighting their own politicians. M. thought that my percentage was much too low."[23] No doubt he was thinking of his chief's eternal struggles. But whichever side one took, it was clear that this continuous friction was too exhausting; the energies which it devoured could have been far better spent.

So Robertson's departure had become essential; but how was it to be achieved? Lloyd George still could not face the simple method of outright dismissal; Robertson was not particularly disposed to help out by resigning. Various suggestions were mooted—Hankey, for instance, proposed that Robertson should be made Commander-in-Chief in India, but Haig, when consulted on this by Lloyd George, pointed out that General Sir Charles Monro was doing excellent work in that capacity and should be left to get on with it. Lloyd George then fell back on an earlier and very curious idea: that Wilson and Robertson should simply change places. Alternatively, the latter could remain as C.I.G.S., but the powers of the office would be sharply curtailed. Either way, it would be Wilson, not Robertson, who had the ear of the Prime Minister, whether as C.I.G.S. or as Permanent Military Representative.

A remarkable scene now followed. Mr. Arthur Balfour, the Foreign Secretary, was reluctant to see Robertson go (and even more reluctant to see Wilson come in) and, believing that Robertson might be unduly influenced by the personal factor, undertook to interview him on behalf of the War Cabinet. The meeting took place on 14 February; Balfour put the alternatives to Robertson:

> I pointed out to him that the Government gave him the alternative of accepting either of the two great Staff appointments connected with the conduct of the War on the Western Front. It seemed to me that they could do no more, and that, on public grounds, he ought to accept.
>
> General Robertson observed repeatedly, and with great insistence, that the fact of his having been offered whichever of the two posts he preferred had, in his view, nothing to do with the question. If his objection had merely been that the powers now given to the Council at Versailles, and therefore to the British Member of it, overshadowed the position of the C.I.G.S., it might conceivably have been worthwhile to transfer his activities from London to Versailles. But this was not his point of view at all. He objected to the new system, and he equally objected to it whether he was expected to take a share in working it as C.I.G.S. or to take a share in working it as Military Member of the Supreme War Council. An objectionable object in the middle of a table (to use his own metaphor) was equally objectionable from whichever end of the table you looked at it. . . .

For over half an hour Balfour tried to get Robertson to change his mind—

> I regret to say with no result at all.
>
> General Robertson was very anxious that the scheme should be so modified that the Military Member at Versailles should be the subordinate and representative of the C.I.G.S. In that case he would be quite ready either to retain the position of Chief of the Staff or go to Versailles.[24]

So that was that. The personal factor did not arise; it was a matter of principle. Robertson was prepared to go to Versailles, with diminished status, because he firmly believed that the status of the Versailles post *ought* to be diminished; he was not prepared to be a C.I.G.S. with diminished status, because he equally believed that the C.I.G.S. was the Government's responsible military adviser, and that the status of his post *ought not* to be diminished. It was one of Robertson's great qualities, to be able to cut through to the heart of matters, and reduce them to such simplicities.

It meant, of course, that he could no longer remain at the centre of direction of the war. "It was," wrote Lloyd George, in a passage unusually mendacious even by the standards of his *War Memoirs,*

> now a question whether the Government of the day should submit to military dictation on a matter where they were by every constitutional precedent the supreme authority. . . . If the Government surrendered, then a military dictatorship would have been an accomplished fact. The Government of the day would have been as impotent in the face of protests or vetoes or orders issued by Robertson here as the German Chancellor and his Ministers had become after July 1916, when confronted by the peremptory messages of Hindenburg and Ludendorff.

That some of Britain's political leaders, including the Prime Minister, had worked themselves into a state of semi-hysteria about "military dictatorship" is unfortunately true; but that is the only truth in Lloyd George's ridiculous and dishonest suggestion.

The dishonesty was very quickly revealed—to anyone who chose to look. There was a last brief flicker of doubt about Wilson, even among his friends; at the twelfth hour Lloyd George offered the post of C.I.G.S. to General Sir Herbert Plumer, who had won fame as the commander of the Second Army in Flanders, and was now commanding the British contingent in Italy. Plumer wasted no time in turning down the offer; like most senior officers, he had great respect for Robertson and no wish to supplant him. So it would be Wilson after all, and Robertson went to the obscurity of Eastern Command in Home Forces. Wilson had been waiting for this news for many days, and had been giving thought to how he should conduct himself in the new situation. On 9 February he discussed the matter with Lord Milner, a member of the War Cabinet with special responsibilities for the Supreme War Council, who had been very active in all these negotiations: "If . . . Robertson refuses Versailles, then Milner and I agreed that he should put in someone junior to me, and let me have a directing voice in Versailles if I was C.I.G.S. The whole thing is rather muddlesome."[25] "Muddlesome" it remained. Four days later, just before the final crisis, Wilson met Robertson himself: "We had a good talk; we differ fundamentally because he wants Versailles to be under him, and I say it cannot be."[26] This was the thought of the day; fearing that Robertson might still hang on as C.I.G.S., Wilson told Derby "that Versailles could not be deputy to anyone." When he became C.I.G.S. himself two days later, however, he quickly discovered the inconveniences of this position. His successor at Versailles was an old friend and fellow Rifleman, Sir Henry Rawlinson—but Rawlinson was also a full general, an army commander and a man of character. Wil-

son soon found himself in conflict with the Permanent Military Representative, and rendered powerless by his own earlier insistence. It was
a retribution from which he was, in the event, rescued by the Germans;
under the weight of their attack in March, Gough's Fifth Army
crumbled and Rawlinson was recalled to the front to replace Gough.
This time Wilson made no mistake. In place of Rawlinson at Versailles
he appointed Major-General the Hon. Sir C. Sackville-West, a relatively junior officer whom Hankey unblushingly describes as "Wilson's
'own man' [who] virtually took his instructions from him."[27] So
Robertson had been right after all.

This was Lloyd George's final contribution to the Army's difficulties
and dangers in 1918: he had replaced at its head a man who was universally trusted (described by Lord Esher as "one of England's first as-
sets in the war"[28]) by one whom he himself later described in these
words:

> [Wilson] had undoubtedly the nimblest intelligence amongst the soldiers
> of high degree. He had also a lucidity of mind and therefore of expres-
> sion which was given to none of his professional rivals. It was a delight
> to hear him unravel and expound a military problem. For that reason
> he was specially helpful in a council of civilians. But he had no power
> of decision. That is why he failed in the field. For the same reason he
> was not a complete success in council. He shrank from the respon-
> sibility of the final word, even in advice.[29]

Meanwhile the days were slipping past, and the hour of truth was at
hand.

Chapter III: Notes

1. (p. 28) Lloyd George: *War Memoirs,* Odhams, 1936, Ch. LXXII.
2. (p. 28) Ibid., Ch. LXX.
3. (p. 29) Ibid. The full text of this speech is given in Appendix II to Ch. LXX.
4. (p. 29) *The Times,* 7 January 1918.
5. (p. 29) Lloyd George, op. cit., Ch. LXXII.
6. (p. 29) *The Times,* 16 January 1918.
7. (p. 30) Lloyd George, op. cit., Ch. LXXII.
8. (p. 30) Sir Auckland Geddes, Director-General of National Service.
9. (p. 31) Rapallo Conference communiqué, 7 November 1917.
10. (p. 33) In April 1917 alone U-boats sank 526,447 gross tons of British ship-
    ping, and there was a real fear that the country might be starved into submis-
    sion. The introduction of convoys reduced the danger, but it should be noted
    that the last three months of 1917 witnessed the sinking of no less than
    694,874 gross tons—still a very formidable figure.
11. (p. 34) French and German divisions in 1914 each consisted of four regi-
    ments of three battalions. To reduce from twelve battalions to nine, one
    merely removed a regiment. This was not possible in the British Army,
    which does not fight by regiments but by battalions, some of them lineal de-

scendants of older regiments (i.e. 1/Oxford and Bucks Light Infantry was the old 43rd, 2/Oxford and Bucks was the old 52nd, etc.). The selection of battalions for amalgamation or disbandment was therefore a complicated matter, with wide ramifications.

12. (p. 34) While General Sir Herbert Plumer was in Italy, commanding the British contingent there, the Second Army went into temporary suspension. It returned to the Order of Battle when Plumer came back to France, on 17 March; General Rawlinson then went to Versailles, and the Fourth Army temporarily disappeared, to return when Rawlinson succeeded Gough on 27 March. The Fifth Army then went into suspension, reappearing on 23 May under General Birdwood.

13. (p. 34) Lloyd George, op. cit., Ch. LXXII.

14. (p. 35) These included some 97,000 Chinese.

15. (p. 36) Sir Edward Spears: *Prelude to Victory,* Jonathan Cape, 1939, p. 36.

16. (p. 37) Stephen Roskill: *Hankey: Man of Secrets,* Collins, vol. i, pp. 445–47.

17. (p. 37) Brig.-Gen. John Charteris: *At G.H.Q.,* Cassell, 1931, p. 286.

18. (p. 37) Robertson to Haig, 9 October 1917; Robert Blake, *The Private Papers of Douglas Haig,* Eyre and Spottiswoode, 1952, p. 259.

19. (p. 37) Major-Gen. Sir C. E. Callwell: *Field-Marshal Sir Henry Wilson: His Life and Diaries,* Cassell, 1927, vol. ii, p. 48.

20. (p. 37) Blake, op. cit., p. 279.

21. (p. 38) Blake, op. cit., p. 282.

22. (p. 38) Lord Esher: *Journals and Letters,* Nicholson and Watson, 1938, iv, p. 179; 14 February 1918.

23. (p. 38) Col. Repington: *The First World War,* Constable, 1920, ii, p. 58.

24. (p. 39) For full text of Balfour's report to the War Cabinet, see Lloyd George, op. cit., Ch. LXXVI.

25. (p. 40) Callwell, op. cit., vol. ii, p. 58.

26. (p. 40) Ibid., p. 60.

27. (p. 41) Lord Hankey: *The Supreme Command 1914–1918,* Allen and Unwin, 1961, vol. ii, p. 797.

28. (p. 41) Lord Esher, *The Tragedy of Lord Kitchener,* John Murray, 1921, p. 129.

29. (p. 41) Lloyd George, op. cit., Ch. LXXVI.

IV

"GERMANY WILL BE RUINED"

"The German accession of morale is not of a permanent character and is not likely to stand the strain of an unsuccessful attack with consequently heavy losses. . . . If Germany attacks and fails she will be ruined." (British G.H.Q. Intelligence analysis, 7 January 1918)

At ten minutes past five on the morning of 21 March, General Sir Hubert Gough, commanding the British Fifth Army, was awakened by the roar of a bombardment "so sustained and steady that it at once gave me the impression of some crushing, smashing power. I jumped out of bed and walked across the passage to the telephone in my office and called up the General Staff. On what part of our front was the bombardment falling? The answer came back almost immediately: 'All four corps[1] report heavy bombardment along their front.'"[2]

The *Kaiserschlacht* had begun. With the ultimate issue of the war now being contested by a great, desperate modern nation, reinforced by the collapse of a once-powerful foe, only one thing could make this a short battle: the swift collapse of Germany's remaining enemies. Neither the British Army, on whom the first blow fell, nor its commanders, were prepared to oblige in that manner. If they did not collapse, not one blow but several would be needed; the battle, once again, would be long-drawn-out; victory would, as Haig believed, "belong to the side which holds out longest." What made this belief the more certain was the knowledge of the Allies that, slow though it might be, each day brought American entry into battle closer; the last reservoirs of manpower were on their side. Thus from beginning to end the *Kaiserschlacht* was a race against time.

The opening was spectacular—one of the great dramatic moments of the war; for the British Army a tragedy comparable to 1 July 1916.[3]

On the main front of attack, held by the British Fifth and Third Armies, and on three diversionary sectors, Flanders (British First Army), Champagne and Verdun (French), the bombardment opened with a single shattering crash. The 6,473 guns and howitzers on the main front were supported by no less than 3,532 trench mortars of all calibres. The effect was devastating; in many places the entire defending force in the "Forward" and "Battle" Zones was annihilated. The 41st Brigade (14th Division, Fifth Army) had one battalion, 8/King's Royal Rifle Corps, in the Forward Zone, 7/Rifle Brigade in the Battle Zone, and 8/Rifle Brigade in reserve. The regimental history of the Rifle Brigade laconically states: "About 4.40 a.m. the enemy bombardment opened. . . . From that moment nothing was heard of, or from, the Seventh Battalion."[4] The same fate befell the 8/K.R.R.C., so that immediately, before any infantry attack developed, the 41st Brigade lost two-thirds of its strength. Similar disasters were taking place all along the Fifth Army front: Forward Zone garrisons were wiped out, headquarters demolished, communications smashed, artillery positions rendered practically untenable by gas shell, forty-two miles of continuous catastrophe. The Third Army had the advantage of holding much stronger positions with stronger forces; nevertheless, it did not escape unscathed. In the sector of the 153rd Brigade (51st Highland Division), for example, "the troops occupying the Forward Zone had been mostly killed, buried by the bombardment, or taken prisoner; the few survivors were not capable of much resistance, and none returned to tell the tale."[5]

Five hours after the opening of this pulverizing bombardment, the German infantry came over in thick fog which extended all along the fronts of the Fifth and Third Armies. In the Fifth Army sector particularly, where the defenders were very thin on the ground, continuous trenches were virtually non-existent, and rear positions pious hopes rather than military realities, great store had been set by mutually supporting machine-gun posts. To be effective, however, these needed to communicate, and preferably to see each other; the bombardment cut out communication, the fog blotted out vision. The German tactic of infiltration succeeded in these circumstances beyond all the dreams of its devisers: British battalion headquarters found the enemy infantry upon them before they were even aware that the attack had begun; posts were surrounded; gunners became aware of close-by shadows in the murk on which they had to fire over open sights. The front crumbled like plaster; each probe loosened a little more for its neighbours; soon the Germans achieved the cherished aim of so many attacks during the war—they reached the gun-line. On 21 March the Fifth Army lost 383 guns; by midnight on the 22nd the Third Army had lost 150. The British line was breached; the Germans poured through. It was no longer a question of assault; it was pursuit.

Now, in this moment of triumph, a cardinal weakness of German tactics was revealed. An officer of the British heavy artillery in the Third Army sector described the scene as the British retreat continued in all its confusion, and the Germans tried to keep up their pressure:

> The roads were fairly full, and this time while it would be wrong to say there was a panic the retreat resembled more of a rout than had previously been the case. Everyone seemed anxious to get away as quickly as possible and regardless of anyone else. . . . A few military policemen dashed up and down on horseback trying to enforce some kind of order, but no one took much notice; had the Germans been able to break through with cavalry or armoured cars the war would have ended for most of us.[6]

But there was no cavalry; there were no armoured cars (see pp. 23–24). In confusion, in great weariness, the British still retreated, but as they did so the Germans were less and less able to harass them or even cause them very much further loss. And on the Somme, the Fifth Army area, the British did at least have one asset to play with: space. Here no objective of great strategic significance lay near the front; the great rail junction of Amiens was forty miles behind the front lines.

General Gough and his neighbour, General Byng, soon put in their Army reserves; Haig sent them what he could from other parts of the front and from G.H.Q. reserve. It all took time, time for plenty of deep anxiety, time for many more setbacks and moments of depression. The truth was that in its low state of manpower the British Army simply did not have any large reserves; Haig looked to his French colleague, Pétain, to supply the bulk of the means required to overcome the crisis. There was a mutual agreement that in such a case as this each ally would come to the help of the other, and Pétain had designated General Humbert to command an army for this very purpose. Gough naturally expected Humbert to bring his army forward as rapidly as possible; he was in for a rude awakening: "Humbert came in to see me, and when I said something to the effect that it was a desperate struggle and that I was glad to see him with his Army, he replied, 'Mais, je n'ai que mon fanion,' referring to the little pennant on his motor with the Army colours. This, however, was not exactly the aid that we were looking for at that moment."[7]

The truth was that Pétain, never an optimist even at the best of times, had allowed himself to be thoroughly misled by a skilful German deception ploy. Despite the scale of the attack on the British (fifty German divisions were identified by British Intelligence in action on the *first day* alone) Pétain believed that the main blow was about to fall on his own armies in Champagne. Accordingly, he was reluctant and slow to part with his precious reserves, and in the absence of an effective force behind the junction of the two allies a serious threat developed. The crises of the battlefield were grave enough; but the gravest crisis of all was now inside the mind of General Pétain.

It came to a head on the night of 24 March. Pétain, looking "very much upset, almost unbalanced and most anxious," came to Haig's Advanced Headquarters:

> . . . He told me that he had seen [General Fayolle][8] today at Mont-didier, where the French reserves are now collecting, and had directed him in the event of the German advance being pressed still further, to fall back south-westwards to Beauvais in order to cover Paris. It was at once clear to me that the effect of this order must be to separate the French from the British right flank, and so allow the enemy to penetrate between the two armies. I at once asked Pétain if he meant to abandon my right flank. He nodded assent, and added, "It is the only thing possible, if the enemy compel the Allies to fall back still further."[9]

Haig was appalled; it suddenly became clear to him that his French colleague was mentally accepting a defeat more disastrous than anything threatened by the darkest days of 1914. He continues:

> From my talk with Pétain I gathered that he had recently attended a Cabinet meeting in Paris and that his orders from his Government are *"to cover Paris at all costs"* [Haig's italics]. On the other hand to keep touch with the British Army is no longer the basic principle of French strategy. In my opinion, our Army's existence in France depends on keeping the British and French Armies united. So I hurried back to my headquarters at Beaurepaire Château to report the serious change in French strategy to the C.I.G.S. and Secretary of State for War, and ask them to come to France.

By the time Haig was back at his main headquarters at Montreuil it was 3 A.M. in the morning of 25 March; by that time his mind had clarified even further. The message to Wilson which he now told his Chief of Staff to draft went considerably further than a simple request to come over to France at once with the Secretary of State. In any case, as he now realized, it was not Lord Derby whom he needed to meet but Lord Milner, Minister without Portfolio, who was in effect the British Minister at Versailles. He was quite clear as to what the purpose of their visit should be: "to arrange that General Foch or some other determined general, who would fight, should be given supreme control of the operations in France. I knew Foch's strategical ideas were in conformity with the orders given me by Lord Kitchener when I became Commander-in-Chief, and that he was a man of great courage and decision as shown during the fighting at Ypres in October and November 1914."[10]

What Haig did not know was that Milner was already in France. The twenty-fifth of March was a day of confusion, as attempts were made to locate the key figures on whom would fall the responsibility of re-shaping the destiny of the Allies. On 26 March they met at Doullens: on the French side, President Poincaré, M. Clemenceau, Pétain, Foch and the French Military Representative at Versailles, Weygand; on the British side, Lord Milner, Wilson, Haig, Lawrence and Major-General A. A. Montgomery, representing General Rawlinson, the British Military Representative at Versailles.

It was an historic occasion. On a cue quickly supplied by Haig, Milner and Clemenceau drafted an agreement entrusting to Foch "the co-ordination of the action of the British and French Armies in front of Amiens." Haig commented: "This proposal seemed to me quite worthless, as Foch would be in a subordinate position to Pétain and myself. In my opinion it was essential to success that Foch should *co-ordinate the action of all the allied armies on the western front* [Haig's italics]. Both Governments agreed to this."[11] Thus there came about at last the formal unity of command which had eluded the Allies throughout the war. Created by the stress of battle, it took the only form that battle conditions would permit—command over all armies by one man belonging to the nation which possessed the reserves. So Foch became what another war would call Supreme Allied Commander. The title of Commander-in-Chief actually followed later, and brought with it the rank of Marshal of France; what mattered on 26 March was the actuality, the single will which would now grip Allied operations. As the meeting broke up, Clemenceau drily remarked to Foch: "Well, you've got the job you so much wanted." Foch replied: "A fine gift! You give me a lost battle and tell me to win it!"

He was wrong in two respects: the battle was not lost, and it was not his personal direction that changed its course. His contribution was his authority and his frame of mind—an attitude which would not even contemplate a "Pétain solution." In practical terms, all that Foch could do immediately was to order the concentration of powerful French reserves in the Amiens area, but long before these could intervene decisively the battle had faded out. Already, on 26 March at Doullens, Byng had told Haig: "In the south near the Somme the enemy is very tired. . . . Friend and foe are, it seems, dead beat and seem to stagger up against each other."[12] Two days later the Germans delivered a powerful blow on the front of the Third Army; it was a complete failure, repelled with crushing loss. This was partly due to poor tactics, partly to well-handled British defence with strong air support; it was also partly due to certain ominous symptoms which were becoming visible in the German Army. On that day Captain Rudolf Binding wrote:

> Today the advance of our infantry suddenly stopped near Albert. Nobody could understand why. Our airmen had reported no enemy between Albert and Amiens. The enemy's guns were only firing now and again on the very edge of affairs. Our way seemed entirely clear. I jumped into a car with orders to find out what was causing the stoppage in front. . . . I . . . took a sharp turn with the car into Albert.
>
> As soon as I got near the town I began to see curious sights. Strange figures, who looked very little like soldiers, and certainly showed no signs of advancing, were making their way back. . . . There were men driving cows before them on a line; others who carried a hen under one arm and a box of note-paper under the other. Men carrying a bottle of wine under their arm and another one open in their hand. Men who had torn a silk drawing-room curtain off its rod and were dragging it to the rear as a useful bit of loot. Men with writing paper and coloured notebooks. Evidently they had found it desirable to sack a stationer's shop. Men dressed up in comic disguise. Men with top hats on their heads. Men staggering. Men who could hardly walk. . . .
>
> When I got into the town the streets were running with wine. Out of a cellar came a lieutenant of the Second Marine Division, helpless and in despair. I asked him, "What is going to happen?" It was essential for them to get forward immediately. He replied, solemnly and emphatically, "I cannot get my men out of this cellar without bloodshed." When I insisted . . . he invited me to try my hand, but it was no business of mine, and I saw, too, that I could have done no more than he. I drove back to Divisional H.Q. with a fearful impression of the situation.[13]

Everywhere the story was the same. On the Fifth Army front—now, with the removal of Gough in undeserved disgrace and his replacement by Rawlinson, renamed the Fourth Army—the Germans were stopped at last just nine miles short of Amiens. Field-Marshal von Hindenburg sadly wrote:

> Our advance became slower and slower. The hopes and wishes which had soared beyond Amiens had to be recalled. Facts must be treated as facts. . . . We ought to have shouted in the ear of every single man: "Press on to Amiens. Put in your last ounce. Perhaps Amiens means

decisive victory. Capture Villiers-Bretonneux whatever happens, so that from its heights we can command Amiens with masses of our heavy artillery!" It was in vain; our strength was exhausted.[14]

On 5 April, after sixteen days of ferocious and critical battle, the "March Offensive" ended. Ludendorff concluded: "The enemy's resistance was beyond our powers. . . . O.H.L.[15] was forced to take the extremely hard decision to abandon the attack on Amiens for good."[16]

The German achievement fell far short of the intentions of those who had planned this mighty stroke with such meticulous skill; nevertheless, it was substantial. A vast bulge had been driven into the Allied line; ground bought by the Allies at a fearful cost in 1916 was now lost again; immense quantities of munitions had been destroyed or captured;[17] nearly 250,000 casualties had been inflicted. The majority of these were sustained by the British Army: a total of 178,000, of whom over 70,000 were prisoners. The French had lost 77,000, which indicates that they must have been doing something, though this was not always apparent to their hard-pressed allies. Such a rate of loss is staggering, and if one adds to it the German casualties (about the same as the Allies') it is easy to see why this event towers above all that had preceded it since the very blackest moments in the early days of the war, in 1914. It represents a human wastage of 31,000 men a day. All that can be said in mitigation is that, by the very nature of this style of warfare, because for much of the time it consisted of the forward movement of a victorious mass, many of the men represented in these dreadful figures were, in fact, taken prisoner, and so survived. But many did not.

Germany had attacked, and she had failed; yet it could not be said that this great military empire was ruined—she was still a long way from that. Whatever satisfaction Foch, in his new exalted station, or British G.H.Q. might have derived from the successful—if horrifyingly costly—outcome of this battle was very soon obliterated by a new German blow, in Flanders. This was where Ludendorff would have preferred to launch his first attack, in all its pride of strength. Only a fear that ground conditions might be unsuitable in March had prevented that, but preparations were already advanced for what had always been envisaged as a supporting attack, and now became an alternative offensive. The blow fell on 9 April, on a narrow front between Armentières and Bethune east of the River Lys, from which the battle takes its name. Once again the Germans employed a massive weight of artillery; once again they were helped by a heavy mist. Other factors also assisted them: one part of the defence system was held by a weak Portuguese corps, in a low state of morale, which broke at once. Many of the British divisions holding the fronts of the First and Second Armies in Flanders were tired and reduced after their exertions in Picardy. And ironically, when the German assault was delivered, it found the going good on ground unusually firm because of the dry spring.

The features of the Battle of the Lys were, first, its steady extension northwards after the break-in on the Portuguese sector at Laventie, until it became, in effect, a fourth Battle of Ypres, with General Plumer controlling the British effort as he had done in the Third Battle ("Passchendaele") the year before; and, secondly, the astonishing powers of resistance displayed by the decimated British units. On the first day the Germans made a penetration of about three and a half miles; during the entire remainder of the month the best they could do was to gain another seven to eight miles, which nevertheless brought them within five miles of the vital rail junction at Hazebrouck, itself only some twenty-two miles from the sea, at Dunkirk. But this was their limit; they could advance no further.

For the men whose task it was to stop them, it was a murderous experience; for their commanders, a period of intense strain. For Haig this was for a long time unalleviated by any useful contribution from Foch. The Allied Commander-in-Chief flatly refused to relieve British divisions in the midst of battle; such a policy, in his view, could lead only to the erosion of reserves. It was a hard doctrine for the front-line infantryman and his supporting gunners. By 11 April the fighting was so grim, the outlook so bleak, that even the normally taciturn Haig felt impelled to make a special appeal to his soldiers. He told them: "There is no other course open to us but to fight it out! Every position must be held to the last man: there must be no retirement. With our backs to the wall, and believing in the justice of our cause, each one of us must fight on to the end. The safety of our homes and the freedom of mankind alike depend on the conduct of each one of us at this critical moment."

On 15 April Foch gave it to Haig as his firm opinion that the Battle of Flanders was *"finie";* in fact it still had fifteen difficult days to run, a period of hardship and danger to the Allied cause. Performances varied: the well-rested and up-to-strength Belgian Army had a good day north of Ypres on 17 April; the French, now at last arriving in force, had a bad day on 25 April, when they lost the pivotal position of Mount Kemmel. The German *Alpine Corps* had a large hand in this achievement—but the same unit had failed against the British on 14 April. The British themselves, their ranks re-filled with young conscripts, some of them only eighteen and a half years old and barely trained, also had their good and bad days—yet an officer of the *Alpine Corps,* which had fought in Serbia, at Verdun, in Rumania and in

Italy, told a British officer after the war: "I think I may say that the defenders on the British front in April 1918 were the best troops of the many with whom we crossed swords in the course of the four and a quarter years."[18] Good and not so good, lucky and unlucky, by 29 April their work was done. The German armies on the Flanders front "had exhausted their powers of attack."[19] General von Kuhl, Chief of Staff to the Army Group Commander, Crown Prince Rupprecht of Bavaria, summed up:

> The storming of Kemmel was a great feat, but, on the whole, the objective set had not been attained. The attack had not penetrated to the decisive heights of Cassel and Mont des Cats, the possession of which would have compelled the evacuation of the Ypres Salient and the Yser position. No great strategic movement had become possible; the Channel ports had not been reached. Our troops on the left flank in the conquered trenches were in a very unfavourable situation, as they were strongly enfiladed by the enemy. . . . The second great offensive had not brought about the hoped-for decision.[20]

So ended the Battle of the Lys. The cost, though less than half that of the slightly shorter "March Offensive" in Picardy, was heavy nevertheless: 76,300 British and 35,000 French casualties. The two offensives together had thus cost the Allies 351,793 men, while the German combined figure is 348,300. These are staggering totals; they mean that in forty days over 700,000 Europeans had become battle casualties.[21] Small wonder if men were everywhere looking over their shoulders for the arrival of the Americans; small wonder if some of them expressed themselves with bitterness:

> When is it reasonable to think that the Americans will be able to put in that immense army of three millions, fully equipped, each man, with a hair mattress, a hot-water bottle, a gramophone, and a medicine chest, which they tell us will get to Berlin and "cook the goose" of the Kaiser? When? If it came next year it might produce the desired military results. But is there the slightest reason to imagine that it will come next year, or the year after, or even the year after that?[22]

Were the Germans, then, winning the race against time? Superficially, it looked as though they might be; on 1 May the total strength of the American Expeditionary Force in France was 23,548 officers and 406,111 enlisted men, formed into seven divisions,[23] and parts of two more, of which only one was in the line. By the end of the month the manpower had swollen to over 650,000, and the number of divisions (according to whose table you read) to sixteen, seventeen or eighteen. But the A.E.F. remained to all intents a paper army. By agreement between General Pershing and Lord Milner, the new American divisions were bringing over only their infantry, machine-gunners, engineers and signal units. Artillery and transport would be provided by the British and French. Accordingly, the reinforcements grew from 64,200 in March and 93,128 in April to 206,287 in May, of whom 176,602 were combatants, 140,024 being infantry. It was thus a collection of some complete, some completing and some deliberately incomplete divisions that Pershing commanded. And his determination not to allow them to be committed to battle in this condition was absolute. His instructions,[24] after all, were perfectly clear:

> In military operations against the Imperial German Government you are directed to co-operate with the forces of the other countries employed against that enemy; but in so doing the underlying idea must be kept in view that the forces of the United States are a separate and distinct component of the combined forces, the identity of which must be preserved. This fundamental rule is subject to such minor exceptions in particular circumstances as your judgment may approve. The action is confided to you and you will exercise full discretion in determining the manner of co-operation.

Fortified by this instruction (and by the historical antecedent of the French themselves when fighting beside the Americans on an earlier occasion[25]), Pershing resisted all requests to disperse his keen, vigorous young soldiers among allies who appeared to them tired, jaded, disillusioned and sometimes cynical, for any other reason than training. And he was freshly fortified in this determination by the resolution of the Fifth Supreme War Council on 2 May: "It is the opinion of the Supreme War Council that, in order to carry the War to a successful conclusion, an American Army should be formed as early as possible under its own commander and under its own flag." How consciously did the assembled statesmen and soldiers of the Allies reflect that the main thing was to get the Americans to France, and let the war itself dictate (as it was bound to do) how they should be deployed? Pershing was a stubborn man, battling for a sound principle—a formidable combination; yet not even he would be able to stand by and see his allies smashed to pieces—the risk to his own army would be too great. So it would be the war that decided the issue, and meanwhile this accelerated flow of Americans across the Atlantic (56 per cent of them in British shipping) was a portent which, Ludendorff admits, took him by surprise.

Germany's heavy casualties had made deep inroads into her accre-

Men of destiny. *Above left:* M. Georges Clemenceau (centre), 'unquestionably the most formidable man in France', with Field-Marshal Sir Douglas Haig in 1918. Clemenceau and Haig were friends from their first meeting; as Haig said, 'friends are discovered, not made'. *Above right:* Mr Lloyd George speaking in Dundee; his rhetorical skill was a powerful factor in 'the rallying of the nation in difficult times'. *Below left:* President Woodrow Wilson in France in 1919; at the World Peace Conference, as in 1918, he fatally displayed 'the arrogance of the high-minded man'. *Below right:* Marshal Ferdinand Foch, Allied Supreme Commander; 'his method was inspirational, not administrative'. At the head of his very small staff was General Maxime Weygand (left), who gave precision to Foch's laconic directives

Lieutenant-General Sir Arthur Currie, commanding the Canadian Army Corps (left), greets General John J. Pershing, Commander-in-Chief of the American Expeditionary Force; 'Pershing was a man obsessed' with the idea of 'a distinct American Army'

Allies. American troops (background, left) in training with the British (including some very young soldiers), May 1918. Pershing was glad of such facilities, but always suspicious of 'the disposition of the British to assume control of our units'

The Second Battle of the Marne, July-
August 1918: 'French tanks added to the
demoralization of the German infantry'.
These are the light Renault models,
weighing only 7 tons, with a crew of two,
but armed only with a single machine gun,
and very vulnerable

General Charles Mangin; 'always of
sanguine temperament', it was Mangin's
Tenth Army which spear-headed the
French advances from July to October

'The first American attack of the war': the
28th Regiment, US 1st Division, advancing
to capture the village of Cantigny, 28 May

10218

'The pendulum-swing of national fortune'. *Above:* French prisoners captured on the Aisne in June. *Below:* Some of the 18,500 German prisoners taken in the Battle of Amiens, 8-12 August, passing others already collected (right) and interested Australians. Harvesting still continues in the fields

tion of strength earlier in the year. This was something which he noted
with dismay. But there was something else, even more worrying:

> Our troops had fought well; but the fact that certain divisions had obvi-
> ously failed to show any inclination to attack in the plain of the Lys
> gave food for thought . . . the way in which the troops stopped round
> captured food supplies, while individuals stayed behind to search houses
> and farms for food, was a serious matter. This impaired our chances of
> success and showed poor discipline. But it was equally serious that both
> our young company commanders and our senior officers did not feel
> strong enough to take disciplinary action, and exercise enough authority
> to enable them to lead their men forward without delay. The absence of
> our old peace-trained corps of officers was most severely felt. They had
> been the repository of the moral strength of the Army.[26]

All the writing on the wall spelt bad news for Germany.

What was to be done? Both Ludendorff and his Army Group Commander in the north, Crown Prince Rupprecht, remained convinced
that Flanders was the key area, where success lay readier to hand than
on any other part of the Western Front. Readier to hand—more
difficult to grasp; because Foch had at last gripped the danger in the
north, and re-deployed his reserves accordingly. A chart at British
G.H.Q. showed that on 1 May there were fourteen French infantry divisions and three of cavalry on the British front, a figure which rose to
sixteen infantry on 8 May and still stood at thirteen on 26 May, despite the lull in the fighting. More French reserves were positioned
behind their own left flank, available for a quick move northwards if
necessary. Before anything effective could be done again in Flanders it
was essential to pull these French divisions to the south, and prevent
them from lending this powerful support to their allies. Ludendorff accepted that his next move would have to be an attack on the French.
The location selected was Champagne, the Chemin des Dames Ridge
of evil memory.

> To battered, battle-weary troops, whose only knowledge of France was
> based upon their experience of the Northern front, the Champagne
> country in the full glory of spring was a revelation. Gone was the de-
> pressing monotony of Flanders, drab and weeping, with its muds, its
> mists, its pollards, and its pavé; gone the battle-wrecked landscapes of
> Picardy and the Somme, with their shattered villages and blasted
> woods. Here all was peace. The countryside basked contentedly in the
> blazing sunshine. Trim villages nestled in quiet hollows beside lazy
> streams, and tired eyes were refreshed by the sight of rolling hills, clad
> with great woods golden with laburnum blossom; by the soft greenery

of lush meadowland, shrubby vineyards and fields of growing corn. Right up to within two miles of the line civilians were living, going about their business of husbandry with characteristic unconcern.[27]

By one of the war's most sickening ironies, the new German blow fell upon four worn-out British divisions which had been sent to a "quiet sector" of the French front in order to rest and recuperate, and in part exchange for the French divisions on the British front. The writer of the idyllic passage quoted above was Captain Sidney Rogerson, 2/West Yorkshire Regiment; he belonged to the 8th Division, which had already been heavily engaged twice. In the "March Offensive" it had lost 250 officers and 4,693 other ranks; in April at Villers Bretonneux, where the Germans had made one last unsuccessful lunge at Amiens with the help of a few tanks, the 8th Division had lost another 133 officers and 3,420 other ranks in four days. Now, once more, it found itself in the cauldron of battle.

There was virtually no warning; Rogerson, at 23rd Brigade Headquarters, was shown a pink telephone slip that had just come in at 3:45 P.M. on 26 May:

> "The enemy will attack on a wide front at 01.00 hours tomorrow, 27th inst."—then followed orders for taking up battle stations.
> For a second we looked at each other in silence. In a flash the whole world had changed. The landscape around us smiled no longer. It was all a grinning reality, a mockery designed to raise our hopes so that they could be shattered the more pitilessly. The sun still blazed down but it had lost its heat. . . . For the third time we were to bear the brunt of an enemy offensive. Surely we who had suffered so much already might have been spared this! It was too much to hope that those of us who had come through so far would again escape. The mercy was that we had little time to indulge in self-pity.[28]

Foch, on his lofty pinnacle, Pétain, the normally hard-headed French Commander-in-Chief, General Franchet d'Espérey, commanding the French Northern Army Group, and General Duchêne, commanding their Sixth Army, were all alike taken by surprise. General Sir Alexander Hamilton Gordon, whose IX Corps contained the ill-fated British divisions, had become apprehensive of German intentions by 22 May, and protested against the French defensive system which crowded men and guns into the cramped space north of the River Aisne, an obvious trap. His protests were brushed aside by Duchêne with a rudeness that invited retribution. It came, with devastating certainty, on 27 May—but it was Hamilton Gordon's soldiers who bore the brunt of it.

The German bombardment, by some 4,000 guns and many mortars, "orchestrated" once more by Colonel Bruchmüller, was of extreme violence and accuracy; the British and French forward positions were obliterated by howitzer and mortar fire, the defending artillery overwhelmed by high-explosive liberally laced with gas. At 3:40 A.M. seventeen German divisions moved forward to storm the Chemin des Dames Ridge. In a matter of minutes the astounding message was received at 23rd Brigade H.Q.: "Can see enemy balloons rising from our front line." Major-General von Unruh, Chief of Staff of the German *4th Reserve Corps,* wrote:

> Against the onslaught of three German divisions, which were quickly followed by two others, it was humanly impossible for the extended and surprised English troops to stand up, and to all inquiries which came through from Army Headquarters and the Crown Prince,[29] we could truthfully answer, "Attack is being carried out according to plan."
> Our losses were remarkably small. The enemy had no time to resist. The English, who could usually be relied upon to hold out in shell-holes, firing to their last cartridge, were given no opportunity by the violence and activity of our combined artillery and trench-mortar fire to display their customary coolness. They were up against "force majeure," and, first blown out of their trenches and then surrounded, sentry-posts, Lewis-gun teams, and whole platoons saw that resistance was hopeless and were reluctantly obliged to surrender. Everywhere one could see groups stumbling down from the high ground to be taken prisoner by our waiting troops.[30]

Similar misfortunes befell the French on the left of the British IX Corps; by the end of the day their 21st and 22nd Divisions had ceased to exist as organized bodies. The breakthrough was complete on a 25-mile front; the Aisne bridges in rear had not been destroyed, so that by evening the Germans had crossed the river, swept over the next ridge, and reached the River Vesle. "This was roughly an advance of ten miles. No such day's work had been done in France since trench warfare began."[31] By 30 May the Germans claimed 50,000 prisoners and about 800 captured guns. Sidney Rogerson wrote:

> It was a crowning mercy that they had no cavalry. How many times during the retreat did we thank Heaven for this! The sight of a few mounted men in the distance would at once start a ripple of anxiety, the word "Cavalry!" being whispered and passed from mouth to mouth down the firing line. Men looked apprehensively over their shoulders, fearful lest horsemen might be already behind them. Cavalry was the one factor which would have smashed the morale of the defence in a twinkling.[32]

By 3 June the Germans stood once more on the banks of the River Marne, as they had done in 1914, near Château Thierry, only fifty-six miles from Paris. The most spectacular—and most equivocal—victory of the war had been won. The cost to the Allies had been severe indeed: to the British, 28,703 officers and men (the unfortunate 8th Division alone lost 7,862), to the French, 98,160. For the latter the moral shock was at least as bad as the casualties. The Chemin des Dames, scene of fierce and tragic action in 1917, was "holy ground" for France; to lose it so quickly after such earlier sacrifices seemed appalling. The reputations of many French commanders were badly dented: Foch's prestige as Commander-in-Chief was scarcely enhanced, and soon it was perceptible that Haig, hitherto under a cloud because of the showy German successes against him in March and April, now gained stature and began to exercise increasing influence on Foch's plans. Pétain was in semi-disgrace; General Guillaumat was recalled from Salonika to replace him, and though this extreme step was not in fact taken, Pétain and the French Army were now placed directly under Foch. Franchet d'Espérey was removed and sent to Salonika, though his resilient energy soon turned his "punishment" into an opportunity for fame. General Duchêne, and some of his corps commanders, were dismissed. New men came in, with new ideas: the brave and skilful Gouraud, and the fiery Charles Mangin, returning from the disgrace he had shared with Nivelle a year before.

These changes were good auguries for the Allies, but there were better ones. On 28 May, when the Battle of the Aisne was at its most critical, away on the Somme a portent was seen: the 28th Regiment of the U.S. 1st Division captured the village of Cantigny, advancing its front about a mile. This was the first American attack in the war. On 1 June the U.S. 2nd Division took up a second-line position to support the defence of Château Thierry, and on the 3rd a machine-gun battalion of the 3rd Division went into action there.[38] On 6 June the 2nd Division counter-attacked at Belleau Wood, beginning a grim American acquaintance with that locality. These were all small affairs, but they had a great significance: the United States Army was in the fight at last. And behind these leading units the Allies had now agreed to concentrate all available shipping resources on bringing over 250,000 more Americans in June and the same number in July. The Germans had lost their race against time.

When the Aisne battle ended on 6 June, Ludendorff once more found himself in a dilemma. For all its flourish, as von Unruh says, "in truth the brilliant offensive had petered out." And it had petered out in an awkward fashion, with the Germans now in a pocket whose "mouth," between Pontoise and Reims, was broad enough (about forty

miles) but which then tapered to a front of only about ten miles at
Château Thierry, thus making it difficult both to supply and to defend. Yet Ludendorff, who never lost sight of his real goal, was not
displeased. "The chances," he tells us, "for a successful execution of an
attack in Flanders against the English, planned as the principal issue of
the whole undertaking, had been essentially enhanced."[34] To the extent
that British troops had been engaged on the French front, and some
French reserves withdrawn from the British front, this was possibly so.
But this southward shift of Allied strength needed to develop further,
and a better defensive line in Champagne had to be established for the
day when O.H.L. transferred the main battle back to Flanders. Another attack was needed to broaden the front. This necessity had been
foreseen, and preparations were already well advanced. It would be
conducted by the *Eighteenth Army* under General von Hutier, who
had shown his offensive skill at Riga in 1917 and in Picardy on 21
March; it would be called the Battle of the Matz.

The German bombardment opened at midnight on 8 June. This time
the French were not taken by surprise—in fact their counterprepara-
tion fire had started ten minutes earlier. Nevertheless the Germans
made good progress on 9 June: an advance of six miles and 8,000 prisoners. The chief reason for this was that, despite wise admonitions by
the Army Group Commander, General Fayolle, most French commanders persisted in crowding men into their forward positions; even
with so many dire examples before them, they found defence in depth
a difficult lesson to learn. However, there was no rout, and though the
Germans gained more ground on 10 June they won no strategic objective and the pace of their advance slowed significantly. On that day
Foch was at Fayolle's headquarters; they had decided to form the latter's reserves into a Tenth Army under General Mangin. They summoned Mangin to join them; meanwhile Foch said to Fayolle: "Mangin *must* attack tomorrow."

Fayolle replied: "That's absolutely impossible in less than two
days!"

Foch then said: "Well, you'll see."

At that moment Mangin arrived. Without any preamble Foch shot at
him the question: "Are you going to attack?"

"Yes, mon général."

"Tomorrow?"

"Yes, mon général."

"Tomorrow morning?"

"I can't fix the exact hour of the attack yet. But I shall be seeing my
five divisional commanders at Pronleroy at 6 o'clock and at 7 o'clock
they'll be off again with some fire up their backsides."

Mangin says: "My two questioners burst into a laugh which surprised me a bit."[35]

Nevertheless, his attack did go in on 11 June, at 11:30 A.M., supported by low-flying aircraft and 144 tanks. It gained some ground, and captured more than a thousand prisoners; on the 12th it made little further progress, and on the 13th the battle ended. Its moral value, however, was out of all proportion to statistical reckonings. Mangin had told his soldiers as they prepared for the attack: "Tomorrow's operation should be the end of the defensive battle which we have been fighting for more than two months. It should mark the definite check of the Germans and the renewal of the offensive on our part."

Always of sanguine temperament, Mangin was being a little over-optimistic now; there were strains and perils yet to come, and more weeks of anxiety for the Allied High Command. But he had struck a new note. It would be heard again.

Chapter IV: Notes

1. (p. 43) From right to left, III (Butler), XVIII (Maxse), XIX (Watts), VII (Congreve); in the Third Army, on the left, three of the Army's four corps were affected: V (Fanshawe), IV (Harper), VI (Haldane).
2. (p. 43) Gen. Sir Hubert Gough: *The Fifth Army*, Hodder and Stoughton, 1931, p. 260. Most accounts say that the German bombardment opened at 4:40 A.M., or thereabouts; General Gough must therefore have been a heavy sleeper, or is mistaken.
3. (p. 43) The opening day of the First Battle of the Somme, on which the British Army sustained over 57,000 casualties.
4. (p. 44) W. W. Seymour: *The History of the Rifle Brigade in the War of 1914–1918*, Rifle Brigade Club, 1936, vol. ii, p. 232.
5. (p. 44) Official History, *1918*, i, p. 221.
6. (p. 45) Arthur Behrend: *As from Kemmel Hill*, Eyre and Spottiswoode, 1963, p. 91.
7. (p. 45) Gough, op. cit., p. 266.
8. (p. 46) Commanding the Groupe d'armées de réserve (G.A.R.).
9. (p. 46) See Robert Blake: *The Private Papers of Douglas Haig*, Eyre and Spottiswoode, 1952, pp. 296–97.
10. (p. 47) Blake, op. cit., p. 297.
11. (p. 47) Blake, op. cit., p. 298.
12. (p. 48) Duff Cooper: *Haig*, Faber, 1935, vol. ii, p. 256.
13. (p. 48) Rudolf Binding: *A Fatalist at War*, Allen and Unwin, 1929, pp. 209–10.
14. (p. 49) Hindenburg: *Out of My Life*, Cassell, 1920, p. 350.
15. (p. 49) Oberste Heersleitung: German G.H.Q.
16. (p. 49) Ludendorff: *War Memories*, Hutchinson, 1919, ii, p. 600.
17. (p. 49) The British lost about 1,000 guns. When Mr. (later Lord) Balfour was informed of this he remarked: "Oh, really? What a bore."
18. (p. 51) Official History, *1918*, ii, p. 304.
19. (p. 51) *Der Deutsche Landkrieg*, ed. Lieut.-Gen. M. Schwarte, quoted in the Official History, *1918*, ii, p. 454.
20. (p. 51) Ibid.

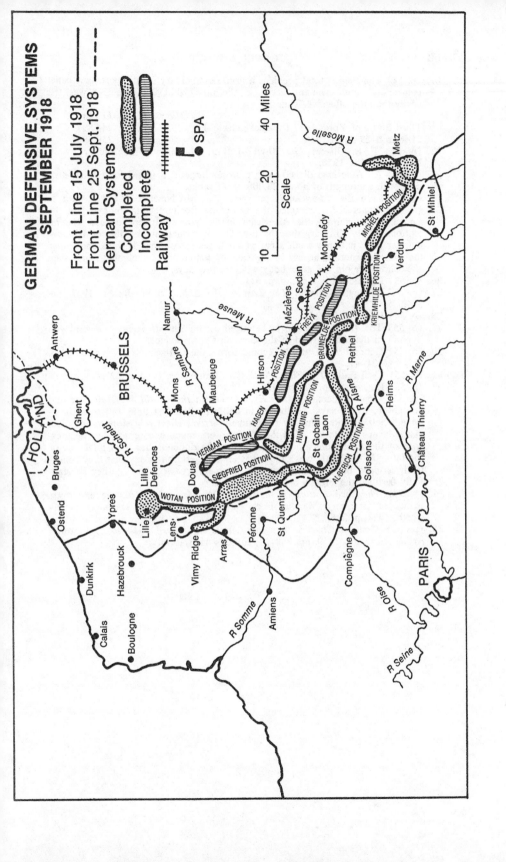

**GERMAN DEFENSIVE SYSTEMS
SEPTEMBER 1918**

Front Line 15 July 1918
Front Line 25 Sept. 1918
German Systems
Completed
Incomplete
Railway

SPA

Scale

10   0   20   40 Miles

HOLLAND

Ostend
Bruges
Antwerp
Ghent

BRUSSELS

R. Scheldt

Calais
Dunkirk
Boulogne
Hazebrouck
Ypres
Lens
Lille
Lille Defences
Douai
Mons
Namur
R Sambre
Maubeuge
Hirson
Mézières
Sedan
Montmédy
Metz

WOTAN POSITION
SIEGFRIED POSITION
HERMAN POSITION
HAGEN POSITION
HUNDUNG POSITION
FREYA POSITION
BRUNEHILDE POSITION
MICHEL POSITION

Vimy Ridge
Arras
Péronne
St Quentin
St Gobain
Laon
Soissons
Rethel
Reims

ALBERICH POSITION
KRIEMHILDE POSITION

R Meuse
R Aisne
R Marne

Amiens
R Somme
Compiègne
R Oise
Château Thierry

PARIS

R Seine

Verdun
St Mihiel
R Moselle

21. (p. 51) The British total provides a grim commentary on the persistent belief (especially in government circles at the time) that the defensive was less costly than the offensive. Thus:

	Days	Losses
Third Battle of Ypres 1917 ("Passchendaele")	105	244,897
21 March–29 April 1918	40	239,793

22. (p. 51) F. S. Oliver: *The Anvil of War*, Macmillan, 1936, letter to his brother, 2 May 1918.
23. (p. 51) An American division was twice as large as a British or French division, with a strength of about 28,000 of all ranks.
24. (p. 52) From the American Secretary of War, Mr. Newton D. Baker; para. 5.
25. (p. 52) Louis XVI instructed the Count de Rochambeau, commanding the French forces helping the Americans in the War of Independence: "the intentions of the King are that the French troops shall not be dispersed in any manner and that they shall serve at all times as a corps d'armée and under the French generals, except in the case of temporary detachments, and then they should rejoin the main body within a few days."
26. (p. 53) Ludendorff, op. cit., ii, p. 611.
27. (p. 54) Sidney Rogerson: *The Last of the Ebb*, Arthur Barker, 1937, pp. 3–4.
28. (p. 54) Ibid., pp. 24–25.
29. (p. 55) The *4th Reserve Corps* belonged to the *Seventh Army* (General von Boehn) in the army group of the German Crown Prince.
30. (p. 55) General von Unruh's account forms the end section of Rogerson, op. cit., pp. 121–47.
31. (p. 55) Cyril Falls: *The First World War*, Longmans, 1960, p. 327.
32. (p. 55) Rogerson, op. cit., p. 112.
33. (p. 56) General Pershing (*My Experiences in the World War*, Hodder and Stoughton, 1931) says: "Although in battle for the first time, our men maintained their positions and by their timely arrival effectively stopped the German advance on Paris." That the French were much encouraged by the presence of the Americans among them cannot be doubted, but the actual role of the latter in the battle was small; it is an exaggeration to say that they "effectively stopped the German advance" but quite true to say that they substantially fortified the French defence.
34. (p. 57) *The Two Battles of the Marne* by Marshal Joffre, the ex-Crown Prince of Germany, Marshal Foch and Gen. Ludendorff; Thornton Butterworth, 1927; p. 236.
35. (p. 58) General Charles Mangin: *Lettres de guerre 1914–1918*, Librairie Arthème Fayard, 1950, pp. 268–69; author's translation.

V

"A PRETTY RIVER, THE MARNE!"

(Remark of Marshal Joffre)

For a month there was a lull on the Western Front—the last lull of the war. It was a time for stock-taking, for coming to a reckoning of profit and loss in this spring of 1918, and working out the chances for the summer. For the British Army there were special problems—the legacy of that fatal lack of understanding between soldiers and statesmen which we have already observed.[1] Manpower was the haunting theme: lack of manpower had hindered the Army's attempts to construct defences at the beginning of the year; lack of manpower had weakened the defence in March and April; lack of manpower, after the loss of nearly a quarter of a million killed, wounded, or taken prisoner in battle, now gravely affected recovery. By May, out of fifty British (United Kingdom) divisions on the Western Front, ten were considered to be "exhausted," and eight of these had to be "reduced to cadre."[2] All this was *before* the attacks on the French, and the further British casualties incurred in these. By the end of the month these fresh losses, and the Government's continuing failure to meet the Army's evident needs, produced a situation which was potentially very grave indeed. Foch set it down in detail in a formal memorandum for the Supreme War Council, in which he said: ". . . at the moment of a decisive effort on the part of the enemy, the strength of the British Army is decreasing day by day. It even decreases more rapidly than that of the American Army increases. . . . The result is a decrease in the total strength of the Allies. This consequence is exceptionally grave: it may mean the loss of the war."

An Anglo-French meeting on 1 June was marked by a vigorous argument, lasting over two hours, between Foch and Lloyd George on the subject of British manpower. Despite all Lloyd George's protestations, Foch raised the spectre of the B.E.F. being reduced to no more than thirty divisions if the present rate of reinforcement continued. He put the blunt question to Lloyd George: "What number of divisions will the British Government maintain?" Haig intervened at this point to remind Lord Milner (now Secretary of State for War) that the War Office had at one stage warned him that it might be no more than twenty-eight. Milner said he thought this was pessimistic. But both British ministers were clearly shaken—so shaken that they agreed to allow an officer from Foch's staff to examine the British manpower figures. Whether it was at the prompting of this officer, or due to a stirring of conscience, or fear, or some other motive, the British reinforcement programme improved markedly from this point onwards, permitting all but one of the cadre divisions to be reconstituted, and others to be brought up to strength. Even so, as Foch says, "from the middle of April to the middle of July, the situation of the British Army remained extremely precarious."[3]

Heavy casualties, great strain, great fatigue, thin ranks as reminders of lost comrades, units broken up and dispersed—all the ingredients of low morale seemed to be present in the B.E.F. In April, May and June G.H.Q. paid close attention to the Army's morale, as revealed in the letters the soldiers were writing home, and in July the Censorship Department reported its findings to the Commander-in-Chief.[4] Here there is only space for a few samples of the many extracts which were put in front of Haig. The compilers of the report admitted that they were giving disproportionate space to adverse, discontented letters in order not to build up an untrue, rosy picture. So we find in a letter of 15 June (unit not mentioned): "We are expecting Fritz over any time now. I think the quicker he drives us out of France the better, it is quite time to end it somehow or other . . . everybody is fed up with the war out here and don't care who wins so long as we can get it over."

From the 17th Division on the same day we hear:

> Good luck I say to anyone who can keep out of this hell. I am surprised to hear that you have joined the Woman's Land Army. Do you realize Maggie you are helping to prolong the war? I suppose you did not think. What does it matter whether we win the war or not? We shall never get it over so long as the women and girls keep relieving men for the Army. That is like fighting our own mothers and our own sisters. Only when there are no men left will the war finish, that is the way the lads look at it out here.

It would have been simply unbelievable if nobody, in what was now largely a conscript army, had felt like this; but it is interesting to note in how many of these pessimistic and depressed epistles the corroboration of "everybody out here" or "the lads out here" is invoked. In fact, however, amazing though it may seem, the majority of "the lads" did not feel like that at all (if they had done, the remaining history of 1918 could scarcely have taken place!). Thus on 22 May we find a man of the Royal Warwicks writing:

> I can bear testimony to the splendid qualities of our troops, they are perhaps the biggest lot of growsers under the sun, but they have their growse and finish with it and always fight well. No task is too great for them to undertake, but they must have their growse with it, it is part of their lives. I really believe as you say that Jerry will not digest the lump he has bitten, on the contrary I think he will receive a severe attack of indigestion from us before long.

The same tough note is echoed on 13 June in the 41st Brigade, belonging to one of the divisions earlier reduced to cadre, and now reconstituted with "B" Category men: "Well we are not downhearted and never will be. Never be under the impression that we are beaten and never let people talk to you on that matter, but I can assure you that every one of our lads are bound to win never mind how long it takes." And from the 74th (Yeomanry) Division, only recently arrived from a very different theatre of war, Palestine, we hear: "There is no getting away from the fact that we are in for a gruelling time and plenty of severe fighting in the near future and may possibly have to give ground in places, but *please do not be alarmed* as Tommy Atkins is on his metal and *all will be well*. We are preparing something for Fritz and very soon it will be our day, and then it will be God help the Huns for they will get *Hell*."

As I have said before, the brave letters of these simple, patriotic, self-sacrificing men are often almost incomprehensible by modern standards of thought and feeling; one perceives a departed race of unassuming heroes—and the modern world professes not to like heroes. Even at the time, in mid-1918, after all they had endured, and in the light of their immediate future prospects, there was something breathtaking about the sentiments expressed. But they do help us to understand how it was that an army which had passed through such a trial, in which its fortunes had sunk to such a low ebb, was able after only a few weeks to embark upon one of the most glorious passages in British military history.

What is also interesting is the evident sense among some of these men, for the most part ordinary soldiers with no special information to enlighten them, that a change was at hand, that this lull in the war was the moment of equilibrium between the ebb and the flood. They could not read their Commander-in-Chief's mind, but had they been able to do so they would have found in it the corroboration of their instinct—while he, reading their letters to those they loved, must, like other British commanders before and after him, have drawn deep draughts of encouragement from his indomitable Army.

Change was indeed at hand: not merely strategic change, the pendulum swing of national fortune in this murderous match, but a stylistic change which would separate the last months of the war from the familiar image of trench warfare as firmly as trench warfare itself had shattered the accepted concepts of war by manoeuvre at the end of 1914. That moral and technological equipoise which had ruled the battlefields for three unspeakable years was on the point of being broken. In neither area, moral nor material, was the change very dramatic in itself; there was no waving of magic wands to transform men's natures or the weapons in their hands, but there was just sufficient transformation of both to bring the balance down on one side—and, as normally happens, once the descent began it accelerated to the point of final rest—the end of the war.

In the technological area, perhaps the most indicative symptom occurred formally on 6 June: the setting up of what was called the Independent Air Force at Nancy under the command of Major-General Sir Hugh Trenchard. This occasion was such a portent for the distant future, so obviously a harbinger of the Strategic Air Offensive of 1941–45, with all the controversy that still surrounds it, that the correct estimate of the I.A.F. in its 1918 context becomes very difficult. The objective of the Force, and the persistence with which it pursued that objective—striking at the German Army in its homeland by attacking its industrial base and thus the morale of the workers in the munitions factories—clearly makes it a part of the war of the future. The manner in which it was born and the equipment which it wielded, however, are rather a different matter.

The origin of the Independent Air Force must be traced, not to far-seeing strategic insight, but to the somewhat less attractive emotions of fear and revenge. It was Germany's development of the powerful Gotha bomber, and the alarm and anger produced by these aircraft in the spring and summer of 1917—especially the attacks on London on 13 June and 6–7 July[5]—that placed the bombing of Germany herself in the forefront of British minds. Despite the protests of its responsible advisers, who were all too aware of the hard struggle for air superiority being waged by the Royal Flying Corps in France, the Government first demanded the withdrawal of two fighter squadrons from the front for home defence, and then, when the attacks were strongly renewed in September, countermeasures by British bombers were decreed. Accordingly the Forty-first Wing was formed in October at Ochey aerodrome, near Nancy, under the command of Lieutenant-Colonel C. L. N. Newall (Chief of Air Staff in 1940 and later Marshal of the Royal Air Force); it consisted of one day-bombing squadron and two of night-bombers, of which one was equipped with F.E.2b's, whose maximum speed was 73 m.p.h., air endurance three and a half hours and maximum load (including crew) 452 lb. At full strength and peak performance, the thirty-six aircraft of the Forty-first Wing were unlikely to bring the German Empire to its knees.

Even when the wing expanded to five squadrons and became VIII Brigade, and when it received its subsequent advancement to an Independent Air Force of three wings (ten squadrons), it was clearly no war-winner. As an American writer says,[6] "This first Bomber Command amply demonstrates the singlemindedness, if not vindictiveness, with which the British undertook to even the score in the last year of the war"—and its efforts (often exaggerated, as were those of Fighter Command in 1940) certainly cheered the public. In its five months of existence the Independent Air Force dropped 543 tons of bombs on Germany (of which 220 tons were on aerodromes); the damage it inflicted cannot be precisely stated, but obviously comprised a high proportion of the 746 Germans killed and 1,843 injured through air action in the whole war[7] and of the 24 million marks worth of damage done. By Second World War standards, of course, these figures are insignificant—the Hamburg "fire-storm" alone is thought to have killed at least 30,000 people in three nights of July 1943—but they should not be scorned. A German authority later said: "The direct destructive effect of the enemy air raids did not correspond with the resources expended for this purpose. On the other hand, the indirect effect, namely, falling off in production of war industries, and also the breaking down of the moral resistance of the nation, cannot be too seriously estimated."[8] As General Trenchard expressed it: "The moral effect of bombing stands to the material effect in a proportion of 20 to 1."

Nevertheless, when all due acknowledgement is made to what the Independent Air Force achieved in 1918, it remains the vision of the future that we chiefly salute, and there can be no doubt that this was largely due to the Force's commander. Trenchard played a greater rôle between the wars than any other senior figure of the First World War in Britain: the Royal Air Force (born in April 1918) was preserved by him and shaped in his image, and a good deal of defence policy with it. He was one of the great leaders; Colonel Repington, visiting his headquarters in April 1917, when he was commanding the Royal

Flying Corps in France, called him "one of the few indispensable men in the army. He has done wonders and deserves immense credit." Visiting him again at I.A.F. headquarters in September 1918, he found Trenchard "the same as ever. Brilliant, full of ideas, alert, combative, and a mine of information." Trenchard on this occasion told Repington (among much else): "It is impracticable to stop the night bomber." This certainly was the voice of the future, the doctrine that "the bomber will always get through" on which the air defence of Great Britain was founded for a long time (too long?), and which was to inspire the Strategic Air Offensive for better or worse.

The future was yet to come; there remained a present indicative, whose signs and omens were becoming daily clearer. It was during this lull of intensive battle in June and July that the first manifestations of the terrible Spanish influenza pandemic of 1918–19 were seen. In the space of some eleven months, this disease killed more people than the war itself. It respected neither social class nor nationality—rich London boroughs had mortality rates as high as (sometimes higher than) those of poor boroughs; at the front, French, British and Germans were all stricken. As the virulence of the pandemic came to its peak in Europe in October, 1,200 people a week were dying in Paris, about 4,000 a week in Britain. But there is little doubt that the Germans, soldiers and civilians alike, suffered more than their enemies, because of the weakening of their resistance to disease caused by years of food shortages and privation. By comparison with a British total of 200,000 deaths by May 1919, over 400,000 German civilians had died, and 186,000 soldiers—a terrible addition to the mortality of the great battles. And probably for the same reason that made the German death-rate worse, influenza struck the Germans sooner: by June they had 1,000–2,000 cases per division; by July battalion rifle strengths were in some places as low as 200–240, company strengths only fifty.[9] The result, it need hardly be said, was a weakening of morale even more significant than the loss of actual numbers, though this was serious enough.

The Allies profited by their opponents' misfortunes. The French, in particular, were very active in minor operations designed to keep the front fluid for a counter-stroke, and improve the jumping-off positions from which it would be launched. Both their First Army, on the right of the British, and their Sixth, to the west of Reims, carried out "coups de main" against selected localities with success. But once more it was the Tenth Army, under the restless prodding of Mangin, that pulled off the best strokes: an attack on 28 June whose progress surprised even

Mangin himself—a useful bridgehead was established and 1,200 prisoners taken; a diversionary operation on 3 July which brought in over
1,000 more—a clear sign of faltering morale in the German Army.
And there were other portents elsewhere: a sample of what the
Australians called "peaceful penetration" carried out by their 2nd Division on 10 June, which collected over 300 prisoners, the final capture
of Belleau Wood by the American Marines on 25 June, and a well-
conducted advance near Ypres by the British 5th Division on the 28th,
taking another 440 prisoners.

French, Americans and British all remained active through the first
part of July, and everywhere the pattern was the same. Best of all,
bringing the greatest encouragement for the future, was the Australian
success at Le Hamel on a date made particularly auspicious by the first
co-operation of the Americans in a British attack: the Fourth of July.
The Battle of Le Hamel was a little masterpiece, casting a long shadow
before it, and for that reason worthy of closer attention; a remarkable
soldier made his high command début in it who certainly deserves notice.

The Australian Army Corps had been formed in November 1917,
but it was not until May 1918 that it was commanded by an
Australian general, and not until August that its five divisions were
united at last into one unit. The commander in question was Lieutenant-General John Monash, and the Australian Corps under his
command was now about to perform some amazing prodigies. Monash
was a type of man which some British regular officers found hard to
understand—as were his brave, skilful, insubordinate soldiers. He was
a Jew, an engineer in civilian life, what some Regulars had been disposed
to dismiss rather sneeringly as a "Saturday-afternoon soldier." Haig,
and others who had played significant parts in creating the Territorial
Army and making it fit for war, knew the worth of such men. Monash
was one who showed how well they had spent their Saturday after-
noons—but in his case much more time than that: he had studied the
military profession in peacetime with a thoroughness that few Regulars
could match. When the war came he moved up from command to command and enhanced his reputation every time his responsibility was enlarged. In the Australian Army, where an officer was never permitted
to hide his weaknesses behind the veils of seniority or tradition, this
was no easy thing to do.

Monash had to earn his success; what was its secret? In a war in
which the main burden of harrowing loss always fell on the infantry, it
is Monash's doctrine of the infantry rôle that probably holds the answer. He later wrote:

I had formed the theory that the true rôle of the infantry was not to expend itself upon heroic physical effort, nor to wither away under merci-
less machine gun fire, nor to impale itself on hostile bayonets, nor to
tear itself to pieces in hostile entanglements . . . but, on the contrary,
to advance under the maximum possible array of mechanical resources,
in the form of guns, machine guns, tanks, mortars and aeroplanes; to
advance with as little impediment as possible; to be relieved as far as
possible of the obligation to *fight* their way forward; to march, reso-
lutely, regardless of the din and tumult of battle, to the appointed goal;
and there to hold and defend the territory gained; and to gather, in the
form of prisoners, guns and stores, the fruits of victory.[10]

This doctrine, so opposed to the common experience of the war,
Monash was now about to turn into a reality. The qualities that helped
him do this were immense thoroughness in preparation, rigid insistence
on secrecy and battle discipline, and formidable force of character; he
was a first-class general in command of first-class troops.

The Australians had fought on the Somme with distinction in 1916;
in 1917 the Ypres Salient—the Battle of Messines in June and the
heavy fighting along the Menin Road Ridge towards Broodseinde in
September and October—had been their theatre. They returned to the
Somme in the crisis of March 1918 and made the area between Villers
Bretonneux and Albert their hunting ground. In May and June their
various essays in "peaceful penetration" persuaded their commanders
that the Germans in this sector were vulnerable to real counter-attack;
their positions, contrary to usual German practice, were not well-en-
trenched—partly, no doubt, because they were expecting to resume
their own offensive before long, but partly also because of the decline
in professionalism in the German Army due to the heavy losses of
officers, N.C.O.s and its best troops in the early battles of the year.
General Rawlinson, commanding the British Fourth Army, to which
the Australian Corps belonged, was already secretly considering such
an attack, and the preparatory blow proposed by Monash fitted in well
with his ideas.

Monash submitted his scheme on 21 June: the recapture of the village of Le Hamel, together with Hamel and Vaire Woods. The object
was to shorten and straighten the Australian line in anticipation of the
general attack later, and to disorganize the Germans and deprive them
of observation. It may sometimes seem to a later generation that First
World War generals tended towards a deluded obsession over such
matters as "straightening the line"; in fact, however, in what remained
from first to last an artillery war, this was an important consideration.
In an offensive, the artillery barrage was vital; everything depended on
its accuracy. In Monash's view, it was a small price to pay for a big

success to call upon the infantry "to undertake, before the battle, such rectifications and adjustments of our front line as would accommodate themselves to a straight and simple barrage line."[11] Even when straight, an artillery barrage was a highly complicated affair, and, as Monash remarks, "to make it conform to the tortuous configuration of our Infantry front line" was to ask of the gunners the virtually impossible—yet this was often done, and there was constant surprise at the resulting confusion and casualties. It was his steady grasp of such fundamental simplicities that put Monash into a very special category of men.

So the line was to be straightened, for future reference. It was a job for one division, and the unit selected was the 4th Australian under Major-General E. G. Sinclair-Maclagan—with certain additions. Over 600 guns and howitzers gave fire support; the machine-gun battalions of the 2nd, 3rd and 5th Australian Divisions lent their aid; there were sixty of the new Mark V fighting tanks and twelve supply tanks of the 5th Tank Brigade (Brigadier-General A. Courage)—a very important element in the plan; and there were to be eight companies drawn from the American 131st and 132nd Regiments, belonging to Major-General George Bell's 33rd (National Guard) Division, which was training in the Australian area. These Americans suddenly found themselves at the center of a small inter-Allied storm.

To Monash, meticulous planning was of the very essence of the art of war. He wrote: "A perfected modern battle plan is like nothing so much as a score for an orchestral composition, where the various arms and units are the instruments, and the tasks they perform are their respective musical phrases. Every individual unit must make its entry precisely at the proper moment, and play its phrase in the general harmony."[12] So each of the eight American companies had its special part to play—they were not supernumeraries, not mere spectators. Consequently, when he learned, two days before the attack, that he was only to be allowed to use four American companies—1,000 men instead of the proposed 2,000—he was far from pleased. (The companies which were to be withdrawn were, he records, also "loud in their lamentations.") However, orders were orders, and the plan was amended accordingly, each American platoon still having its particular rôle. It is not difficult to imagine Monash's feelings when, at four o'clock in the afternoon of 3 July, the very eve of the battle, Fourth Army Headquarters informed him—without explanation—that no Americans were to be used at all.

It is possible that some British corps commanders, brought up in the tradition of obedience, might have left it at that; some certainly would not have done so, and Monash had no intention of meekly accepting this dangerous interference. He arranged an immediate meeting with his Army commander, General Rawlinson, who was an imaginative and sympathetic officer. "It was a meeting full of tense situations," says Monash.

> I well knew that . . . the withdrawal of the Americans would result in untold confusion and in dangerous gaps in our line of battle. . . . I could not afford to take the further risk of the occurrence of something in the nature of an "international incident" between the troops concerned, whose respective points of view about the resulting situation could be readily surmised. So I resolved to take a firm stand and press my views as strongly as I dared, for even a corps commander must use circumspection when presuming to argue with an army commander.

In effect, with what "circumspection" we know not, Monash argued that, at this late hour, it was a question either of keeping the Americans in, or of calling off the battle.

Rawlinson agreed, but explained that his orders came from the Commander-in-Chief—and Haig was absent from his headquarters and could not be located. However, Rawlinson went on trying, and at last was able to speak to Haig who told him that "he had directed the withdrawal of the Americans in deference to the wish of General Pershing, but that, as matters stood, he now wished everything to go on as originally planned." So Monash, by perseverance and determination, had his way, and saved his plan. As he said later, "It appeared to me at the time that great issues had hung for an hour or so upon the chance of my being able to carry my point." To the extent that the battle of 4 July set a pattern for the future, it was an important factor in this transitional phase of the war, and Monash was right. Pershing, however, saw the thing in another light. "The incident," he wrote,[13] "though relatively unimportant in itself, showed clearly the disposition of the British to assume control of our units, the very thing which I had made such strong efforts and had imposed so many conditions to prevent. Its immediate effect was to cause me to make the instructions so positive that nothing of the kind could occur again."

Which was a pity, because the attack on 4 July was an unqualified success, as uplifting to American spirits as to Australian and British. Monash's attention to detail and insistence on secrecy were entirely rewarded. "No battle within my previous experience," he wrote, "passed off so smoothly, so exactly to timetable, or was so free from any kind of hitch. It was all over in 93 minutes." Advancing through a heavy ground mist, the Australians and Americans quickly overran all their objectives; they captured 41 German officers, 1,431 other ranks, 2 field guns, 171 machine-guns and 26 trench mortars. The Australian casualties were 51 officers and 724 other ranks, while the Americans lost 6 officers and 128 other ranks. The Battle of Le Hamel is often forgotten when the roll of the great holocausts of the First World War is being called, and that, too, is a pity, because it was a textbook victory, "the perfection of team work" as Monash described it. British G.H.Q. was sufficiently impressed to publish the complete text of the Australian Corps battle plan, with an official commentary, as a General Staff brochure. This document concluded

> The success of the attack was due:
> (a) To the care and skill as regards every detail with which the plan was drawn up by the Corps, Division, Brigade and Battalion Staffs.
> (b) The excellent co-operation between the infantry, machine gunners, artillery, tanks and R.A.F. . . .

It was in this area of co-operation—teamwork—that Le Hamel offered the most significant omens for the future. For the immediate future there was a most encouraging lesson to be learned from the co-operation of infantry, tanks and artillery. The tanks at Le Hamel were used as an infantry weapon, advancing, as Monash says, "level with the infantry, and close up to the barrage." Some had argued that this was impossible: the Mark V tanks stood eight feet eight inches high, and it was feared that many would be hit by low-trajectory British shells. In the event, one-third of the losses suffered by the tanks in the action *were* due to being hit by their supporting artillery, but as the total put out of action from all causes was only three the success of the experiment was not disputed. For the more distant future, there was an even more useful innovation: the collaboration of machine-gunners and the R.A.F. An important feature of consolidation in any advance was the rapid advance of the machine-guns to the captured positions; but it was not just the guns that had to go forward—they needed ammunition, and machine-guns devour ammunition in vast quantities. At Le Hamel, for the first time in history, a solution to this serious problem was attempted by air supply, and the R.A.F. successfully dropped 100,000 rounds to the Australian machine-gunners during the battle—a practice which was soon to be generally adopted.

Allied relations, despite General Pershing's apprehensions, also profited by this victory. The fine bearing and enthusiasm of the men of the American 131st and 132nd Regiments who took part greatly impressed the Australians—not, by and large, people easily impressed. The American performance on 4 July extracted a compliment out of proportion to its scale. An Australian company commander ended his report to his colonel: "United States troops are now classified as Diggers."[14]

And now the moment of decision was at hand: the war was about to turn upon its hinge. Germany's losses between March and July had been enormous—the British Official Historian estimates them at about a million—and still the yearned for victory remained beyond the sky-line. Manpower was running out; time was running out. But there was just time—and just enough strength—for one more throw, one more attempt to crack the Allied line beyond repair. The question, once again, was *where?* "Again and again," says Ludendorff, "our thoughts returned to the idea of an offensive in Flanders. . . . But an offensive at this point still presented too difficult a problem." He meant that the British Army had recovered too well in the lull since April; its reserves were now too strong for a quick decision. They had to be drawn away from the critical point, so once more the prescription was an offensive on both sides of Reims, threatening Paris. If that succeeded, it was hoped that "there would be a very decisive weakening of the enemy in Flanders." The victory at Reims could then be followed up, about a fortnight later, by the decisive stroke against the British in the north. But it meant two blows, not one. Did Germany have sufficient strength for that? And what would her enemies be doing? These questions— and others besides—were about to receive summary answers.

It was not in Foch's nature to be content with the defensive for long. It was not in Mangin's nature to be content with it at all. The Generalissimo and the Tenth Army commander had a good rapport, they spoke each other's language at this stage of the war, and between them they were to prove more than a match for the ingrained caution of General Pétain. Foch was hatching a counter-stroke on the grand scale; Mangin was to be its chief executive, supported by the able Degoutte and his Sixth Army. Pétain was instructed to dispose his forces accordingly; it only remained to pick the time.

Information crossed the lines freely during these days, and from French deserters (whose chagrin at the subsequent unfolding of events may be imagined) the Germans learned that a counter-attack was com-ing. Their own preparations were obvious to their soldiers and difficult to conceal entirely from the Allies; airmen reported that there was so much movement of small parties of men behind the German lines that they looked like ants' nests disturbed. On both sides the sense of approaching a climax was acute; Captain Rudolf Binding wrote on 12 July: "The atmosphere about us remains charged; it is as if the tension in each one of us could not be high enough."

France's national day seemed to offer as good a cue as any, but to the surprise and relief of the Germans 14 July came and went quietly. They could go ahead with their own plan unhindered. Binding, a staff officer scheduled for liaison duties, wrote that evening:

> To-night is the fateful one. It looks as if the enemy suspected nothing, but that is hardly credible. The dust-clouds over the roads, which mark the path of the troops and transport even in the morning, would alone be sufficient to give us away. We move late in the evening, and between one and two o'clock hell breaks loose. The preparation for this hell consisted mainly of paper: the road to it was paved with paper. If we fire off as much ammunition at the enemy as we had paper fired at us he will have a bad time.

The French were not taken by surprise; prisoners and deserters gave them the information they needed, right down to the timing of the German barrage, so that they were able to anticipate this by about half an hour, to the consternation of the German infantry. East of Reims, twenty-five divisions of the German *First and Third Armies* attacked General Gouraud's Fourth Army; west of Reims eighteen divisions of the *Seventh Army* attacked General Berthelot's Fifth Army (which included two American divisions and two Italian). The artillery support was once again massive—probably about 5,000 guns in all, once more directed by the able Colonel Bruchmüller. And there were even tanks: twenty of them opposite Gouraud, five opposite Berthelot—but there is no record of their having any influence whatever on the battle. This was the last German onslaught of the war—though no one was to know that. What many could quite easily see, however, was that from the very beginning things went badly wrong. When he next put pen to paper, on 16 July, Rudolf Binding wrote from his "bivouac among brushwood":

> I have lived through the most disheartening day of the whole War, though it was by no means the most dangerous. This wilderness of chalk is not very big, but it seems endless when one gets held up in it, and we are held up. Under a merciless sun, which set the air quivering in a dance of heat, and sent wave after hot wave up from the grilling soil, the treeless, waterless chalk downs lay devoid of all colour, like stones at white-heat. No shade, no paths, not even roads; just crumbling white streaks on a flat plate. Across this wind rusty snakes of barbed wire. Into this the French deliberately lured us. They put up no resistance in front; they had neither infantry nor artillery in this forward battle-zone, the full use and value of which they had learned from Ludendorff. Our guns bombarded empty trenches; our gas-shells gassed empty artillery positions; only in little hidden folds of the ground, sparsely distributed, lay machine gun posts, like lice in the seams and folds of a

garment, to give the attacking force a warm reception. The barrage, which was to have preceded and protected it, went right on somewhere over the enemy's rear positions, while in front the first line of real resistance was not yet carried.

After uninterrupted fighting from five o'clock in the morning until the night, smothered all the time with carefully directed fire, we only succeeded in advancing about three kilometres. . . .[15]

Few narratives so clearly convey the sense of defeat, shocking because it was so unexpected. The credit for the French success lies very largely with General Gouraud. In 1915, commanding the French contingent at Gallipoli, Gouraud had lost an arm and had both his legs broken; his fighting spirit was, if anything, enlarged by these calamities. He was a general who cared deeply for his men, and was held by them in great affection. His careful and skilful application of "defence in depth" in July 1918 saved many lives, and what the British Official History calls his "inspired leading" during the battle made the German defeat absolute in the sector east of Reims.

West of Reims, the Fifth Army's interpretation of "defence in depth" was less successful. Despite tough resistance by the American 3rd Division near Château Thierry (where the right flank of the Sixth Army was also attacked) the Germans made progress on a wide front. The two divisions of the Italian II Corps suffered particularly heavy casualties, and for a time the position of the Fifth Army appeared to be critical. Impressed by the German penetration south of the River Marne, Pétain ordered the return of troops (including the American 2nd Division) who were on their way to Mangin for the French counter-stroke, which would therefore have to be postponed. The relationship between Pétain and Mangin was by now beginning to resemble a tug of war, and the man in the middle, pulled alternately each way, was General Fayolle, commander of the Reserve Army Group. Foch was at Fayolle's headquarters, on his way to see Haig, when he learned what Pétain had done, and if he had done nothing else in the war his immediate countermanding of Pétain's order and insistence that the counter-attack should be delivered as planned would deserve the gratitude of all his allies and compatriots. Yet so full of ironies is history that it was on this very day that Clemenceau, supposing him to have lost his grip, was talking of replacing him. Fortunately such matters take a little time, which was all that Foch needed.

It was characteristic of the man that when he met Haig that day the latter found him "in the best of spirits." They were about to resolve a sharp disagreement which had been going on between them for some time and was made all the more intractable by the fact that they were both right. Foch wanted direct and immediate British help in the Champagne battle, which he sensed was a turning point of the war. If Haig agreed, he would leave himself with only seven reserve divisions on the British front; facing him, according to the close and accurate scrutiny of G.H.Q. Intelligence, Prince Rupprecht of Bavaria had

35 reserve divisions on 31 May
42   "   "   on 8 June
28   "   "   on 25 June
23   "   "   on 16 July

(the last figure would rise again to twenty-six before events in Champagne produced a significant alteration). And, as we know, Champagne was for Ludendorff merely a curtain-raiser for the decisive blow in Flanders. On the other hand, Champagne was the theatre of a battle actually in progress, as Foch pointed out: "Foch agreed with me [about the threat to the British front] but said his first object was to hold up the present attack at all costs as soon as possible. He only wanted my divisions as a reserve in case of necessity, and they would be in a position *ready to return to me at once* in case the British front was threatened. Under these circumstances, I agreed to send the next two divisions as arranged."[16] And so it came about that four British divisions, 15th, 34th, 51st and 62nd, forming XXII Corps under Lieutenant-General Sir Alexander Godley, would take their place beside the French, Americans and Italians to make the crisis of the war a truly international occasion.

Haig and Foch normally resolved their difficulties amicably, as they did on 15 July. They conducted their business without political interference, but that could not always be avoided. On this occasion Haig had come to the meeting with a telegram from Wilson in his pocket, saying that the Government were anxious about the Flanders front, and the movement of British reserves away from it: "[the War Cabinet] rely on the exercise of your judgment . . . as to the security of the British front after the removal of these troops." Haig wryly noted the shifts of the political mind which one day would tell him to "carry out loyally any instructions issued to you by the C. in C. Allied Forces" and on another day tell him to "use my judgment": "This is a case of 'heads you win and tails I lose.' If things go well, the Government take credit to themselves and the Generalissimo; if badly, the Field-Marshal will be blamed!" This is one of the things that high command is about.

Meanwhile, at the front along the Marne, there was heavy fighting on the 16th. The Germans made little progress, and even when they made progress they lost some of the ground won to French counter-attacks in which the American 3rd and 28th Divisions played an important part. On General Gouraud's front they were driven back in several places. Their bridgehead over the Marne was becoming precarious, the river crossings being under more or less continuous shell fire and air attack. On the 17th Gouraud advanced a little further; west of Reims there was stalemate, attacks and counter-attacks cancelling each other out. Both the German *Seventh Army* Headquarters and the Crown Prince's *Army Group* were now convinced that the Marne bridgehead was a liability. They urged immediate withdrawal—a sorry outcome, after only three days, to an effort intended to herald final victory. Reluctantly, at midnight, O.H.L. agreed to a gradual retirement, but delayed giving the final order in the hope that at least the tip of the salient containing Reims itself might be pinched out.

Ludendorff himself was absent. He was in Mons, seeing whether, in this bleak hour, Flanders might come to the rescue of Champagne instead of the other way about: "In the night of the 17th–18th I myself went to the Headquarters of the *Army Group* of Crown Prince Rupprecht, to review once more the state of their preparations. The attack was intended as a continuation of that which had been suspended at the end of April . . . its objectives being the possession of the commanding heights between Poperinghe and Bailleul, as well as the high ground round Hazebrouck." Already heavy artillery, mortars and aircraft were on their way north for the Flanders attack that Haig had been awaiting so long. But it never came. Ludendorff says: "During the discussion with the Army Group of Crown Prince Rupprecht on the morning of the 18th I received the first news that, by means of an unexpected tank attack, the French had pierced the line south-west of Soissons."[17]

It was a good deal more than "an unexpected tank attack"; it was the carefully prepared and well-concealed counter-offensive of the French Tenth and Sixth Armies striking from the west. As in September 1914, in the very same area, the Germans in over-confidence had opened a vulnerable right flank to a counter-blow, and as in 1914 the French Generalissimo was gratefully accepting the gift. The Tenth Army threw sixteen divisions (including two American) into the assault, supporting them with 1,545 guns, 346 tanks and 581 aircraft. The Sixth Army used eight divisions (two American), 588 guns, 147 tanks and 562 aircraft. This substantial air weapon was, like the ground forces, international; it included IX Brigade of the Royal Air Force and an American squadron of great renown. All of them would have their work cut out in the days ahead.

King George V visits Fourth Army Headquarters at Flixecourt, 13 August: (1) General Sir Henry Rawlinson, Commanding Fourth Army; (2) General Debeney, Commanding French First Army; (3) General Weygand (behind); (4) Marshal Foch; (5) Lieutenant-General Sir Herbert Lawrence, Haig's Chief-of-Staff (behind); (6) King George V; (7) Field-Marshal Sir Douglas Haig, British Commander-in-Chief; (8) General Pétain, French Commander-in-Chief; (9) General Fayolle, Commanding the French Army Group (G.A.R.)

'All Australian battalions were now very weak': an Australian platoon (only sixteen men) receives its instructions. Companies often went into battle only fifty strong, battalions two hundred and fifty to three hundred; but it will be noted that this platoon has three Lewis guns

' "Whippets", a name likely to conjure up misleading images': the Medium Mark A ('Whippet') tank weighed 14 tons, carried a crew of three and four Hotchkiss machine guns. Its maximum (road) speed was 8.3 m.p.h. A 'Whippet' is here seen at Proyart, 23 August, with what appears to be a Mark V burning in the background

'Collaboration between "Whippets" and cavalry proved to be an illusion': Canadian cavalry resting on 10 August. Even when open warfare returned in the final stages, cavalry was largely ineffective; there was a 'hiatus in the mobile arm'

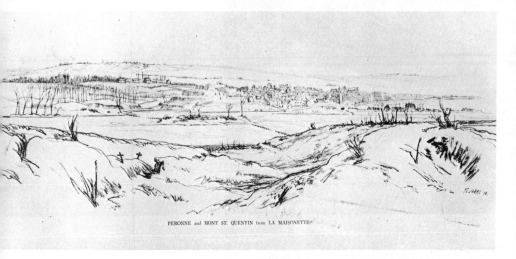

'A famous fortress of the Western Front': Mont St Quentin, just outside Péronne, captured by the Australian 2nd Division on 31 August. Field sketch by Captain F. E. Hodge

'. . . the most formidable task ever faced by Australian infantry': moving up a trench for the attack on Mont St Quentin, 31 August

'. . . brave, skilful, insubordinate soldiers': Australians resting in a barn, gambling, their favourite diversion. General Monash said: 'The Australian Army is a proof that individualism is the best and not the worst foundation upon which to build collective discipline'

'A first-class general in command of first-class troops'. Lieutenant-General Sir John Monash, commanding the Australian Army Corps, presenting a Victoria Cross. Out of fifty V.C.s won in the Fourth Army during the last 'Hundred Days', twenty were won by Australians

The centre and spearhead of the Tenth Army's attack were the American 1st and 2nd Divisions on either side of the crack Moroccan Division. The establishment of an American division in 1918 was about twice that of a French or British division, so this constituted a very powerful assault force. Its impact was fierce and overwhelming:

It was 4.35, the morning of July 18.

Miles of close-laid batteries opened with one stupendous thunder. The air above the tree-tops spoke with unearthly noises, the shriek and rumble of light and heavy shells. Forward through the woods, very near, rose up a continued crashing roar of explosions, and a murk of smoke, and a hell of bright fires continually renewed. It lasted only five minutes, that barrage, with every French and American gun that could be brought to bear firing at top speed. But they were terrible minutes for the unsuspecting Boche. Dazed, beaten down, and swept away, he tumbled out of his holes when it lifted, only to find the long bayonets of the Americans licking like flame across his forward positions, and those black devils, the Senegalese, raging with knives in his rifle-pits. His counter-barrage was slow and weak, and when it came the shells burst well behind the assaulting waves, which were already deep in his defenses.[18]

The Americans of the 1st and 2nd Divisions were soldiers of a kind not much seen on the battlefields of Europe since 1914. They were regulars—in the 2nd Division half of them were Marines—tall men, strong and fit, relaxed but disciplined, mostly good shots, good marchers, adept in all the skills of their profession of arms which, it must be said, though philanthropists lament, the majority of them had embraced with pleasure and now pursued with stern satisfaction. "There is no sight in all the pageant of war like young, trained men going up to battle," wrote one of their officers. Trained they were indeed, as the old 1914 B.E.F. had been trained, as the magnificent German Army which had supplied the war's driving force for all these years had been trained, as the Frenchmen who once before had turned the course of the war beside the River Marne had been trained. But high-explosive shell is no respecter of training: the bursting shell tears a platoon of perfectly disciplined Guardsmen to pieces as indifferently as a rabble of raw recruits; the raking machine-gun, looking for its targets, does not stop to examine their badges. In a war of endless destructive novelty, no training can be comprehensive or give much protection; every occasion is a training for itself. Once again, on the wooded slopes of the Soissonais, the war took on a new aspect and produced fresh novelties.

Machine-guns raved everywhere; there was a crackling din of rifles, and
the coughing roar of hand-grenades. Company and platoon commanders lost control—their men were committed to the fight—and so
thick was the going that anything like formation was impossible. It was
every man for himself, an irregular, broken line, clawing through the
tangles, climbing over fallen trees, plunging heavily into Boche rifle-pits.
Here and there a well-fought Maxim gun held its front until somebody—
officer, non-com, or private—got a few men together and, crawling to
left or right, gained a flank and silenced it. And some guns were silenced by blind, furious rushes that left a trail of writhing khaki figures,
but always carried two or three frenzied Marines with bayonets into the
emplacement; from whence would come shooting and screaming and
other clotted unpleasant sounds, and then silence.[19]

All along the front of the Tenth Army and the left flank of the Sixth,
such scenes were repeated, and the Germans quickly gave way. In
many places the French tanks, carefully concealed until the moment of
action among the thick foliage of the Forest of Villers Cotterêts, added
to the demoralization of the German infantry. Over 200 of these tanks
took part in the battle on 18 July; they were of the light Renault
model, weighing only seven tons, carrying a crew of two protected only
by thin armour plate, and armed with a single machine-gun. They are
often referred to (by Ludendorff for one) as "fast"; all such things
are relative, but even by 1918 standards it seems a curious word to use
about a vehicle with a road speed of 6 m.p.h. That they contributed to
the victory on 18 July and on the next day cannot be doubted, but the
cost was high: sixty-two hit by German artillery fire on the 18th, fifty
more on the 19th.

At the end of the afternoon of the 18th the tug of war between Mangin and Pétain resumed in characteristic fashion. At six o'clock Pétain
and Fayolle arrived at Mangin's command post; Mangin spread out a
map at the foot of a tree, and showed them the day's results, explain-
ing the nature of the fighting. Pétain said—and to Mangin it seemed
almost reluctantly—that it was a great success, and that he had not
even dared to hope for so much, but . . . but that he had not one single division to give to back up the Tenth Army's achievement. Mangin
protested and entreated: it was essential to follow up a success like
this, unthinkable to let it just fade out. Pétain replied: "I haven't got
anything. I know what a seducer you are, but this time I can be very
firm, because having absolutely nothing myself, there is nothing I can
give you."

The argument became sharp between them, Mangin at one point
going so far as to say that it would have been better not to launch the
attack at all than to break it off like this. Pétain, no doubt withdrawing

into the icy shell which was always his armour when displeased, curtly repeated that he had nothing to give. He was sorry, but there it was; and he added: "Besides, I am obliged to consider that the Germans are still south of the Marne. That's what concerns me most, and what will have to be put right. On this front we must take up a position of defence in depth and be content with improving the present line."

Mangin retorted that the best way to clear the Germans out of the Marne bridgehead was to exploit to the limit the success already won. Pétain merely repeated once more that he had nothing, not a single division, to give to the Tenth Army, and with that he and Fayolle left the command post.

But Mangin was a man not easily crushed. He thought over the scene for a while, then said to his chief of staff: "What it comes to is this: General Pétain says he is not going to give me anything, but he hasn't *ordered* me to stop the attack; so we'll go on with what we've got, and the attack will continue tomorrow. Make out the orders accordingly." And then, in shrewd self-defence, he sent for Foch's liaison officer, and told him the whole story. Mangin knew that Foch would approve of what he was doing, and the liaison officer was sent off post-haste to find the Generalissimo and make sure that there would be no formal orders from Pétain through Fayolle to break off the attack.

This was by no means the last clash of wills between Pétain and his combative subordinate. And Mangin had no hesitation in enlisting—or trying to enlist—powerful allies. In these days of newly kindled hope there was a steady flow of highly placed personages to the front, among them President Poincaré and Clemenceau. It was a few days later that Clemenceau said to Poincaré: "Mangin is annoying. He is always complaining. He spoke to me about Pétain in inadmissible terms, and even advised me not to keep him. I replied that this was none of his business; besides, Pétain could not be replaced easily. Of course, Mangin does not think so, but he is quite mistaken if he believes that he would be appointed Commander-in-Chief. That is out of the question."[20]

Pétain and Mangin were both patriotic Frenchmen; both wanted to win the war. Their dispute was largely a clash of temperament: Pétain's great quality as a soldier was realism, but in him it easily turned to pessimism; Mangin was aggressive to his finger-tips and had a nose for victory. But the reverse side of that, as Pétain no doubt remembered with bitterness, was the somewhat slapdash over-confidence which had caused the French Army such dreadful losses in the deadly spring of 1917, and led to the mutinies which he, Pétain, had then had to bring under control. The scar of that experience remained with him for the rest of his life. In 1918 there was Foch to

stiffen his fibre; in 1940 there was no one, and the consequences were
as we know.

So the attack was resumed on the 19th, and by the end of that day
the main victory was complete—though the battle itself would continue
until 3 August. In these two days Mangin had advanced over six miles,
taking 15,000 prisoners and 400 guns. And the Germans were retreating at last. Their rearguards fought with all that tenacity which the
German soldier can summon up in adversity to confound his enemies:
their artillery reacted to every thrust with violent barrages, their
machine-gunners were ubiquitous and deadly, their airmen indefatigable. But they were retreating; slowly, obstinately, but definitely retreating, first from the Marne bridgehead, then, as in 1914, to the
Aisne and the Vesle. But how obstinately they fought is to be seen in
the casualties they inflicted. The American 2nd Division, when it was
relieved on the night of 19 July, had lost 5,000 men; the 1st Division
fought on for two more days, by which time its reckoning was 7,200.
When it was relieved by the British 15th Division, the incoming
Scottish soldiers were saddened to find so many of these splendid spec-
imens of manhood lying dead in swathes where the German machine-
guns had caught them, just like so many of the fine, valiant young men
of Kitchener's armies in 1916. The difference was that the Kitchener
armies mostly went into battle relatively raw, and these Americans
were highly trained; but they were trained for General Pershing's idea
of "open warfare," which he believed would save American youth from
the bloody stalemate of the trenches. Only no one had explained that
to the men behind the German machine-guns.

The entry of General Godley's four divisions into the battle was no
mere token gesture of inter-Allied solidarity. Fighting in pairs—the
51st and 62nd in the Fifth Army passing straight through the remains
of the Italian II Corps into a hard attack, the 15th and 34th in the
Sixth Army on the left—they struck at the hinges of the now shrinking
German salient. The freshest cadet at a military academy could see the
strategic significance of these hinge areas; if they gave way the German
divisions trying to extract themselves from the central bulge would be
doomed. The German command, of course, knew that too, so that no-
where was the defence more stubborn, and the achievement of the
XXII Corps, though never as outwardly brilliant as the Franco-
American onset of the first two days, was correspondingly all the more
worthy—a fact handsomely acknowledged by the French, but scarcely
noticed in Britain.

On the eastern side in particular, the 51st and 62nd Divisions encountered difficulty from the first, advancing over the open country of

the Ardre valley, flanked by wooded ridges whose spurs offered ideal positions for machine-gun defence. The corn was standing two feet high on much of this ground, and most accounts dwell on the difficulty of reconnaissance because of this, and the advantage it conferred on the defence, giving concealment to marksmen and machine-guns. Ludendorff, on the other hand, speaks of the "small, low, fast tanks, that allowed the use of machine guns above the corn" and adds: "Our machine guns were hindered by it except when they were mounted on special tripods." The truth probably is that the terrain and the corn that covered it doled out advantages to both sides more or less equally according to local circumstances. It is Pershing who comes nearest to this when he says: "It was harvest time and the ripening grain that covered the rolling landscape gave excellent cover for the enemy's infantry and machine guns and also helped to hide our advance." As on so many occasions during the First World War, it seems unprofitable to look for the causes of loss very far beyond the quality of the enemy who inflicted it and the technical character of the war itself.

By the end of the battle the four British divisions had suffered well over 13,000 casualties; the French had lost over 95,000 men. Between them, the Allies had captured more than 29,000 officers and men, 793 guns and no less than 3,723 of the machine-guns which had held them up so often; French Intelligence estimated the total German loss at 168,000, which may well be about right. Certainly British observers commented on the large number of German dead found as they advanced, and the Americans came away from the battle with the sense of having killed a great many of their enemies. It was another severe blow to Germany—severest of all, however, not on the stricken fields where their dead and wounded lay, but in the minds of their leaders.

Ludendorff, in particular, was overwhelmed by this defeat. One historian[21] speaks of his "intellectual dislocation," a dismay so deep that he could no longer reason, no longer sift the significant from the insignificant, no longer make the fundamental decisions which were called for if Germany was to save something from the wreck of her high hopes. He was "in a gruesome state of nerves" which distressed his staff and all who came into contact with him. But one decision he *had* to make; it was forced on him without options: he had to abandon the Flanders attack. The hope of final victory lay in Flanders; this decision meant the end of that hope. Small wonder if Ludendorff was overwhelmed. Towering, solid, bull-necked, hard eyes glaring out of his heavy features, Field-Marshal von Hindenburg now supplied the stiffening for Germany, the inspiration for her brave but now despondent soldiers. Yet Hindenburg himself, under the granite of his outward impassivity, was torn by terrible emotions:

> We could have no illusion about the far-reaching effects of this battle and our retreat. . . .
> From the purely military point of view it was of the greatest and most fateful importance that we had lost the initiative to the enemy. . . .
> The effect of our failure on the country and our allies was even greater. . . .
> How many hopes, cherished during the last few months, had probably collapsed at one blow! How many calculations had been scattered to the winds.[22]

Hindenburg knew, Ludendorff knew, Foch knew. On 7 August Foch issued an Order of the Day to his armies:

> Four years of effort aided by our faithful Allies, four years of trial stoically accepted, commence to bear their fruit. . . .
> Yesterday I said to you: Obstinacy, Patience, your American comrades are coming. To-day I say to you: Tenacity, Boldness, and Victory must be yours.

Looking back on the battle later he expressed the essential, the fact that made this the turning point of the war: "Since July 18th the control of events had passed into our hands."[23] But it was left to Marshal Joffre, looking down at the placid waters of the unassuming river, to utter the final word: "Une jolie fleuve, la Marne."

Chapter V: Notes

1. (p. 61) See Chapter III, especially pp. 32–35.
2. (p. 61) In effect, the infantry ceased to exist, the battalions being reduced to mere "caretaker" companies of ten officers and forty-five other ranks; artillery, machine-gunners and engineers remained available for action with other divisions.
3. (p. 62) Marshal Foch: *Memoirs*, trans. Col. T. Bentley Mott, Heinemann, 1931, p. 350.
4. (p. 62) See John Terraine: *Impacts of War, 1914 and 1918*, Hutchinson, 1970, pp. 171–76.
5. (p. 64) In the 13 June raid 162 people were killed and 432 injured; in the 7 July raid 57 were killed and 193 injured.
6. (p. 65) R. H. Fredette: *The First Battle of Britain, 1917–1918, and the Birth of the Royal Air Force*, Cassell, 1966, p. 221.
7. (p. 65) Compared with the British total of 1,414 killed and 3,416 injured.
8. (p. 65) Major Grosskreutz in *Die Luftwacht*, October 1928, quoted in the

British Official History, *The War in the Air*, by H. A. Jones, O.U.P., 1937, vi, p. 153.

9. (p. 66) After 1 July the establishment of a German infantry battalion was reduced from 980 to 880: 750 in the four rifle companies, 180 in the machine-gun company.

10. (p. 68) Lieut.-Gen. Sir John Monash, *The Australian Victories in France in 1918*, Angus and Robertson, 1936, p. 96.

11. (p. 69) Ibid.

12. (p. 69) Compare: "To watch a highly-skilled, experienced, and resolute commander controlling a hard-fought battle is to see, not only a man triumphing over the highest mental and physical stresses, but an artist producing his effects in the most complicated and difficult of all the arts." (Field-Marshal Sir William Slim: *Defeat into Victory*, Cassell, 1956, p. 447).

13. (p. 70) John J. Pershing: *My Experiences in the Great War*, Hodder and Stoughton, 1931, p. 475.

14. (p. 72) C. E. W. Bean; *The Official History of Australia in the War of 1914–1918*, Angus and Robertson, 1942, vi, p. 333.

15. (p. 74) Rudolf Binding: *A Fatalist at War*, Allen and Unwin, 1929, p. 234.

16. (p. 75) Robert Blake: *The Private Papers of Douglas Haig*, Eyre and Spottiswoode, 1952, pp. 318–19.

17. (p. 76) Ludendorff: *My War Memories*, Hutchinson, 1919, ii, p. 667.

18. (p. 77) John W. Thomasson Jnr.: *Fix Bayonets!*, Scribner's, 1926, p. 94.

19. (p. 78) Ibid., pp. 98–101.

20. (p. 79) *The Memoirs of Raymond Poincaré*, trans. Sir George Arthur, Heinemann, 1929.

21. (p. 81) Correlli Barnett: *The Swordbearers*, Eyre and Spottiswoode, 1963, p. 342.

22. (p. 82) Hindenburg: *Out of My Life*, Cassell, 1920, p. 386.

23. (p. 82) *The Two Battles of the Marne*, by Marshal Foch, Marshal Joffre, the ex-Crown Prince of Germany and Gen. Ludendorff, Thornton Butterworth, 1928, p. 194.

"THE WAR MUST BE ENDED"

(Kaiser Wilhelm II, 11 August 1918)

At the centre of the understanding of the remainder of the First World War is the fact that from 18 July one side was directed by a man whose nerve and judgment were seriously impaired—Ludendorff— while the other side was directed by two men whose confidence was growing day by day, and whose touch was becoming ever more sure— Foch and Haig. From 3 August, when the Second Battle of the Marne came formally to its end, these two men together controlled—inasmuch as it was humanly possible to control—the progress of the war to its sudden end. Foch's rôle was to co-ordinate the actions of the Allies, and to inspire in all of them the spirit of co-operation without which they would not be able to succeed. Haig's rôle was to provide the spearhead of victory, 100 days of practically unceasing successful attacks unparalleled in British military history.

Because of the aura surrounding the phrase "unity of command" (and its value is indisputable); because of the successes associated with the office of Supreme Allied Commander during the Second World War; and because of the disgraceful venom with which Haig's reputation was later assailed, the real nature of supreme command in 1918 has largely been concealed. Thus Lloyd George, in his *War Memoirs*, could hardly bring himself to say a good word for Haig, but condescendingly admitted that "He did well in the concluding stages of the 1918 campaign— under Foch's supreme direction." That Foch's supreme direction was an asset to the Allies is undoubtedly true, but this kind of remark serves better to hide than to display its nature. General Monash (for whom Lloyd George professed great admiration) expressed the matter very differently:

It has come to be an article of faith that the whole of the successive stages of the great closing offensive of the war had been the subject of most careful timing, and of minute organisation on the part of the Allied High Command, and of our own G.H.Q. Much eulogistic writing has been devoted to an attempted analysis of the comprehensive and far-reaching plans which resulted in the delivery of blow upon blow, in a prescribed order of time and for the achievement of definite strategical or tactical ends.

All who played any part in these great events well know that it was nothing of the kind; that nothing in the nature of a detailed time-table to control so vast a field of effort was possible. All commanders, and the most exalted of them in a higher degree even than those wielding lesser forces, became opportunists, and bent their energies, not to the realisation of a great general plan for a succession of timed attacks, but upon the problem of hitting whenever and wherever an opportunity offered, and the means were ready to hand.[1]

Anyone conjuring up a vision or recollection of the massive apparatus of inter-Allied staffs in the Second World War will be very wide of the mark regarding Foch. His method was inspirational, not administrative, and to operate it he used a small staff of no more than twenty officers, of whom a proportion would always be absent on liaison work. He did not give orders to the armies serving under him in the sense that their own commanders-in-chief could give orders; he had no powers to punish if they disobeyed. So what *could* he do? ". . . by persuasion he could stimulate or restrain commanders-in-chief, decide upon the policy to follow, and thus bring about those concerted actions which result in victory, even when the armies concerned are utterly dissimilar."[2] In the next phase of the great drama, which was to follow the thunder-clap of the Marne with the swiftness of an echo, we may see the method working out to every satisfaction.

It is first necessary to go back in time, to May, before the second phase of the German offensives fell upon the French Army. It was 16 May; the German attacks in Flanders had only recently died away, and threatened to revive at any moment; the British Army was pathetically weak and vulnerable. Foch and his Chief of Staff, Weygand, visited Haig to discuss how the Army could be strengthened—the everlasting manpower problem. And then they turned to another subject: "Foch also explained to me an offensive project which he wishes to carry out if the enemy does not launch his big attack within the new few weeks. I agreed with his general plan, and said I would study my share of the undertaking and let him know. But he must not write his plan nor allow the French commanders to talk about it. Success will depend mainly on secrecy."[3]

It was entirely characteristic of these two men that at such a depressing juncture of the war they should be considering an offensive. And not merely considering: the next day Haig, with his own Chief of Staff, went to Rawlinson's headquarters behind the Somme front: "I told Rawlinson to begin studying in conjunction with General Debeney[4] the question of an attack from the French front south of Roye. I gave him details of the scheme." Despite Haig's urging not to commit himself to paper, Foch followed this up with a "Directive" on 20 May; in view of the state of the British forces, the operation would be mainly French, with the British in a supporting rôle and contributing a strong force of their new tanks. General Debeney was no Mangin; if there was fire in his belly it gave only a dull glow. Rawlinson did not come away from his discussions with his French neighbour with any feeling of exhilaration, and told Haig so. But all these minor problems were, of course, to be swept into obscurity in the crises of the great German onslaughts on the Aisne and the Matz. And no doubt it was just as well that this delay was imposed; it gave time for the British Army to regain its strength, and it put Haig in a better position when the moment came.

Neither Foch nor Haig lost sight of their offensive scheme in the dark days that followed. Not unnaturally, as the French coped with their successive crises, Foch's mind turned readily to the possibilities of bringing relief by launching the offensive on the Somme—or, indeed, anywhere else that seemed to offer reasonable prospects. Haig, however, had his attention fixed on Crown Prince Rupprecht's reserves. As we have seen, although far from reassured, he sent what he could spare to Champagne to repel the final German thrust, and when the counter-stroke came he was quick to sense the turn of the tide. All his military instinct now informed him that things had changed: the Australian "peaceful penetrations," the brilliant stroke at Le Hamel, another British success at Meteren—all pointed the same way. Rawlinson wanted to follow Le Hamel with a similar enterprise. Haig said "not yet"; it was necessary to conserve the Army's strength for the big occasion, and he could feel that this was near. He watched the events in Champagne carefully. On 22 July he wrote:

> I had a paper prepared today for Foch giving my plans. Unless Rupprecht's reserves are reduced in some way, I can only go in for small local attacks. If Rupprecht attacks British Second Army, I propose to counter-attack and regain Kemmel if possible—Fifth and First Armies will co-operate in this.
>
> If Rupprecht does not attack me, but his reserves are drawn off elsewhere, I recommend a surprise attack to improve our position east of

Amiens. I have prepared this proposal in some detail. I am taking the paper with me tomorrow to hand to Foch on Wednesday at our meeting.

Every piece of information that came in strengthened his intention. The next day:

> As we are fairly well prepared to meet an attack by Rupprecht upon my Second Army, it is most likely that the attack won't be delivered. So I am prepared to take the offensive and have approved of an operation taking place on Rawlinson's front, and steps have been taken to make preparations very secretly in order to be ready, should the battle now being fought out on the Marne cause the situation to turn in our favour.

Two meetings with Foch in the next three days settled the matter. The rôles of the armies were now reversed: after their heavy losses in the battles of Champagne, and with a manpower problem now as serious as that of the British two months earlier, the French would not be the leaders. A strongly reinforced British Fourth Army would be doing most of the work, with the French supporting. Recognizing this—and certain other considerations also—Foch came to an important conclusion:

> It could be assumed that by the time this operation took place our victory in the Soissons region would have yielded most of the results to be expected from it. Therefore good reasons existed for hurrying forward the offensive south of the Somme, so as not to allow the enemy any respite. Finally, for the purpose of ensuring perfect co-operation between the British Fourth Army and the French First Army, which were to act together, and of securing the greatest possible energy in execution, I asked Sir Douglas Haig to take personal command of the two Armies.[5]

Haig simply noted: "I am pleased that Foch should have entrusted me with the direction of these operations."

The Fourth Army assembly for the coming battle was of extreme complexity, and was performed with wonderful precision. At the core of Rawlinson's preparations was the concentration of three formations, the presence of any one of which would, if known to the enemy, have given the game away. He had, already under command, the British III Corps and the Australian Corps; to these were to be added the Canadian Corps, the Cavalry Corps and the largest number of tanks to be assembled for one battle during the whole war. In the rolling empty uplands of the Somme plateaux, almost devoid of cover, it was no easy matter to conceal the gathering of such forces as these. Yet it was done.

Once more, in the proceedings of 1918, we seem to glimpse a distant future. In 1944 an essential preliminary to the Allied landing in north-west Europe was an elaborate deception plan designed to persuade the Germans that the invasion would take place in the Pas de Calais, rather than Normandy or Brittany. An important element in this plan was a careful build-up of false radio signals suggesting a massive concentration against the Pas de Calais; this was so successful that the German *Fifteenth Army* in that area continued to receive priority for reinforcement *even after* the landings had taken place. The blueprint for such a ploy was drawn up in July and August 1918.

The Canadian Army Corps occupied a special position in the B.E.F. in the summer of 1918. It was the irrevocable policy of the Canadian Government, from the moment that the corps was formed in September 1915, that the Canadian divisions should always fight together. By 1918 there were four of them, of very high quality. But the crises of the great defensive battles of the year did not call for the intervention of such a large unit: single divisions, even brigades, to fill gaps and paper over cracks, were what the local commanders needed, and while the Australian Government reluctantly allowed its corps to be split up to provide these, the Canadian did not. This was infuriating at the time, but paid dividends now, with the Army going over to the offensive. The Canadian divisions were fresh and intact—a powerful accession of strength. Not surprisingly, they were concentrated in the area of greatest danger—Flanders. The problem was to get them to the Somme without the Germans being aware of the move.

And the solution was technological: radio—wireless, as it was then called—provided the necessary deception. While the main body of the Canadian Corps was making its move, two battalions and some signal units went to the Second Army area, and there the signallers started a flow of dummy radio traffic suggesting a corps build-up which in turn would indicate an imminent attack. The ruse was less successful in 1918 than in 1944; it was a difficult matter to pull divisions out of the line without the enemy noticing, and German Intelligence did indeed notice the departure of two Canadian divisions. But where to? As the Canadian Official History says: "If the enemy was not fully deceived, at least he was confused."[6] Complete radio silence on the Somme until the battle began helped this confusion, as did the extension of the Australian front to screen the Canadian build-up. When zero hour came the Germans were definitely not expecting to meet a Canadian attack.

Indeed, they were not expecting an attack at all. On 4 August Ludendorff issued the following Order of the Day:

> I am under the impression that, in many quarters, the possibility of an enemy offensive is viewed with a certain degree of apprehension. There is nothing to justify this apprehension provided our troops are vigilant and do their duty . . . we should wish for nothing better than to see the enemy launch an offensive, which can but hasten the disintegration of his forces. . . .

This over-confident document is a tribute to the skill of the Fourth Army staff and the discipline of its soldiers. Throughout the army area signposts urged all comers: "KEEP YOUR MOUTH SHUT," and the same message was pasted into every soldier's pay book. "Nothing attracts attention to an offensive more than a large number of officers with maps looking over the parapet and visiting Observation Posts," said a Fourth Army Instruction; reconnaissance of the German lines was accordingly severely restricted. No troops or transport were permitted to march *towards* the front in daylight except where absolutely necessary for normal reasons. Some units were even detailed to allow themselves to be seen marching *away* from the front. The Royal Air Force patrolled ceaselessly to make sure that nothing untoward was being revealed. By all these assorted means, and others besides, the Fourth Army achieved its surprise.

It was, nevertheless, the edging southwards of the Australian Corps to screen the Canadians, and the corresponding extension of the front of the British III Corps on the left, that deceived the Germans most. Certainly, this apparent thinning of the front seemed to offer them promising opportunities. On 29 July, the eve of their relief by III Corps, the Australians carried out one more act of "peaceful penetration" in the Morlancourt sector. From their point of view it was delightfully successful: three officers, 135 other ranks and thirty-six machine-guns captured. From the point of view of III Corps the Australian frolic was less of a blessing. On 6 August, while the 18th and 58th Divisions were carrying out reliefs, they were heavily attacked by a fresh division of Württembergers. The Germans took over 250 prisoners, and regained much of the ground won by the Australians. Next day there was heavy fighting on the III Corps front, as the British reacted in their turn. The details of all this are relatively unimportant; what mattered was the dislocation and the fatigue to the

troops concerned—because this was the day on which G.H.Q. decided
that the main attack would go in on 8 August.

Zero hour, by agreement between Rawlinson and Debeney, was 4:20
A.M. for the British, forty-five minutes later for the French. The
French would not be using tanks, and so would need a short preliminary bombardment. The British decided to dispense with this, relying
on their 342 heavy Mark V and 72 Medium Mark A tanks. The latter
are generally referred to as "Whippets," a name which is liable to conjure up misleading images. The Whippet weighed only fourteen tons,
carried a crew of three and an armament of four Hotchkiss machine-
guns, and had a range of eighty miles, as compared with thirty-five for
the Mark V—but there all resemblance to dogs of the greyhound breed
ceases: the maximum (road) speed of a Whippet was 8.3 m.p.h.,
which is scarcely a gallop (the Mark V's was 4.6 m.p.h.). There was
also a long Mark V Star model, valuable for crossing wide trench obstacles, and capable of lifting twenty to twenty-five men. Unfortunately, owing to a design defect which lodged the radiator inside the
tank without compensating ventilation, there was a hazard from fumes
and carbon monoxide poisoning which meant that "having been so lifted
they required a considerable time for recovery."[7] One hundred and
twenty supply tanks completed Rawlinson's array of armour.

It was yet another of 1918's hints at things to come that this concentration of armour on the ground was matched (indeed, exceeded) by a
concentration in the air. On the Fourth Army front no less than 800
aircraft were assembled, 376 of them fighters; one squadron was allotted to work with the tanks—a clear pointer to 1939. The French contribution was even more powerful; General Debeney had requested the
support of the Air Division, hitherto operating in Champagne, and as
fighting was now dying down in that area Pétain had agreed. The
accession of this powerful unit of over 600 planes brought Debeney's
total air strength to 1,104, the Allied total to 1,904. To this the Germans could initially oppose only 365 aircraft. Nevertheless the Royal
Air Force did not go altogether happily into battle; July had been a
month of particularly sad losses—Major James McCudden, killed acci-
dentally on 9 July, and Major Edward Mannock shot down by ground
fire on 26 July. McCudden comes fourth in the list of British
aces, with fifty-seven kills; Mannock tops the list with seventy-three,
but it was his quality as a formation leader that entitled him to the
claim "that he was the greatest fighting pilot of the war."

Preparations (except where III Corps was still making good the setbacks of 6 August) came to completion: the Canadians moved into line
on the British right, the Australians gathered in the centre; the Cavalry
Corps, three divisions strong, closed up; the tanks were standing by;

Rawlinson's 2,070 guns and howitzers were ready to fire. The Germans seemed unsuspicious. At about 3 A.M. ground mist began to form in the river valleys, soon spreading to the higher ground, and thickening as zero hour approached. This was not an unmixed blessing—in particular it hampered R.A.F. co-operation—but, as with the Germans on 21 March, it was the attackers who stood to gain most from bad visibility, the defenders who would be most hampered.

At 4:20 A.M. the British barrage came down with crackling precision, and the long lines of tanks and infantry advanced through the murky half-light. Not until the mist cleared in the bright August sun (about 10 A.M.) could they actually see the effect they were producing, but they began to have the "feel" of it straight away. Except in the III Corps area there were no checks, no untoward halts. The forward movement, necessarily slow in the mist, continued steadily; the supports, coming up behind, never entangled with the front divisions, but passed through them according to plan, dead on time and without a hitch. By seven o'clock the Australians were all on their first objective; by half past ten on their second; by eleven o'clock the Canadians were up alongside. As the mists cleared and the sun burst through, a remarkable sight was seen in the wide spaces of the centre of the field:

> . . . the whole Santerre plateau seen from the air was dotted with parties of infantry, field artillery, and tanks moving forward. Staff officers were galloping about, many riding horses in battle for the first time. . . . Indeed, at this stage there was more noise of movement than firing, as the heavy batteries . . . were no longer in action; for the infantry had gone so far that it was no longer possible for them to shoot. . . . No enemy guns seemed to be firing and no co-ordinated defence was apparent. . . .[8]

By 1:30 P.M. the main fighting was over. The Australians had occupied all their objectives, except on their extreme flanks where their neighbours were behind them; the Canadians had advanced almost eight miles.

It had been a sensational day, though not devoid of hazards. By common consent the tanks had done marvels. Against German infantry and machine-guns they had proved irresistible, and countless infantry lives had been saved by their action. The German artillery, on the other hand, had not suffered the loss of morale that the year's high casualties had brought about in the infantry. They stuck to their guns, often shooting at tanks at point-blank range. Ten tanks of the 1st Battalion attacked Le Quesnel in the Canadian sector; nine were set on fire by direct hits from field guns at seventy yards. A line of twelve tanks, topping the crest of a rise which marked their start-line with the 5th Australian Division, had six knocked out immediately by field guns at a range of half a mile, and three more shortly after that. Even without enemy action, the tank crews had much to endure, the experience of one 14th Battalion tank being typical: "With the prolonged running at high speed the interior of the tank rapidly became unbearable through heat and petrol fumes, and the crew were forced to evacuate it and to take cover underneath. At this moment two of the crew were wounded, one was sick, one fainted and one was delirious."[9]

Much had been expected of collaboration between the Whippets and the cavalry, but this proved to be an illusion. Where German resistance collapsed, the tanks could not keep up with the horses, but where machine-gunners rallied it was the tanks alone that made progress. By themselves the Whippets were very successful, taking batteries in the rear, supporting patrols and mopping up, many of them experiencing adventures similar to, though it would scarcely be possible to equal, those of the legendary "Musical Box."[10] The armoured cars of the 17th Battalion, once the long, straight Roman road which bisects the battlefield was cleared, plunged deep into the German back areas, shooting up infantry and transport and capturing four officers of the *LI Corps* staff, taken by surprise at a meal. The armour did well on 8 August; it had shown once more, as at Cambrai in November 1917, that it was most effective for breaking *into* the enemy's front. What the technology of 1918 did not permit, however, was exploitation of a break-*through*.

Nevertheless, in the centre victory was complete. The Canadians captured 114 officers, 4,919 other ranks, 161 guns and uncounted hundreds of machine-guns and mortars; their losses were about 3,500. The Australians captured 183 officers, 7,742 other ranks, 173 guns and hundreds of smaller trophies. Their losses were under 3,000. Only on the flanks was there any flaw. After a difficult day on 7 August, trying to win back its lost ground, III Corps had spent a bad night against an alert enemy. There was much German shelling, particularly with gas, which caused many casualties and further dislocation. Surprise in this sector was out of the question; the enemy were as strong as the attackers; tanks were much less numerous, and the steep, well-wooded ground was less suitable for them.

The main objective of III Corps was the Chipilly Spur, thrusting its high promontory into the channel of the Somme, which is here compelled to make a wide southward bend. Unless taken, this spur would prove a serious handicap to the left of the Australian advance; but to take it proved beyond the powers of the 58th Division. The advancing

Australians were caught in enfilade by machine-guns and field artillery sited on the spur; they suffered their most serious casualties and their only failure at this point. Further to the left the 18th Division also failed to progress beyond its first objective.

When every allowance is made for the special conditions that applied to the III Corps front, there remains a contrast between the performances of these divisions and that of the Dominion troops so marked that a further explanation has to be sought. One does not have to look very far: all the divisions of III Corps had had a hard year, all had suffered heavily in the March and April battles.[11] "Thus," says the Official History,

> there was not only a shortage of experienced officers and N.C.O.s, but the ranks of the infantry units had been filled up with young recruits from home. These convalescent divisions had not entered with great enthusiasm on the hard task of preparing a field of battle, in the hours of darkness and in bad weather. The reasons given them for the moves and reliefs had an unexpected effect. Believing that the French were not doing well on the Marne and that, bad omen, they were to take over more front, as the III Corps (with the 18th and 58th Divisions in it) had done before March 1918, the willing co-operation usually exhibited before an attack was absent.[12]

To this should be added the damage done by the German spoiling attack. At bottom it all amounted to an understandable degree of war-weariness; similar phenomena were observed during the campaign in north-west Europe in 1944–45.

Such sentiments were not confined to the British. In the French sector, where the going was very much easier, the absence of "push" was even more marked. General Debeney's instructions to his Army had been vehement in the French manner: ". . . the attacks will be conducted with but one preoccupation, to achieve the greatest rapidity in a succession of forward bounds. . . . Alignment is not to be sought; it is forbidden to wait for neighbouring divisions . . . the attacks will be pushed on and continued until night; from the very first day the troops must go 'very far.'"

This did not occur. Starting three-quarters of an hour after the Canadians, whose advance naturally eased their progress on the left, the French moved so deliberately that when the Canadian line halted it was five hours before the French came up abreast of it. General Debeney was found by Sir Douglas Haig during the afternoon "almost in tears because three battalions of his Colonial infantry had bolted before a German machine gun." This is possibly a sardonic over-statement, but it is clear that the French First Army was not performing well. In Champagne the French had shown much more dash, and they would show it again before the war ended. But Debeney was no Mangin, and the French Army in 1918 was not of the same calibre as the ardent men who had flung themselves at the enemy in 1915, 1916 and in Nivelle's fiasco.

In another sector of the battle there was also disappointment. When the morning mist cleared the great Allied air fleet came into action and "the battle-field became alive with aeroplanes."[13] At first the R.A.F. devoted itself to close co-operation with the advancing soldiers, and some spectacular feats were performed, including the capture of a great railway gun in conjunction with the 5th Australian Division. Low-flying aircraft attacked machine-gun posts, stampeded horse-drawn transport, shot up staff cars and scattered infantry formations—all this adding greatly to the strain on German nerves. At midday, however, there was a change of bombing policy which produced severe and costly air fighting. Reports came in that roads leading to the Somme bridges behind the German lines were becoming congested with retreating troops and transport. If the bridges could be destroyed there seemed to be a wonderful chance of inflicting total disaster on the German *Second Army,* and the R.A.F.'s bombers were accordingly ordered to concentrate on this task.

No less than 205 sorties were made against the Somme bridges on 8 August, and from the first the German reaction was most violent. The German pilots, says the Official History, "fought generally with a reckless courage to take toll of the bombers, even though they could not prevent the attacks. . . . The only means by which the German fighting pilots could redress in some degree their inferiority in numbers was to spend the minimum of time upon the ground. Many of them were in the air on the 8th of August for ten hours, taking part in combat after combat."[14] Only those who have endured such an ordeal can know what it does to a man.

Among the German squadrons taking part in this tremendous fight was the famous "Richthofen circus," now commanded by Hauptmann Hermann Goering. Goering's policy differed from Richthofen's: the latter never hesitated to break off a fight if he thought conditions unfavourable—hence the apparent indestructibility of the "circus." Goering, however, "a leader of proved worth, was possibly gifted with a temperament more offensive in quality than that of his predecessor, or it may be that the German air service, sensing that the whole background of the war was changing, was impelled to throw its weight into the battle heedless of cost or danger."[15] For the "Richthofen circus" the result was tragic: it was "fought almost to destruction." The "circus" had to be withdrawn from the battle, and though reinforced by new young pilots it was never again the dangerous instrument of war that it had once been. Nevertheless, its self-sacrifice was not wasted: thanks to its efforts and those of the other German pilots engaged, no vital damage was done to the Somme bridges, while the Royal Air Force sustained a loss of forty-five aircraft shot down and fifty-two more so badly damaged that they had to be written off. This represents 13 per cent of the total engaged, and 23 per cent of the bombers—a striking tribute to the Luftwaffe's quality.

No deficiencies on the part of the Allies, however, and no achievement of the German Air Service, could disguise the real significance of 8 August. The German Official Monograph on the battle sums it up:

> As the sun set on August 8th on the battlefield the greatest defeat which the German Army had suffered since the beginning of the war was an accomplished fact. The position divisions between the Avre and the Somme which had been struck by the enemy attack were nearly completely annihilated. The troops in the front line north of the Somme had also suffered seriously, as also the reserve divisions thrown into the battle in the course of the day. The total loss of the formations employed in the *Second Army* area is estimated at 650 to 700 officers and 26,000 to 27,000 other ranks. More than 400 guns, besides a huge number of machine guns, trench mortars, and other war material had been lost. . . . More than two-thirds of the total loss had surrendered as prisoners.[16]

Ludendorff wrote:

> August 8th was the black day of the German Army in the history of the war. . . . Our war machine was no longer efficient. Our fighting power had suffered, even though the great majority of divisions still fought heroically. The 8th of August put the decline of that fighting power beyond all doubt and in such a situation as regards reserves, I had no hope of finding a strategic expedient whereby to turn the situation to our advantage. . . .[17]

The Australians just said: "It was a très bon stunt."

Always, on the Western Front, attackers faced the same problem: how, having broken into the enemy's line, to maintain momentum, drive the thrust home. No one had yet found the answer, not the French in 1915 in their great offensives in Artois and Champagne, nor the Germans in 1916 at Verdun, nor the British at Arras and Cambrai in 1917, nor the French in that year under Nivelle. Even in March 1918 the Germans could only drive the British front back; they never broke through. The Battle of Amiens was no exception to the rule. It was to continue for three more days, but each one saw slower progress, harder going against stiffening German resistance. And each day, as the Germans withdrew, the line of battle came nearer to the area of the old 1916 battlefield, a wilderness of collapsing trenches and craters, with jungles of rusty wire and all kinds of hideous débris under the weeds: an awful place to fight in.

The second day of the battle was crucial: at that stage no fresh reinforcements had yet reached the Germans and to all intents and purposes there was a gap in their line facing the Canadian and Australian Corps. Both of these fine formations did their best, but eager though they were they were unused to open warfare conditions. Staffs and commanders, used to the intricate network of telephone communications which had been evolved during years of static trench warfare, were at a loss in the open; it was the breakdown of communications which brought frustration on 9 August more than any other factor. The furthest advance was made by the Canadians—just over three miles; as on the previous day, the French effort was disappointing; on the front of III Corps, on the other hand, a valuable success was gained with the capture of the Chipilly spur by the 58th Division, in which the American 131st Regiment gave decisive help. German losses in men and guns were exceptionally heavy in this sector.

Nevertheless, the day's results were in general disappointing, and it will be useful at this stage to probe a little mythology. Because tanks had achieved great successes on 8 August the idea has persisted that they were war-winners, that had they been better used they could have brought the war to an earlier end. The ninth of August reveals the sterner truth: 414 fighting tanks had rolled into action on 8 August— the full available strength of the Tank Corps; there were no reserves. The reason for this strange disposition is very simple: the original planning for the Battle of Amiens had envisaged a much more limited operation than that which actually transpired, an attack whose main purpose was the disengagement of the Paris-Amiens railway. For this an advance to what was called "the Amiens Defence Line" between Méricourt and Hangest was prescribed, with a further advance "in the direction of" Chaulnes and Roye (the old British front line of 1917). On 3 August, however, Foch told Haig that he was considering bringing in the French Third Army on the right of the First; he was anxious that there should be no delay on the "Amiens Defence Line" and urged a more distant objective. Haig pointed out that his Operation Order of 29 July had mentioned Ham, fifteen miles beyond the old British front, and across the Somme: "This he thought satisfactory. . . . More than once he expressed the opinion that the 'Germans are breaking up,' and was anxious lest they should fall back before I could get my blow in."

Accordingly, two days later, Haig met Rawlinson, Debeney and Lieutenant-General Kavanagh, commanding the Cavalry Corps. He told them:

> I thought that the Fourth Army orders aimed too much at getting a *final* objective on the old Amiens defence line, and stopping counter-attacks on it. This is not far enough, in my opinion, if we succeed at the start in surprising the enemy. So I told Rawlinson (it had already been in my orders) to arrange to *advance as rapidly as possible* and capture the old Amiens line of defence . . . and to put it in a state of defence; *but not to delay;* at once reserves must be pushed on to capture the line Chaulnes-Roye. The general direction of the advance is to be on Ham.

Fourth Army orders were amended accordingly; the battle thus became a virtually unlimited operation. But Tank Corps dispositions had been arranged in a quite different sense, and at this late stage (5 August) it was impossible to change them without creating great confusion. In any case, the rapid advance now envisaged required the maximum number of tanks to take part. As we have seen, the 414 present on 8 August did splendidly—but on 9 August only 145 were available. On 10 August (to round off this revealing story) the number had shrunk to eighty-five. By 11 August, says a Tank Corps historian,[18] "the Tank Corps reserves were used up, and the Tanks and their crews were almost fought to a standstill. They had had three days of continuous fighting and marching, and of the 38 Tanks which went into action on the 11th there was not one but badly needed overhauling. The crews were completely exhausted." On 12 August only six tanks were able to fight. The German empire was not going to be overthrown by six tanks, any more than by Trenchard's ten bomber squadrons at Nancy.

Yet numbers are only a part of the story; by 11 August no less than 688 tanks had been in action, and 480 had been handed over to Tank Corps Salvage Units, too badly damaged to be mended in their units. "Very few of the remaining tanks were actually fit for a long action, and all required a thorough overhaul."[19] This was bad enough, but there was something else, far more serious:

> It is very often not realized what is meant by the exhaustion of the crews; this in the case of tanks does not merely mean bodily fatigue. The crews of one battalion after some hard fighting became absolutely exhausted and most of them physically ill. The pulses of one crew were

taken immediately they got out of their tank; the beats averaged 130 to
the minute or just twice as fast as they should have been. Two men of
one crew temporarily lost their reason and had to be restrained by
force, and one tank commander became delirious. In some cases where
infantry were carried in the tank, they fainted within three-quarters of
an hour of the start. At the time the physical strain on crews accentu-
ated by the extreme heat was not fully appreciated by commanders of
some formations.[20]

It is clear that both mechanically and humanly, the tank of 1918 was
not a war-winning weapon; certainly the later stages of the Battle of
Amiens would have to be conducted without any significant contribution from it.

Those later stages may be briefly summarized as a steady slowing up
of the advance, through fatigue and stronger resistance. The critical action now lay more in the minds of the commanders than in the proceedings at the front. On the Allied side, this expressed itself as a
sharp dispute between Foch and Haig. Haig had for some time considered extending his front northwards by bringing in Rawlinson's neighbour, Byng, with his Third Army, and General Sir Henry Horne's First
Army to the north of that. A visit to the front on 10 August convinced
him that the time had come to transfer the main action to north of the
Somme in the direction of Bapaume. This brought him into conflict
with Foch, who came to see him on the 10th:

> He wishes the advance to continue to the line Noyon-Ham-Péronne,
> and to try to get the bridgeheads on the Somme. I pointed out the
> difficulty of the undertaking unless the enemy is quite demoralized, and
> we can cross the Somme on his heels . . . we must expect German
> reserves to arrive very soon in order to check our advance. My plan to
> advance my left on Bapaume and on Monchy-le-Preux will then be-
> come necessary. In Foch's opinion the fact of the French 1st Army's
> and now the 3rd French Army's getting on without meeting with
> serious opposition shows the enemy is demoralized. I agree that
> some German divisions are demoralized, but not all yet![21]

The next day Haig notes: "Morning reports show enemy's opposition is stiffening on the battle front." He now gave Byng a precise instruction "to break the enemy's front, in order to outflank the enemy's
present battle front." Once more he received a visit from Foch (whose
whole technique of supreme command lay in these personal exhortations, sometimes inspiring, sometimes less so): "After a talk, he
approved (in view of the increased opposition) of my reducing my
front of attack. . . . He asked me to attack with my Third Army. I

told him that three weeks ago I had discussed with Byng the possibility of the Third Army co-operating and today I had seen Byng and given him definite orders to advance as soon as possible on Bapaume."

Foch was still not entirely satisfied—he hated to give a defeated enemy any respite—but from the lofty eminence of his high office he was less able to judge the difficulties of maintaining pressure than commanders on the spot. He continued to urge that the Fourth Army and the French First Army should press their advance pending Byng's intervention. But the army commanders themselves had little relish for this strategy; on 13 August Debeney asked Haig for a postponement of further operations, and a little later that day Haig heard that Rawlinson "considered that the attack would be very costly. I sent word to say that if he had any views to express to come and see me in the morning."

The meeting with Rawlinson on 14 August led to a critical development in Haig's relations with the Generalissimo. Rawlinson, with memories of the 1916 Somme battle graven on his mind, had been uneasy for several days; as far back as 10 August he had verged on the insubordinate when ordered to press forward. He asked Haig: "Are you commanding the British Army or is Marshal Foch?"[22] Now, on the 14th, he showed Haig aerial photographs of the German defences, and a report from the Canadian commander, Lieutenant-General Currie, in which he gave his opinion that "to capture the position in question would be a very costly matter" and said that he "was opposed to attempting it." As these statements coincided with Haig's own views, he ordered the date of the next attack (16 August) to be postponed, though artillery preparation was to continue vigorously, and informed Foch of this decision. No sooner was it taken than news came of a German withdrawal on the Third Army front; this was merely a tactical expedient to straighten an awkward line, but it was yet another indication of the need to set that front in motion as soon as possible.

The fourteenth of August was a busy day for all concerned. No sooner did Foch receive Haig's message than he reacted with predictable vigour. Haig received his response by telegram at 5:30 that afternoon: "Understand perfectly the necessity for effective artillery preparation in view of serious hostile resistance but see no necessity for delaying Fourth Army and First French Army attack to coordinate with Third Army attack. First French Army and Fourth Army attacks should be carried out as soon as possible followed as quickly as possible by Third Army attack."

Neither Foch's tactics nor his strategy had ever been marked by subtlety; he was always a general who sought to impose his will on the enemy by relentless hammering. Haig's idea of unlocking the front

south of the Somme by new thrusts north of it was not Foch's style,
though he was quite happy to see the battle extending both northwards
and southwards. With this in mind he was already planning to bring in
the indefatigable Mangin with his Tenth Army on the right of the
French Third. He also still believed that the French First Army was
capable of making useful progress on the 16th. He despatched another
"Most Urgent" telegram to Haig at 9:10 P.M.: "In view of the dispositions now taken by the French First Army and of the artillery preparation already under way, any postponement of the movement against
Roye, decided upon for the 16th, would have most serious consequences." He continued in somewhat peremptory terms (*"Je vous
demande donc instamment . . ."*) to require that the Fourth Army
should "give its support to the First French Army on the 16th up to
Hattencourt, unless this is utterly impossible on the part of the troops
forming the right wing of the Fourth Army, which you will let me
know without delay."

To this Haig replied early the next morning: "Nothing has happened
. . . to cause me to alter my opinion on the situation on the Roye-
Chaulnes front. I therefore much regret that I cannot alter my orders
to the two Armies in question. I hope to be with you at Sarcus today
at 3 p.m."[23]

By the time Haig arrived at Sarcus, Foch's headquarters, the Generalissimo had had a chastening interview with Debeney: "He told me
that the projected attack on Roye would certainly be difficult, and he
felt that even assuming his forces to be sufficient for making it, they
would be too weak to keep it going."[24] Then Haig appeared, and once
more explained his strategy:

> Foch now wanted to know what orders I had issued for attack: when I
> proposed to attack. Where, and with what troops?
>
> I told Foch of my instructions to Byng and Horne; and that Rawlin-
> son would also co-operate with his left between the Somme and the
> Ancre when my Third Army had advanced, and when by reason of this
> some of the hostile pressure (which was still strong on that sector) had
> lessened.
>
> I spoke to Foch quite straightly and let him understand that *I was re-
> sponsible to my Government and fellow citizens for the handling of the
> British forces* [Haig's italics]. F's attitude at once changed and he said
> all he wanted was early information of my intentions so that he might
> co-ordinate the operations of the other Armies, and that he now
> thought I was quite correct in my decision not to attack the enemy in
> his prepared position. But notwithstanding what he now said, Foch and
> all his Staff had been most insistent for the last five days that I should
> press on along the South bank and capture the Somme bridges above
> Péronne, regardless of German opposition, and British losses.[25]

'. . . a portent for the distant future': a Handley Page 0/400 long-range bomber of the Independent Air Force. Carried sixteen 112 lb bombs or one 1,650 lb bomb; crew, four or five; maximum speed, 97.5 m.p.h.; ceiling 8,500 feet; air endurance, eight hours

'. . . unlikely to bring the German Empire to its knees': an F.E.2b of the Independent Air Force; maximum speed, 73 m.p.h.; air endurance three and a half hours; maximum load (including crew), 452 lbs

'...a temperament more offensive in quality': Hauptmann Hermann Goering, who commanded the 'Richthofen Circus', which was 'fought almost to destruction' on 8 August

. . very tough, resilient battle practitioners': supports of the 4th Canadian Division moving up for the battle the Canal du Nord, 27 September

. . the picture of the changing war': 60-pounder guns (medium artillery) out in the open, supporting a anadian advance through unscarred country; infantry marching along a road in the background

'. . . a good locality to leave alone': sketch by Captain F. E. Hodge, showing Bellenglise, with the bank of the St Quentin Canal cutting in front of the village, and belts of the barbed wire, which was the feature of the Hindenburg Line

'. . . some of the most powerful defences in existence': the barbed wire obstacle of Bellicourt, objective of the American II Corps on September 29

Foch confirms this account in his memoirs: "I definitely came around to the opinion of Field-Marshal Sir Douglas Haig, and I modified my orders of August 12th for the Somme operations."[26]

This passage between the two Allied leaders needs to be narrated in full, because it sets the tone of their relations for the rest of the war. From now onwards it was Haig's armies which would play the leading part, and, partly for this reason but also because their fundamental accord was sound, Haig's opinions would influence Foch profoundly. The Sarcus conference and all that followed it gives the lie direct to Lloyd George's malicious faint praise: "[Haig] did well . . . under Foch's supreme direction" (see p. 84).[27] On the contrary, it would be more accurate to say that Foch did well with Haig's support and counsel.

There were critical deliberations on the German side also, during this period, but they were of a different order. The German commanders very quickly realized that something had gone seriously wrong; that the magnificent German Army was no longer what it had been. Some of them attributed this to a contamination spread by troops coming from the Russian front, where they had been infected by revolutionary propaganda. There was some confirmation of this in the letters they sent home, examined by the Army censors. Thus, in one letter: "The war will end when the great capitalists have killed us all." And in another: "You at home must strike, but make no mistake about it, and raise revolution, then peace will come."

On 10 August, as reserves began to reach the front in larger numbers, one fresh division, the *38th,* found men in front of them "falling back in disorderly flight, among them drunken Bavarians, who shouted to the *94th Regiment,* 'What do you war-prolongers want? If the enemy were only on the Rhine—the war would then be over!'" The *263rd Reserve Regiment* relieved part of the *1st Reserve Division,* which was "pouring back"; "some of its men shouted 'We thought we had set the thing going, now you asses are corking up the hole again.'" The *Alpine Corps,* entering the line, found complete confusion: "individuals and all ranks in large parties were wandering wildly about, but soon for the most part finding their way to the rear . . . only here and there were a few isolated batteries in soldierly array, ready to support the reinforcing troops."

These were the unpalatable matters to be digested at a meeting of the German war-lords at Advanced General Headquarters at Avesnes on 11 August. Ludendorff frankly admitted that a heavy defeat had been suffered, and reported the shouts of "Blacklegs!" and "War-prolongers!". This prompted the Kaiser and the German Crown Prince to ask whether perhaps too much had been asked of the soldiers; Ludendorff replied that the collapse of morale on 8 August could not

be accounted for by fatigue. He offered his own resignation, but neither Hindenburg nor the Kaiser would accept it. He says: "The Emperor gave me quite special proofs of his confidence in those days. I
was deeply moved, but remained anxious as to whether His Majesty really read the whole situation aright." Yet it was at this very meeting
that the Kaiser himself said: "I see that we must strike a balance. We
have nearly reached the limit of our powers of resistance. The war
must be ended."

"Thus," says the British Official History, we see that "the collapse of
Germany began not in the Navy, not in the Homeland, not in any of
the sideshows, but on the Western Front in consequence of defeat in
the field." It is strange how generations of clever men have failed to
notice this.

The question for the German leaders after 8 August was not whether
to end the war, but how to end it. For the next three months they
would vainly seek some "position of strength" from which to negotiate;
Foch and Haig were determined that they should not find it. In this, it
must be said, they were much assisted by Ludendorff; if anyone was
not reading the situation aright, it was he. The local commanders
urged retirements to avoid further disasters, but were overruled—only
to be forced to carry out these very manoeuvres under less favourable
conditions later. General von Lossberg, Chief of Staff of a new army
group formed to co-ordinate the threatened fronts, proposed that all
reinforcements should be placed in the Hindenburg Line, which should
be prepared immediately for defence. "Ludendorff would not
agree. . . . He was opposed to voluntary retirements to shorten the
line, because, although they economized divisions, they allowed the
enemy to do the same and to accumulate reserves; besides, they had a
bad effect on morale and encouraged the enemy."[28] This inability to
make hard decisions in good time, coupled with a tendency to swing
back into absurd optimism, followed by even more disintegrating pessimism, was the fruit of the "intellectual dislocation" which had afflicted
Ludendorff since 18 July and would remain with him to the end (see
p. 81).

Further evidence of this was soon forthcoming—and evidence also
of serious weaknesses both in the German High Command and in the
Central Alliance. Two conferences took place, on 13 August and 14
August, at General Headquarters at Spa (ironically lodged in the
Hotel Britannique). The first of these was attended by Chancellor von
Hertling and Foreign Secretary Admiral von Hintze.[29] Ludendorff told
Hindenburg that it was necessary to give these dignitaries the full
truth, which he still saw in very black terms: "tantamount to a vote of
no-confidence passed by the German Army on the Supreme Com-

mand."[30] In other words, there could be no military solution to Germany's problems, either offensive or defensive, "and so the termination of the war would have to be brought about by diplomacy."[31] Yet at the same time Ludendorff expressed determination to hold on to Belgium and large areas of western Russia—aims which could not fail to stultify any diplomatic approach. And already he was embarking on a calculated process of exculpation which was to have tragic consequences for Germany and for Europe in the future—transferring the blame for defeat from the Army and the High Command to failures in the Fatherland.

The next day there was an Imperial Conference presided over by the Kaiser, at which all these matters were gone over again. It was now that a distinct difference of attitude between Ludendorff and Hindenburg became apparent: "The Field-Marshal took a more optimistic view of the military situation than I did." Hindenburg told the Kaiser that "it would be possible to succeed in remaining on French soil and finally thereby to subject the enemy to our will." Did he really believe this? One view (encouraged by his memoirs) is that he only spoke like this to cheer up what would otherwise have been more like a gathering of mourners at a funeral. Sir John Wheeler-Bennett says however: "The truth is that at this time the Marshal really knew very little of what was going on about him. Separated by an army of officials from a nation which regarded him with almost superstitious adoration, he lived in an entirely false atmosphere of optimism, and Ludendorff saw to it that only those had access to him who represented the nation's 'will to victory,' a will which was slowly growing weaker." This kind of artificiality was a fault of the German system of command by figurehead, and put them at a further disadvantage vis-à-vis the Allies. On the other hand, artificial or not, Hindenburg's calm and resolution would help to some extent to offset Ludendorff's panics and vacillations in the days to come.

For the time being, however, it did not have much effect. Admiral von Hintze addressed the Imperial Conference in the terms expressed by Ludendorff to him the previous day: "He was manifestly moved; tears stood in his eyes. The Emperor was very calm. He agreed with Secretary of State von Hintze and instructed him to open up peace negotiations, if possible, through the Queen of the Netherlands." So ended the Imperial Conference. In effect it had achieved nothing, because no firm hand gripped Germany's destiny at this moment of crisis. A diplomatic solution had been agreed on, but not its implications: there was no attempt to bait the proposed peace negotiations with attractive morsels, no proper consideration of the time factor— diplomacy would await "a lull in the fighting." Even von Hintze, so apparently clear-headed at Spa, soon dried his tears and a week later was telling the Reichstag "there is no ground for doubting our victory."

The end of the Imperial Conference did not terminate the proceedings at Spa on 14 August; the Germans had visitors. That afternoon Emperor Karl of Austria arrived with his Foreign Minister and his Chief of the General Staff, General Arz von Straussenburg. The Austrians gave their opinion that "somehow or other the war must be ended as soon as possible." But what ought to have been a fine opportunity for the two Germanic powers to reach agreement on peace terms was missed; their accord broke down on diverging views of the Polish question—or, to put it more bluntly, on their clash of greed. And when Ludendorff asked for more Austrian divisions for the Western Front (two had already arrived), General Arz said "that the Austro-Hungarian Army was no longer in a condition to hold out through the coming winter; that was my last interview with this General whom I held in the highest esteem both as a man and a soldier."[32] For the two emperors, also, this was a last meeting. But, more significantly, what the Spa gathering demonstrated beyond all doubt was the absurdity of the belief, cherished by Lloyd George and others including even so astute a public servant as Lord Hankey, that Germany could be overthrown by "knocking away the props." There were no props; by 1918 Germany was the sole prop of all her allies, and her defeat in the field meant that she could no longer perform this service for them. Their collapse, one after another, would not be long delayed.

The interval between the great actions of the war was brief enough, and fully occupied with preparations. On the British front these were not without their complications. As far back as 12 August, Pershing had warned Haig that "he might have to withdraw the five American divisions which are training with British divisions. I pointed out to him that I had done everything to equip and help these units of the American Army, and provide them with horses. So far, I have had no help from these troops (except the three battalions which were used in the battle near Chipilly in error)." Haig was understandably irritated at the prospect of losing this important force on the eve of a major offensive effort. Yet, as usual, he was capable of taking the larger view, and recognized the validity of the American desire to concentrate all their units on a front of their own. Pershing wrote: "He . . . said that although he needed our troops he realised my position and my reasons for their withdrawal. He then concluded, in his frank, straightforward way: 'Pershing, of course you shall have them, there can never be any difference between us.' "[33]

In the event, however, Pershing contented himself with a formal request (on 16 August) for only three of the five divisions; Haig informed Foch of this, pointing out that the British line would have to be shortened by some 18,000 yards (a three-division frontage) in compensation. With the axis of the battle now shifting northwards, Foch had transferred General Debeney's army back to French command, but on receiving Haig's information he ordered the French First Army to extend to the north, releasing the Canadian Corps to act first as a reserve, then once more as shock troops.

Fearing a large-scale German withdrawal (the very manoeuvre against which Ludendorff set his face so firmly), Foch chafed at all delay with mounting impatience. He was barely mollified by a smart little victory on the Second Army front on 18 August. British casualties were 671, and 697 German prisoners were taken. Haig commented, "It seems the rule now to capture more prisoners than we have casualties." He himself, nevertheless, shared some of Foch's anxiety; he had a sense of lost opportunities during the Fourth Army's operations, and feared that the same might occur when the Third Army's attack began. On 19 August he visited General Byng: "He explained his plan, which I thought was too limited in its scope. I told him that his objective was to break the enemy's front, and gain Bapaume as soon as possible. . . . Now is the time to act with boldness, and in full confidence that, if we only hit the enemy hard enough, and combine the action of all arms in pressing him, his troops will give way on a very wide front and acknowledge that he is beaten."

Mangin was already on the move again. On 18 and 19 August his Tenth Army made successful preparatory attacks between Soissons and the River Oise, which impelled Foch to write to Haig: "The enemy has everywhere been shaken by the blows already dealt him. We must repeat these blows without losing any time. . . . Therefore I assume that the attack of your Third Army, postponed already until August 21, will be launched that day *with the utmost violence,* carrying along with it the divisions of the First Army lying next to it and your Fourth Army in its entirety." The next day saw the opening of the Battle of Noyon, a brilliant success for Mangin with over 8,000 prisoners being taken—"another black day" for Ludendorff, with "heavy and irreplaceable losses." And now the British were also ready to resume.

The twenty-first of August, like so many of those assault days of the summer of 1918, opened with dense fog, giving way later to brilliant sun and intense heat. The Third Army's attack on this day, like Mangin's on the 18th and 19th, had been conceived as a preparatory affair, which was to cause some heartburn later. On the right Byng's front overlapped the 1916 Somme battlefields north and east of the ruined town of Albert, with such ominous place-names as Contalmaison, Ovillers, Pozières (where the Australians had made their grim début on the Western Front) and Thiepval of dreadful memory. On his extreme left the front touched the Arras battlefield of 1917. Between these two cratered areas, however, was a zone which, although devastated in the German withdrawal of that year, was considered to be reasonable going, satisfactory for the use of tanks.

Viewed as a preliminary, the Third Army's attack on the 21st was successful—in its limited fashion. In front of IV and VI Corps the Germans fell back on a front of 3,000–4,000 yards "according to plan," which meant hard fighting against their rearguards, especially their artillery and machine-guns. The latter from now on became, in the words of the British Official History, "the hard core of the resistance." But what halted the Third Army on 21 August was not so much the enemy (despite the contrary belief of the Bavarian Official Account) as the Third Army's own plan for a strictly limited advance. And for the 22nd, while the left wing of the Fourth Army cleared Albert, the plan prescribed no further advance by the Third Army, only preparation. Indeed, it was the Germans who attacked on this front that day, though with conspicuous and costly lack of success. But Haig, sharing Foch's apprehensions, was becoming more and more discontented with such deliberation.

On the 21st Haig had had an important visitor—Winston Churchill, Minister of Munitions. Churchill described to him the proposed munitions programme for 1919: "I told him we ought to do our utmost to get a decision this autumn. We are engaged in a 'wearing-out battle,' and are outlasting and beating the enemy. If we allow the enemy a period of quiet, he will recover, and the 'wearing-out' process must be recommenced. In reply, I was told that the General Staff in London calculate that the decisive period of the war cannot arrive until next July." Haig was not concerned with "next July"; it was his vision of imminent victory, conceived during the Battle of Amiens, that now guided him, and made him much regret the Third Army's halt on 22 August. That day he addressed his army commanders:

> I request that Army Commanders will, without delay, bring to the notice of all subordinate leaders the changed conditions under which operations are now being carried on, and the consequent necessity for all ranks to act with the utmost boldness and resolution in order to get full advantage from the present favourable situation.
> The effect of two very severe defeats, and the continuous attacks to which the enemy has been subjected during the past month, has been to wear out his troops and disorganise his plans. . . .
> To turn the present situation to account, the most resolute offensive is

everywhere desirable. Risks which a month ago would have been criminal to incur, ought now to be incurred as a duty.

It is no longer necessary to advance in regular lines and step by step. On the contrary, each division should be given a distant objective which must be reached independently of its neighbours, and even if one's flank is thereby exposed for the time being. . . .

The situation is most favourable; let each one of us act energetically, and without hesitation push forward to our objective.[34]

Whether or not inspired by this Order, the British offensive now gathered evident momentum, reflected in headlines and news stories as surprising to the long-disappointed British public as they were agreeable. Thus, on 23 August *The Times* bannered its main news:

NEW BRITISH STROKE
Albert Taken
All Objectives Gained

The first leader said: ". . . a continuous battle of varying intensity is now being waged over nearly half the Western Front, and even 1914 now furnishes no parallel for the present extent of the conflict."

Next day the main news page announced:

BRITISH FRONT ABLAZE
A General Attack
Storm Of Many Villages
Mangin Still Advancing

This was the announcement of the resumption of the Third Army's attack towards Bapaume on 23 August; with the Fourth Army alongside, the British offensive front was now thirty-five miles long. The weather was about to change, but on 23 August the heat was still intense, recalling the sweltering days of the retreat from Mons in the same month of 1914. For the advancing infantry and the gunners at their heavy work this was bad enough; for the tank crews (Byng had about 100 tanks in action) it was purgatory. In some instances entire crews of Mark Vs became unconscious through heat and fumes. The 3rd Battalion's history records:

The heat temporarily put several Whippets out of action as fighting weapons. On a hot summer's day one hour's running with door closed renders a Whippet weaponless except for revolver fire. The heat generated is so intense that it not only causes ammunition to swell so that it jams the gun, but actually in several cases caused rounds to explode inside the tank. Guns became too hot to hold, and in one case the temperature of the steering wheel became unbearable.

Despite the heat and everything the Germans could do, 23 August was a day of success on both army fronts: 8,000 prisoners were taken —2,000 of them by Monash's implacable Australians. On the 24th and 25th, in cooler weather with low clouds impeding air operations, the advance continued. *The Times* announced:

FALL OF SOMME STRONGHOLDS
Bapaume Menaced

and a special correspondent wrote:

> These are great days. It surely must be that they will even loom greatly in history, but they are certainly great to live in. . . . The sweep of our advance is so rapid that no man can say where our advanced line as a whole may stand at any given moment, for every half-hour brings news that this or that village is in our hands, or that an airman has seen the khaki figures somewhere where we never dreamed that they had reached. . . . When one remembers what the names of Thiepval, and Fricourt, and Mametz and Contalmaison meant in the old days of 1916, and Le Sars and Warlencourt, it is difficult to realize that we have again swept over all that ground between Friday night and Sunday morning. . . .

The first leader on that day (26 August) observed with some wonder: "The arrival of our forces at the outskirts of Bapaume yesterday set the seal on a wonderful weekend, and brought into view possibilities which were certainly not in sight a week ago."

This was no less than the truth, but what the editor of *The Times* did not know when he wrote it was that the horizons of the battle were about to widen even further. The operations of the Third and Fourth Armies between 21 and 29 August are known as the Battle of Albert;[35] on 26 August the First Army opened, in its turn, the Battle of the Scarpe. Haig recorded: "Today has been a most successful one. The capture of Monchy le Preux at the cost of 1,500 casualties was quite extraordinary. The enemy knew the value of this position in his system of defences and so devoted much labour to strengthening it since he retook it from us [in March]."

For the rest of the month the two battles continued, jointly presenting to a bewildered public an unfamiliar image of war:

27 August: BATTLE FRONT SPREADING
28 August: ALLIES SWEEP FORWARD
29 August: LINE FLUNG FORWARD
30 August: THE FLOWING TIDE

On 29 August the New Zealand Division, whose standard of excellence in this war matched that of its successor under General Freyberg in the next, entered Bapaume, "an honour," said *The Times,* "they had well earned." On this day the Battle of Albert formally ended—though these formal "openings" and "closings" of First World War battles are often mere historians' conveniences: for the fighting men this one merely merged into what historians call the Battle of Bapaume. All three armies, First, Third and Fourth, continued to fight hard during the four days of this engagement, but the laurels undoubtedly go to the Australian 2nd Division for its capture of Mont St. Quentin, just outside Péronne, on 31 August.

Along the line of the Somme opposite Péronne the Australians faced obstacles that would have daunted most men: beside the river on the western bank ran a canal; the river itself was a series of streams running through a marsh about 1,000 yards wide; all the bridges were down; and across the river, brooding over this whole sector, commanding all the approaches to the Somme and all possible bridgeheads as well as the town of Péronne, a mile to the south, was Mont St. Quentin. This 140-foot-high hill, crowned by a ruined village and a stark clump of tree trunks, its bare, empty slopes seamed with old trenches and belts of rusty wire, was "a veritable bastion," "a famous fortress of the Western Front." None appreciated the importance of this position better than the German High Command, which ordered it to be defended at all costs. The Australian Official History remarks: "The task ahead was in some ways the most formidable ever faced by Australian infantry."

Fortunately, just north of Mont St. Quentin, the Somme bends sharply to an east–west alignment, and here the Australian Corps was astride it. This meant that the high ground could be approached without making new (and inevitably costly) river crossings by frontal assault. Two battalions of the 5th Australian Brigade were detailed for the attack—an apparently trifling force for such an occasion, since all Australian battalions were now very weak, averaging about 300 rifles each. This meant that the attack would be carried out by "eight very tired companies comprising some 550 rifles, with a handful of machine gunners and four companies of 200 in close support."[36] However, this absurdly small force of infantry enjoyed massive artillery backing—five

field brigades and four heavy. In the Australian Corps, as in the rest of
the B.E.F., the proficiency of the artillery and its domination of the
enemy were continuing features of the final offensive. On 31 August it
was the guns that made success possible.

And the success was breathtaking. To conceal their scanty numbers
the Australians made a tremendous noise as they charged the German
positions in the murky half-light of 5 A.M. German accounts tell how
the Australians came upon them suddenly from front and flanks, driving them from one position to another and arriving in each as fast as
the defenders. "It all happened like lightning, and before we had fired
a shot we were taken unawares." "It was all the work of an instant. We
were overrun."[37] Over 700 prisoners were taken—more men than the
Australians had put into the attack. By 8 A.M. Monash was able to report complete success to Rawlinson, who was at first "totally incredu-
lous," as was Haig when he first heard the news. But both recognized
"that the event was calculated to have a most important influence upon
the immediate course of the war."[38]

So August ended with a flourish for Haig's army. During the month
the Fourth Army had taken 29,752 prisoners, the Third and First Armies another 33,827, and 870 guns had been captured. The signs of
victory were manifest all along the front. But there was always another
side to the story. Even in defeat, even with morale evidently crumbling, the German Army was never easy to overcome—even after such
a shock as Mont St. Quentin it rallied sufficiently to make fifteen
counter-attacks. Every success had its price, and for the Fourth Army
the price of continuous success in August was 52,996 officers and men;
for the Third and First Armies (to 3 September) the casualty list totalled 55,716.

Nevertheless, this *was* victory, quite clearly recognizable on the
other side of the line. "It has often been asked," says the British
Official History, "why Ludendorff called the 8th August 'the black day
of the German Army.' The defeat was not decisive. It would have been
truer if he had said that 'August was the black month of the German
nation.' It was the decline in morale in the army and the nation rather
than in the fighting powers of the troops after the change of fortune
which occurred in August, which was decisive." German histories go
somewhat further; thus the Bavarian:

. . . the German front ached and groaned in every joint under the increasing blows delivered with ever fresh and increasing force [*sic*].
Heavy losses in men, horses and material had been suffered, and the ex-
penditure of man-power had reached terrifying proportions. The Ger-

man divisions just melted away. Reinforcements, in spite of demands and entreaties, were not forthcoming. Only by breaking up further divisions [10 in August] and regiments in the field could the gap be more or less filled. The number of companies in a battalion was reduced to three. The general and continuing crisis in the situation made it impossible to afford units the necessary rest and change, or even let them have their baggage trains up occasionally. In the circumstances, the troops deteriorated both spiritually and physically. For the most part they were burnt-out cinders.

It was impossible to conceal all this from the German public. Even before the Battle of Albert opened, Theodor Wolff, a level-headed commentator in the *Berliner Tageblatt,* was writing: "The military failure in the West, which has been announced with sensible frankness, has excited a propensity for all sorts of serious discussions. No sane person in Germany will now want to paint everything in all shades of grey; but there is certainly no longer any demand for the eternal rosy-red. . . ." However, a well-run-in propaganda machine does not easily go into reverse, nor does a cultivated taste for sweeteners quickly die away. In the *Frankfurter Zeitung* a few days later we find a very different note:

> During these weeks of the counter-offensive we remain without anxiety for the German front, which is strong and strategically indestructible. If at certain places the enemy has been able to push so far forward, this is due solely to the fact that our strategy as a whole (including, that is to say, the disposition of our troops and the assignment of reserves to threatened points) is still, so to speak, essentially switched on to our offensive plan of campaign, which is of course only interrupted for the time being. It sounds paradoxical, but it is pretty certainly true to say that our reverses have proved so considerable just because our position as a whole is so strong and so dominates the enemy. . . .

Only for a little while longer would the German public be able to comfort itself with such delusions.

On the Allied side the communiqués told a different story: on the day the New Zealanders entered Bapaume the French Third Army took Noyon; Mangin's Tenth Army on its right was fighting a battle which, even by his standards, was "très dure." French casualties during August totalled nearly 100,000, over 85,000 of them in the First, Third and Tenth Armies. They had taken over 31,000 prisoners and 890 guns. The persisting British belief that the French were not doing much at this stage is clearly quite wrong; there was nevertheless, in even their best performances, a certain haphazardness, suggesting a lack of overall direction, which Haig found worrying.

What Haig knew with depressing certainty was that he was wielding Britain's last army. On 27 August he was discussing the perennial topic of manpower with the Adjutant-General; the War Office had warned that in view of the manpower shortage the B.E.F. might expect to find itself reduced by nineteen British divisions. This would leave forty-two for the next year's campaign—thirty-two British and ten from the Dominions. But even this figure was very doubtful since, as we have seen, Australia was already having great difficulty in maintaining her five divisions in the field. In the light of all this, Haig became more and more convinced as each day went by of the importance of ending the war in 1918. Long, wordy memoranda from the War Office, in which Sir Henry Wilson discoursed on the campaigns of 1919 and even 1920, irritated him profoundly and provoked such marginal comments as: "What rubbish! Who will last till 1920—only America?!" But if the war *was* to be won in 1918, if the fine efforts of the British Army were not to be thrown away, it would have to be by the co-ordinated, concentric blows of *all* the Allies.

On 25 August Haig had received a cordial and friendly note of congratulation from Foch on the progress of his armies. Replying to this and thanking the Generalissimo on the 27th, Haig pointed out that his own strongest offensive front was in the St. Quentin–Cambrai area, but that to extract the full benefit from an advance in this region there should be a converging attack towards Mézières from the Franco-American sector; and that it was high time the Americans took a larger part in these climactic events. Two days later he had another meeting with Foch:

> We discussed the whole situation. Foch was very pleased with what the British Army had done. As regards our future plans, he is "in full agreement with me." I noted, however, that *since he received my letter,* he has decided to put in the American attack down the left bank of the Meuse toward Mézières instead of against the St. Mihiel Salient which was his original plan. Pershing is still preparing for the latter operation. F. will tell him as soon as possible of the change.

This was not quite correct. Foch saw Pershing the next day (30 August) and explained to him the new plan; it meant that the attack on the St. Mihiel Salient which the Americans had been carefully preparing would now be on a reduced scale—a limited operation with strictly defined objectives. The main American effort would be made later alongside the French Fourth Army in the Argonne. If Pershing felt unable to carry out both these tasks he was at liberty to cancel the St. Mihiel stroke; but

> "The attack west of the Meuse will be maintained at all costs
> as regards direction,
> as regards the importance of the forces engaged,
> as regards considerations of time."[39]

For the purpose of this offensive Foch proposed that, over and above the purely American contribution, some twelve to sixteen American divisions should reinforce the French Second and Fourth Armies. Pershing's reaction was predictable.

The accounts of this important meeting on 30 August and its consequences as presented by the two protagonists are only just reconcilable; Pershing's is revealing, not always intentionally. He was clearly shocked by Foch's proposals. It was barely three weeks since the American First Army had come into existence with a sector of its own.[40] All his thinking was directed to the strengthening of that army by bringing together more American divisions, and creating a Second Army as soon as possible. Foch's suggestion of placing a large number of American divisions under French command could not fail to provoke a most obstinate reaction; not only would this interfere with the organization of America's own Armies, said Pershing, but it would have a bad effect on the American troops. "American officers and soldiers alike are, after one experience, no longer willing to be incorporated in other armies."[41]

The change in strategy also shocked Pershing, and he must have shown it, for (as he relates) Foch then said to him:

> "I realise that I am presenting a number of new ideas and that you will probably need time to think them over, but I should like your first impressions," which I did not hesitate a moment to give.
> I said, "Well, Marshal, this is a very sudden change. We are going forward as already recommended to you and approved by you, and I cannot understand why you want these changes."

The briefest inspection of the changed plan seemed to Pershing to show that he would be left "with little to do except hold what will become a quiet sector after the St. Mihiel offensive. This virtually destroys the American Army that we have been trying so long to form."

It did nothing of the kind, of course; the last thing that Foch wanted (with or without Haig's prompting) was to leave the young fresh American Army on a quiet sector. But Pershing was a man obsessed, and the long and at times evidently acrimonious discussion which now followed shows the depth of his obsession. It also shows the worlds apart of the Frenchman scenting victory and peace after four and a half years of a war which had wrecked a part of his country as large as Holland and virtually bled her white, and the American who, despite the fact that his own country had been at war for sixteen months, was only now sniffing the battle and dreaded being balked of worthwhile achievement. It came to this: "Marshal Foch then said, 'Do you wish to take part in the battle?' I replied, 'Most assuredly, but as an American Army and in no other way.' He argued that there would not be time, whereupon I said, 'If you will assign me a sector I will take it at once.' He asked, 'Where would it be?' I replied, 'Wherever you say.'"

Again one has the sense of men inhabiting different worlds, worlds divided by much more than the Atlantic's 3,000 miles, divided by experiences and emotions which had not been shared in the way they had been shared by Foch and Haig. Foch knew only too well, and reminded Pershing, that the Americans lacked almost everything except enthusiasm and numbers: they lacked artillery, they lacked aircraft, they lacked tanks, they lacked transport; above all they lacked experienced commanders and staff officers, categories which cannot be improvised in a short time, as the British had learned to their cost. Pershing's proud replies to Foch were founded on the belief that much of this experience was related only to trench warfare and was not really needed; his dashing young men possessed the key which would unlock these rigid battlefields once they were off the mark. Foch, with memories of what the same sort of pride had cost France in 1914 and 1915, and Britain in 1916, could only beg him to take time into account and urge the need for the new plan, but Pershing was adamant:

> I was provoked to say: "Marshal Foch, you have no authority as Allied Commander-in-Chief to call upon me to yield up my command of the American Army and have it scattered among the Allied forces where it will not be an American army at all." He was apparently surprised at my remark, and said, "I must insist upon the arrangement," to which I replied, as we both rose from the table where we sat, "Marshal Foch, you may insist all you please, but I decline absolutely to agree to your plan. While our army will fight wherever you may decide, it will not fight except as an independent American army." . . .
>
> He said he was disposed to do what he could toward forming an American army. He then picked up his maps and papers and left, very pale and apparently exhausted, saying at the door, as he handed me the memorandum of his proposal, that he thought that after careful study I would arrive at the same conclusion he had.

In the event, as was usually the case with discords among the Allies, compromise prevailed. In war, this is not always an entirely satisfactory solution. Thus, as we shall see, conceding to Pershing an attack at St. Mihiel to be followed by an immediate regrouping west of the Meuse did not prove to be an unmixed blessing either for the Allies or for the Americans themselves. On the other hand, the Americans *were* about to fight on an important scale, and Pershing *did* relax his adamant posture to the extent of allowing a third of his men to continue to take part in British, Belgian and French operations.

The episode is instructive; it reveals (taken in conjunction with Haig's earlier representations on 15 August) the limitations of supreme command in 1918. Foch might well look "pale and exhausted" after such confrontations; it says much for his temper and his manners that relations with his powerful subordinates were generally quickly repaired after such scenes. What it also throws light on is the special difficulty which confronts coalitions in making war—a difficulty often ignored by politicians trying to regulate strategy by counting heads. Here the Germans had an advantage; it is difficult to think of anyone on their side saying, "Field-Marshal von Hindenburg, you may insist all you please, but. . . ." Homogeneity in an army is a precious asset; from Marlborough to Eisenhower the examples multiply of how difficulties mount without it.

Meanwhile for Foch and Haig, as September came in, there was other urgent business to consider; it concerned the Hindenburg Line.

Chapter VI: Notes

1. (p. 85) Lieut.-Gen. Sir John Monash: *The Australian Victories in France in 1918*, Angus and Robertson, 1936, pp. 152–53.
2. (p. 85) Marshal Foch: *Memoirs,* trans. Col. T. Bentley Mott, Heinemann, 1931, pp. 209–11.
3. (p. 85) Duff Cooper: *Haig*, 1935, ii, p. 297.
4. (p. 86) Commanding the French First Army on the right of the British.
5. (p. 87) Foch, op. cit., pp. 436–37.
6. (p. 88) Col. G. W. L. Nicholson: *Canadian Expeditionary Force 1914–1918*, Queen's Printer, Ottawa, 1962, p. 389.
7. (p. 90) Col. H. C. B. Rogers: *Tanks in Battle,* Seeley Service, 1965, p. 69.
8. (p. 91) Official History, *1918*, iv, p. 51.
9. (p. 92) C. and A. Williams-Ellis: *The Tank Corps,* George Newnes, 1919, p. 200.
10. (p. 92) See Appendix B.
11. (p. 93) Between 21 March and 5 April casualties in the four divisions of III Corps had been:
    12th Division   3,510
    18th Division   5,435
    47th Division   4,471

58th Division 2,234
The 58th Division was engaged again at Villers Bretonneux on 24–25 April, when it suffered a further 3,530 casualties.

12. (p. 93) Official History, *1918*, iv, p. 75.
13. (p. 94) Official History, *The War in the Air*, by H. A. Jones, vi, p. 437.
14. (p. 94) Ibid., pp. 442–43.
15. (p. 94) Ibid., p. 443.
16. (p. 95) *Die Katastrophe des 8 August 1918*, Oldenburg: Stalling.
17. (p. 95) Ludendorff: *My War Memories*, Hutchinson, 1919, ii, pp. 679 and 684.
18. (p. 97) Williams-Ellis, op. cit., pp. 210–11.
19. (p. 97) Royal Armoured Corps Papers, Bovington: "Short Report on Tank Corps Operations."
20. (p. 98) Ibid.
21. (p. 98) Duff Cooper, op. cit., ii, p. 345.
22. (p. 99) Official History, *1918*, iv, pp. 135–36.
23. (p. 100) O.A.D. 900/27, Haig to Foch, 15 August 1918.
24. (p. 100) Foch, op. cit., p. 446.
25. (p. 100) Robert Blake: *The Private Papers of Douglas Haig*, Eyre and Spottiswoode, 1963, pp. 323–24.
26. (p. 101) Foch, op. cit., p. 447.
27. (p. 101) Churchill gives this explanation of Lloyd George's attitude: "The part the Prime Minister had played in establishing unity of command led him unconsciously to dwell upon the brilliant conceptions of the Generalissimo, and to view only in a half light the potent forward heave of the British Army without which the results would have been mediocre. The Press and public at home followed the lead thus given. . . ." (*The World Crisis*, Odhams, ii, p. 1373). Yet, as we have seen, it was Haig who played the chief part in bringing about *effective* unity of command, and whose armies, as Churchill says, "bore the Lion's share in the victorious advance, as they had already borne the brunt of the German assault."
28. (p. 102) Official History, *1918*, iv, p. 161, quoting General von Kuhl, *Entstehung. Durch Fuhrung und Zusammenbruch der Offensive von 1918* (Berlin: Deutscher Verlag).
29. (p. 102) Von Hertling replaced Michaelis on 1 November 1917, von Hintze replaced von Kuhlman on 9 July 1918.
30. (p. 103) Sir John Wheeler-Bennett: *Hindenburg: The Wooden Titan*, Macmillan, 1967, p. 157.
31. (p. 103) Ludendorff, op. cit., ii, p. 686.
32. (p. 104) Ibid., pp. 687–88.
33. (p. 104) John J. Pershing, *My Experiences in the World War*, Hodder and Stoughton, 1931, p. 545.
34. (p. 107) Official History, *1918*, iv, Appendix XX.
35. (p. 108) Official nomenclature; at first this was called the Battle of Bapaume, but later that title was transferred to the sequel, 30 August–3 September.
36. (p. 109) Australian Official History, vol. vi, p. 816. In a referendum in December 1917 Australia rejected conscription. As in Britain, the eagerness which had inspired the wonderful voluntary effort of 1914 and 1915 had now died away, and recruiting figures were quite inadequate for such a large force as five divisions. It must be remembered that throughout 1918 the Australian Imperial Force faced that most depressing of prospects, the breaking up of units.
37. (p. 110) History of the Alexander Guard Regiment, quoted in the Official Australian History, vi, p. 817.
38. (p. 110) Monash, op. cit., p. 186.

39. (p. 113) Foch to Pershing, 31 August; Foch, op. cit., p. 464.
40. (p. 113) According to Pershing the U. S. First Army was formally created on 24 July, but the order only became effective on 10 August.
41. (p. 113) This and subsequent quotations are from Pershing, op. cit., pp. 568–73.

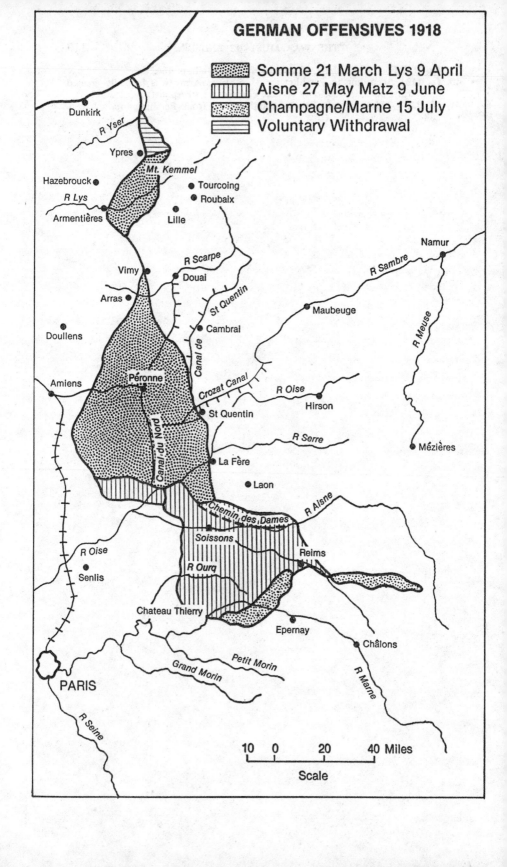

GERMAN OFFENSIVES 1918

Somme 21 March Lys 9 April
Aisne 27 May Matz 9 June
Champagne/Marne 15 July
Voluntary Withdrawal

Dunkirk

R Yser

Ypres

Mt. Kemmel

Hazebrouck

Tourcoing
Roubaix

R Lys

Armentières

Lille

Namur

R Sambre

Vimy

R Scarpe

Douai

St Quentin

Arras

Maubeuge

R Meuse

Doullens

Cambrai

Canal de

Amiens

Péronne

Crozat Canal

R Oise

Hirson

Canal du Nord

St Quentin

R Serre

Mézières

La Fère

Laon

R Aisne

Chemin des Dames

Soissons

Reims

R Oise

R Ourq

Senlis

Chateau Thierry

Epernay

Châlons

PARIS

Petit Morin

Grand Morin

R Marne

R Seine

10   0   20   40   Miles

Scale

VII

"MEN WHO HAVE BURIED THEIR DEAREST HOPES"

"The Field-Marshal and I parted with a firm handshake, like men who have buried their dearest hopes, and who are resolved to hold together in the hardest hours of human life as they have held together in success." (Ludendorff, evening of 28 September 1918)

The first day of September brought Haig a telegram from the Chief of Imperial General Staff, Sir Henry Wilson. It was marked "H.W. Personal," and it read as follows:

> Just a word of caution in regard to incurring heavy losses in attacks on Hindenburg Line as opposed to losses when driving the enemy back to that line. I do not mean to say that you have incurred such losses, but I know the War Cabinet would become anxious if we received heavy punishment in attacking the Hindenburg Line, without success.
>
> Wilson.

Haig commented:

> It is impossible for a C.I.G.S. to send a telegram of this nature to a C.-in-C. in the Field as a "personal" one. The Cabinet are ready to meddle and interfere in my plans to an underhand-way, but do not dare openly to say that they mean to take the responsibility for any failure though ready to take credit for every success! The object of this telegram is, no doubt, to save the Prime Minister [Lloyd George] in case of any failure.[1] So I read it to mean that I can attack the Hindenburg Line if I think it right to do so. The C.I.G.S. and the Cabinet already know that my arrangements are being made to that end. If my attack is successful, I will remain on as C.-in-C. If we fail, or our

losses are excessive, I can hope for no mercy! I wrote to Henry Wilson in reply.[2] What a wretched lot of weaklings we have in high places at the present time!

Haig's strictures are understandable; but what we have here is an example of the suggestive power of words and names. The name of Field-Marshal von Hindenburg was revered in Germany; to his fellow countrymen it had a satisfying ring of iron. In Britain it was by no means revered, but it had taken on an ominous sound, and the system of fortifications associated with it in the British mind had also become a thing of dread. It was as though the grim-faced Prussian marshal would be found squatting there in person, with nameless engines of destruction awaiting those who had the temerity to attack him.

There were, indeed, good grounds for apprehension; the obstacle in the path of the British armies was undoubtedly formidable. It is not always realized that its very existence was an admission of an earlier German defeat. Field-Marshal von Hindenburg was appointed Chief of Staff with Ludendorff as his First Quartermaster-General on 20 August 1916; on 5 September they paid their first visit to the Western Front. What they found shocked them deeply. The Battle of Verdun was now in its 197th day, with the French more and more on the offensive; the Battle of the Somme was in its sixty-seventh day, and coming to its climax. German losses in these two battles were extremely heavy, both in men and material. Looking to the future, says Ludendorff, the new High Command "had to face the danger that 'Somme fighting' would break out at various points on our fronts, and that even our troops would not be able to withstand such attacks indefinitely, especially if the enemy gave us no time for rest and the accumulation of material. Our position was uncommonly difficult, and a way out hard to find."

The solution adopted reversed all previous German military doctrine. Hitherto, with the single much-regretted exception of the retreat from the Marne to the Aisne in September 1914, it had been their inflexible rule never to make a voluntary withdrawal. At the Battle of the Somme Hindenburg's predecessor, General von Falkenhayn, had instructed the army commander concerned: "The first principle in position warfare must be to yield not a foot of ground; and if it be lost to retake it by immediate counter-attack, even to the use of the last man." The present author has counted not less than 330 German attacks or counter-attacks in accordance with that principle in the course of the Battle of the Somme, but it took Hindenburg and Ludendorff no time at all to perceive that this could not go on. Germany was facing manpower bankruptcy. Accordingly, says Ludendorff, "the construction had been begun as early as September of powerful rear positions in the West. . . . Whether we should retire on them, and how the positions would be used, was not of course decided in September, 1916; the important thing then was to get them built."

And now, two years later, they were to be put to the test. The British use of the word "line" in this connection is misleading. Describing the key sector before the attack in 1918, a German general, von Ardenne, wrote:

> Englishmen call our defensive front the Hindenburg line, and thereby show they fail to grasp the real character of our defences. We have no line, but a complicated, four-sided system of redoubts and fortifications extending from Cambrai to La Fère, a distance of nearly forty miles. The system, however, has a depth of twenty-five miles, so that, instead of having to penetrate a line, the enemy has to destroy a granite block with an area of one thousand square miles before he arrives at a position to deploy his forces in complete freedom and direct his attacks to high strategic ends.[3]

Each section of the defences was called by the German word *"stellung,"* which means "position." The one described above by General von Ardenne with bombastic exaggeration was the "Siegfried Stellung," covering Cambrai and St. Quentin. Other parts also enjoyed names from the Ring Saga: what the British called the "Drocourt-Quéant Switch" (prolonging "Siegfried" to the north) was the "Wotan Position"; south of St. Quentin and west of Laon was the "Alberich Position";[4] in Champagne came the "Brunhild Position," and behind the Argonne, as far as Metz, the "Kriemhilde Position." Of them all, the "Siegfried" was the oldest and most elaborate, while the "Kriemhilde" was least heavily fortified, because the ground before it was naturally suitable for defence.

Strong as "Siegfried" undoubtedly was, General von Ardenne's "granite block a thousand miles square" has to be dismissed as a figment of his imagination. According to General Sir Frederick Maurice, its depth was about ten miles (which is quite enough); an important feature was its intricate layout of wire entanglements: "They were often arranged in geometrical patterns, so that the angles could be swept by machine-gun fire, and there were, in places, as many as eight or nine belts of barbed wire in front of the trenches."[5] In September 1918 these dense belts of wire were red with rust, but, says the Official History, "no troops who saw it before rust had touched it will forget the sinister impression made by its blue sheen in the light of afternoon."

General von Ardenne is also incorrect in saying that the British commanders did not understand the character of the defences they were about to attack. The exact opposite is true. A German corps headquarters captured on 6 August supplied the Fourth Army with a most valuable document, revealing every detail of the position between the River Oise and Bellicourt. It showed all the trenches and wire belts, every battery, every observation post, every sound-ranging and flash-spotting location, every artillery and infantry headquarters, every dugout, every machine-gun position. In addition, it revealed the whole rear organization: ammunition and supply dumps, railheads, billets, camps, communications and power installations, balloon sheds and landing grounds. "It has fallen to the lot of a few commanders," says the Fourth Army's history, "to be provided with such detailed information as was furnished by the German memorandum."[6]

However intimate their knowledge of it, by whatever name one called it, the barrier in front of the British armies was still no joke. One did not need to be a deep student of war to see that hard fighting lay ahead; neither Haig nor his soldiers balked at it. Once more the Commander-in-Chief told his generals: "the enemy would be engaged by the Allied Armies on a very wide front from now on, and that there was no risk of any *heavy attack* by the enemy. We were therefore justified in taking very great risks in our forthcoming operations. . . ." As regards his own responsibilities, he shouldered them with his habitual calm; as regards the enemy, the thing that mattered was to give them no respite.

Foch's strategy now expressed itself in a famous slogan: *"Tout le monde à la bataille!"*, which may be satisfactorily translated as "Everyone go to it!" For the time being, however, this was more an idea, or a hope, than a reality; barring only the ever-restless Mangin on the Aisne it was Haig's armies that "went to it" virtually unaided. This meant, as the British Official Historian points out, that "Strategically the main offensive was made at the wrong place, because the Army that was most fighting-fit happened to be holding that front." What it came to, in other words, was that once more the decisive battle would take the form of a head-on assault on the most powerful of the German defences. As I have said elsewhere:

This is not to be hypercritical of Foch; given the general state of the French Army (despite numerous magnificent rallies by individual formations), and given Pétain's overall frame of mind, in addition to the continuing unpreparedness of the bulk of the Americans, it is hard to see what else he could have done. If he had not taken advantage of Haig's attacks, the great likelihood is that there would have been no advance at all, and no victory in 1918. Nevertheless, the criticism stands that, so long as the Allies attacked, Foch was not greatly concerned about how or where.[7]

On 2 September it was once more the turn of the British First Army, with the Third Army in a supporting rôle. This time the objective was the Drocourt-Quéant Line (abbreviated to "D-Q," German "Wotan") south-east of Arras. The D-Q Line was strong and heavily wired, but did not have the depth of the main Siegfried position further south. Nevertheless, it was a very fine achievement by the Canadian Corps to break through this line at every point attacked in the course of one day, and the results were far-reaching. Even Ludendorff's obstinacy was now overcome; when the field commanders urged a large withdrawal, "we had to admit the necessity for this measure." Carried out over the next eight days, and involving four armies, the withdrawal meant that the whole of the territory won in the great March offensive would now be abandoned. Still further to the north a similar retirement was taking place from the area won in April, with the British Fifth and Second Armies closely following.

Foch and Haig were running well together now, yet despite Foch's invincible optimism it was the Scotsman who had the clearer vision. On 3 September Colonel Repington visited the Generalissimo, whom he found "in great form. He was plainly dressed in blue, with brown gaiters and boots, and no spurs or decorations. He did most of the talking. . . ." Repington gives us a vivid impression of Foch's rapid, staccato speech, punctuated with energetic gestures:

Je les attaque. . . . . Bon. Je dis, allez à la bataille. Tout le monde va à la bataille. Bon. Je ne les lâche pas, les Boches . . .

(I attack them. Good! I say, "Into battle!" Everyone goes into battle. Good! I don't let go of them, the Boches. So—they're not let off. Good! They don't know what to do. I do know. I don't have a plan. I watch what happens. Good! Something does happen. I exploit it. They're chased with a sword in their backs. Good! They give way. The battlefront widens. Good! They're attacked all along it. Things are warming up. Good! I keep going. I push them. We hammer them everywhere. This will go on for six weeks. I shan't do anything silly. But I shall push them. In the end they'll be worn out. Good! We'll take prisoners and guns. Good! We'll chase them with the bayonet. Tic! [He makes a lunge at an imaginary Boche.] We kill them. Toc! [He pretends to fire at a Boche.] They're off balance. Germany is disillusioned. . . .")

This was fine, ebullient stuff—yet it was in the course of this same interview that Foch told Repington that he was thinking of the campaign of spring 1919: "he intended to make his great effort by April

1." The next day Foch met Haig, who recorded: "He is most hopeful, and thinks the German is nearing the end." The two generals were using the same phrases, but they were not meaning the same thing. When Churchill (always drawn to the sound of guns) came to see Haig on 8 September, "I told him that I considered that *the Allies should aim at getting a decision as soon as possible* [Haig's italics]. This month or next, not next spring or summer as the Cabinet proposed."

What with Wilson's ineffable telegram (Haig was not much mollified by a letter on 3 September saying: "How famously you are getting on. You know how pleased I am, how pleased we all are. . . .") and what he gleaned from Churchill and other visitors, Haig was now certain that a dangerous gap existed between his own views and the Government's. On 9 September he and his Chief of Staff, General Lawrence, went to London, and the next day Haig saw Lord Milner at the War Office:

> I had specially asked for this interview, and I stated that the object of my visit was to explain how greatly the situation in the field had changed to the advantage of the Allies. I considered it to be of first importance that the Cabinet should realise how all our plans and methods are at once affected by this change.
>
> Within the last four weeks we had captured 77,000 prisoners and nearly six hundred guns.[8] There has never been such a victory in the annals of Britain, and its effects are not yet apparent. The German prisoners now taken will not obey their officers or N.C.O.s. The same story of indiscipline is told me of the prisoners from our hospitals. The discipline of the German Army is quickly going, and the German officer is no longer what he was. From these and other facts I draw the conclusion that the enemy's troops will not await our attacks in even the strongest position.
>
> Briefly, in my opinion, the character of the war has changed. What is wanted now at once is to provide the means to exploit our recent great success to the full. Reserves in England should be regarded as reserves for the French front, and all yeomanry, cyclists and other troops now kept for civil [sic] defence should be sent to France at once.
>
> If we act with energy now, a decision can be obtained in the very near future.

Haig had put his cards on the table. This keen sense of a change in the atmosphere, the style, the tempo of a war—as a true sailor senses a coming storm, or a change of wind—is an attribute of real generalship, but it calls for powers not merely of perception but also of decision. Feeling victory now at last truly within his grasp, Haig was naturally fearful of ambitious programmes for the next year which would divert manpower and material resources needed in the immediate battle. He knew that Churchill was directing his munitions schedules towards an output of 10,000 fighting tanks and 10,000 tracked vehicles for transportation, supported by thousands of aircraft, for the 1919 campaign. Ten thousand tanks without crews would, of course, be useless—tank crews required careful training in a difficult task; the diversion of manpower immediately needed in France implied by Churchill's scheme was quite appalling. Haig also knew that a revolutionary new tank (the Medium D; it was on this tank that General J. F. C. Fuller based his famous "Plan 1919," a blueprint of blitzkrieg) was already in production. Unfortunately only one came off the production line in 1918; meanwhile, what were badly needed were more Mark Vs and Whippets. Haig wanted to finish the war, and was prepared to take risks in order to do it soon; the Government saw things differently.

Their point of view is not difficult to understand. The war had held many disappointments, many hopes had been deferred, making many hearts sick. Haig had a reputation for optimism which, in civilian eyes, the grim battles of attrition of 1916 and 1917 did not justify.[9] How could they be sure that he was right now? In any case, *not* to prepare against the eventuality of another year of war would have been a dereliction of duty. It was a matter of striking a balance between the immediate and the distant future, a delicate decision calling for considerable mutual trust between the Government and its military chiefs. As between the Prime Minister and the Commander-in-Chief, this simply did not exist: Lloyd George could not bring himself to believe that Haig was capable of winning decisive victories, nor did he believe that the war would be won in the West.

Furthermore, this was a Government whose nerves were shaken in other ways. It was aware of a bad mood in the country, a compound of sheer war-weariness and fright at the German successes earlier in the year. This expressed itself in agitation against enemy aliens in Britain which, after four years of war, reached a pitch of almost unbelievable hysteria. In July the largest crowd seen since the outbreak of war gathered in Trafalgar Square to demand immediate internment of all aliens. Reluctantly the Government responded with some tightening of the law, but this did not satisfy the scare-mongers. On 24 August there was another mass meeting in Hyde Park, and a petition over two miles long, with 1,250,000 signatures, was carried to 10 Downing Street, demanding immediate internment of every alien without any distinction. To his credit, Lloyd George did not allow himself to be carried away or intimidated.

And there were other problems, even graver. In July there had been a strike of munitions workers in Coventry and Birmingham which only ended when the Government threatened to conscript the strikers into the Army. On 30 August there was a one-day police strike, which understandably caused much anger and alarm. And as September came in there were ominous signs of a strike by the railwaymen, which did, indeed, take place in South Wales on the 13th, spreading to the other regions on the 24th. It was against this background of disturbance throughout the nation that the Government surveyed the progress of the war and the demands that it was likely to make in the most sensitive area of all—manpower. Haig came away from his talk with Milner on 10 September feeling reassured—"Lord Milner fully agreed and said he would do his best to help"—but he was misled by the blandness of the politician. The Government remained unconvinced.

Yet the signs that would bring conviction were multiplying. Haig returned to France on the 12th, a day big with events. His own Third Army made another short stride forward (known as the Battle of Havrincourt) against stiff German opposition. By comparison with earlier and later feats this was not a particularly showy success, yet to at least one participant it had the look of another turning point. General Byng remembered it in a conversation with Colonel Repington after the war:

> He reckons his most important day with the 3rd Army to have been the capture of Havrincourt by the 56th Division[10] in September 1918. He supported it quickly with two other divisions, and the Boches threw two of the old Vionville divisions[11] of their 3rd and 10th Corps, Brandenburgers and Hanoverians, against him with two more in reserve. They were well beaten, and the heart was out of the enemy afterwards.

So the Third Army's achievement was even greater than it looked on 12 September, while on its flanks the First and Fourth Armies also made small advances. But the main action of the day, which gives it its place in history, occurred far away to the east, beyond Verdun, in the St. Mihiel Salient.

Ever since 1914 the German salient at St. Mihiel had locked in the eastern flank of the Verdun fortress area in the same way as the Messines Ridge had locked in the south side of the Ypres Salient, until it was stormed by General Plumer's Second Army in June 1917. St. Mihiel was a long way from the sea and the ports of disembarkation, yet this was the area selected by both the French and the American High Commands from the earliest arrivals of American troops in France for their first major operation. It was a long time coming; the final decision for an American offensive at St. Mihiel was taken on 10 August 1918—sixteen months after America's declaration of war on Germany.

And now the time had come. There was to be no mistake about it; this was America's own battle, and nothing must be allowed to spoil it. The First Army was commanded by Pershing himself, with no less than 550,000 men under command in its twelve divisions, and 110,000 Frenchmen also attached. At 1 A.M. on 12 September the fire of 3,010 pieces of artillery proclaimed the opening of the battle; Pershing wryly notes that not one of these guns was of American manufacture, though 1,681 were manned by American crews, the rest by the French. On the southern face of the salient, where the main American attack went in, zero hour was 5 A.M.; the Franco-American attack on the western face came three hours later. Once more dense mist favoured the attackers, though hampering the work of the air forces. Pershing enjoyed complete air superiority—nearly 1,400 aircraft including Trenchard's Independent Air Force and the French Air Division of 600 planes. He had hoped for some British heavy tanks, but so great were the demands now being made on the Tank Corps that none could be spared. The French, however, supplied 267 of their light tanks, of which 154 were manned by Americans.

From the first the attack went well. Colonel Repington was at Pershing's headquarters that day, and wrote in his diary:

> The main attack was wonderfully successful and attained its three objectives with rapidity, Thiancourt being gained, 9 kil. distant, by 11.30 a.m. The secondary attack also gained Dommartin, and at the close of the afternoon it looked as though the Americans might make a good bag in the salient and might also have taken a good number of guns. The defence was not good, and many Boches surrendered freely.

The promise of a "good bag" was amply fulfilled: some 15,000 prisoners and 460 guns, thanks to the irresolution of the German High Command which had known that an attack was coming, but could not bring itself to evacuate the salient in time.

Pershing was naturally delighted. The 7,000 American casualties were saddening, but nothing could take away from the achievement of this Army, some of whose divisions had never before taken part in an offensive. To their general, "this striking victory completely demonstrated the wisdom of building up a distinct American army." Despite all the difficulties and irritations for the Allies implied in that build-up, Pershing is undoubtedly right. As Repington, who had spent the previous day inspecting their training camps, perceived, ". . . the Americans fight better by themselves. Everything has to be, and so is, American. The pride of race is very strong. The Americans are earnest serious people, even the private soldiers, who have nothing of the

devil-may-care light-heartedness of our men. They have come here to
do or die and are as keen as mustard, but still very serious and quiet
about it all. They are in truth Crusaders."

The congratulations poured in. From the President of the United
States, ". . . The boys have done what we expected of them and done
it in a way we most admire. We are deeply proud of them and of their
Chief . . ." From the Generalissimo, "The American First Army,
under your command, on this first day has won a magnificent victory
by a manoeuvre as skilfully prepared as it was valiantly executed . . ."
And from the British Commander-in-Chief, "All ranks of the British
Armies in France welcome with unbounded admiration and pleasure the
victory which has attended the initial offensive of the great American
Army under your personal command. . . ."

There was only one flaw. On 13 September Repington toured the
battlefield, noting that "all goes exceedingly well," but then, "Returning later to view the American jumping-off ground and the battery positions, we found the country roads much blocked with troops and
transport of all kinds. The Staff work failed here, and for miles transport congested all the approaches. One enterprising Boche air squadron, flying low, could have played the deuce on these roads, but not
one came."

This scene, unfortunately, was an omen for the future, a hint of what
might come when the Americans redeployed for their next offensive,
west of the Meuse, with very little time either to make or to execute
their plans.

As September wore on, every day brought fresh evidence of the collapse of German morale, amply confirmed by captured documents. On
3 September, we find a secret Order of Ludendorff saying:

> An increase has recently taken place in the number of complaints re-
> ceived from home that men on leave from the front create a very un-
> favourable impression by making statements actually bordering on high
> treason and incitement to disobedience. Instances such as these drag the
> honour and respect of the individual as well as of the whole Army into
> the mud, and have a disastrous effect upon the morale of the people at
> home.

An Order of the *38th Division* on 8 September said: "Every opportunity and all means must be used to restore the old discipline among the
troops. . . ." A week later an Order of the *94th Infantry Regiment*,
belonging to the same division, indicated the alarm of the German
commanders at the dwindling steadfastness of their troops: "Every

commander and every man is to be most minutely instructed in the importance of holding the outpost and forward zones as long as possible and of retaking them if lost. In case of an attack on a large scale, the main line of resistance must be held absolutely intact." When morale is collapsing, however, exhortations are useless. In one of his last letters home (he was killed on 23 September) a Scottish sergeant wrote:

I have seen prisoners coming from the Battles of the Somme, Mons and Messines and along the road to Menin; then they had an expression of hard defiance on their faces; their eyes were saying: "You've had the better of me; but there are many others like me still to carry on the fight, and in the end we shall crush you." Now their soldiers are no more than a pitiful crowd. Exhaustion of the spirit which always accompanies the exhaustion of the body. They are marked with the sign of the defeated.

To Haig, further back, confident of early victory though he was, these signs were less obvious. He was aware of the high cost of victory —out of over 600,000 casualties sustained by the B.E.F. since 21 March, 180,000 came during the period 8 August to 26 September— and above all he was aware of the great test that lay ahead. Accordingly, he held the impatient Rawlinson on a tight rein, telling him to rest his men as much as possible for the next battle, the attack on the Hindenburg Line itself. The Third Army's success at Havrincourt, however, encouraged him, and the next day he gave his consent to Rawlinson's plan for clearing the German outpost positions on the high ground in front of the main Hindenburg position. Some stubborn resistance already encountered indicated that a set-piece operation would be needed. Very few tanks could be spared, in view of future needs, so once more it would be artillery that would have to prepare the way. The Fourth Army deployed 1,488 guns, but in order to preserve surprise there was to be no preliminary bombardment; instead the guns would provide concentration shoots at zero hour and a creeping barrage to protect the infantry advance. Three hundred machineguns were also assembled; they were a normal ingredient of the barrages of 1917 and 1918, but in the roar of the guns their presence was often unnoticed. On this occasion, because of an error of synchronization of watches, some of them opened fire too soon, much to the amazement and gratification of the infantry, who described the sound they made as resembling the tearing of a huge sheet of calico or the firing of a million rifles. The effect of all 300 may be imagined.

Zero hour for this new battle (whose official name is Epéhy) was 5:20 A.M. on 18 September. All three corps of the Fourth Army[12] took part, supported by the right-hand (V) corps of the Third Army on their left and in theory by the French First Army on their right. This aid, however, did not materialize, with the result that IX Corps, on that flank, made less progress than was hoped for. III Corps, at the other end of the Fourth Army's front, also ran into difficulties attacking the stubbornly held villages of Epéhy and Peizière. In the centre, however, where General Monash's indefatigable Australians were stationed, success was complete and dramatic. Two divisions, the 1st and 4th, took part in the attack, a total of some 6,800 infantry (battalion strengths averaged about 400); during the day they captured 4,243 prisoners, 76 guns, 300 machine-guns and 30 trench mortars. The Australians took all their objectives, advancing to a distance of 5,000 yards on a front of four miles. Their casualties amounted to 1,260 officers and men. As the Fourth Army's history says, "these figures speak for themselves."[13] Rawlinson reported to Haig that German officers were now saying frankly that their men would not face the Australians.

The full tally for 18 September was over 9,000 prisoners and 100 guns. The next day brought Haig a characteristic communication from Sir Henry Wilson:

> My General,
>   Well done! You must be a famous General!
>
> Henry.

To this Haig replied:

> My dear Henry,
>   Very many thanks for your kind little note of yesterday. No, certainly not! I am not nor am I likely to be a "famous General." For that must we not have pandered to Repington and the Gutter Press? But we have a surprisingly large number of *very capable* generals. Thanks to these gentlemen and to their "sound military knowledge built up by study and practice until it has become an instinct" and to a steady adherence to the principles of our Field Service Regulations Part I are our successes to be chiefly attributed.

As Duff Cooper says: "The hour of triumph is as true a test of character as the hour of disaster. To treat both those impostors with the same equanimity is the hallmark of greatness of mind." And one may add that if one is seeking the quality that made Haig an outstanding general one need not look much further than his phrase, "steady adherence to principles." It was his refusal to depart from sound principle in any circumstance that brought him and his army through to these days of glory.

The Battles of Havrincourt and Epéhy signalled an unmistakable message; yet still the politicians remained sceptical. Lord Milner was in France, and on 21 September he was at G.H.Q. Haig records:

> I had another talk with Milner. He states recruiting is bad, and that if The British Army is used up now there will be no men for next year. He was quite satisfied that I should do what I deemed best in the matter of attacking or not. I pointed out that the situation was most satisfactory and that in order to take advantage of it every available man should be put into the battle at once. In my opinion, it is possible to get a decision this year; but if we do not, every blow that we deliver now will make the task next year much easier.

Despite all the evidence of his eyes and ears, Milner remained unconvinced. Two days later he was back in London talking to Wilson, who noted in his diary: "He thinks Haig ridiculously optimistic and is afraid that he may embark on another Paschendaele [sic]. He warned Haig that if he knocked his present army about there was no other to replace it. Milner saw many generals in France and they were all most optimistic. The manpower is the trouble,[14] and Douglas Haig and Foch and Du Cane[15] can't understand it."

It is curious—and indicative of the strain upon government in the fifth year of a modern war—that the War Cabinet did not sense the crescendo and the elation that accompanied it. This was not just a matter of the Western Front. The large Allied army—French, British, Serbians, Greeks, Italians and Czechs—which had been locked up in Salonica since 1915 was at last on the move under the command of the dynamic General Franchet d'Espérey. With their German support reduced to only three battalions and a number of artillery batteries, the war-weary Bulgarians put up only slight resistance. As Ludendorff said, with some bitterness: "The Bulgarian Army went home." The collapse was complete, and now there was nothing that Germany could do about it:

> We could not answer every single cry for help. We had to insist that Bulgaria must do something for herself, for otherwise we, too, were lost. It made no difference whether our defeat came in Macedonia or in the West. We were not strong enough to hold our line in the West and at the same time to establish in the Balkans a German front to replace the Bulgarian, as we should have had to do if we were to hold that front in the long run.[16]

The end came quickly: on 25 September, beaten everywhere, the Bulgarians asked for an armistice; on 29 September it was signed. In his book, *The Supreme Command 1914–1918*, published as late as 1961, Lord Hankey celebrates this moment with an outbreak of capital letters: "THE FIRST OF THE PROPS HAD FALLEN." But, as we have seen, this was simply not the case. Germany herself was the prop, and it was the steady pressure of the Allies, particularly the British, on the Western Front that prevented her from continuing to prop up her ally. It is no denigration of General Franchet d'Espérey's competent offensive to point out that Bulgaria was really defeated in France.

The same was true of Turkey. On 19 September General Allenby opened the Battle of Megiddo in Palestine. A brief glamour seemed to return to war on this front, with cavalry making wide flanking movements across country littered with biblical associations (the German commander, Liman von Sanders, was nearly captured in Nazareth) and crossing the Plain of Armageddon, and Colonel T. E. Lawrence's Arabs closing on Damascus. By 25 September the Turks were in full flight; the British had taken 45,000 prisoners and 265 guns. On 29 September Hankey wrote in his diary: "The Turks have lost practically their whole Palestine army with all its material. They cannot hope to replenish this material if Bulgaria goes out and they can hardly send any troops, if they are likely to be threatened by an Allied Army marching on Constantinople from Bulgaria . . ." Turkey's plight was not yet quite so disastrous as Bulgaria's, but, like Bulgaria, only one thing could have saved her: large reinforcements of German troops. None, of course, could be forthcoming, and though the Germans present performed prodigies they were, as Ludendorff says, "limited in numbers, and could only keep the Turkish Army together for a time." Turkey, too, was being defeated in France.

This anticipates; the climax of the war was fast approaching, and these developments in secondary theatres were only part of a larger pattern. Only once, in over four years of war, had the Allies succeeded in co-ordinating their efforts against the Central Powers. That was in September 1916, when a major Anglo-French effort on the Somme (including the first use of tanks) coincided with a final offensive burst by General Brusilov's Russian armies in Galicia, Rumania's entry into the war, and the launching of the Seventh Battle of the Isonzo by the Italians. Germany and Austria-Hungary found themselves hard pressed by these attacks, but though 1916 was undoubtedly the turning point of the war it was not, unfortunately, the end of it. Now, two years later, in September 1918, co-ordination would be tried again.

So close was the accord between Foch and Haig at this stage that it is very difficult to see where one's responsibility ended and the other's began. Both had been looking north for some time, and on 9 September Foch had visited King Albert of the Belgians to ask him to command an Anglo-Franco-Belgian offensive in Flanders. The British contribution, with Haig's entire approval, was to be General Plumer's Second Army. Pershing, as we have seen, had already been given the outline of the future American rôle. It was just a matter of timing. On 21 September Haig held a conference with his army commanders who were all in a buoyant mood. He told them:

> As regards our own operations, the objective of the main British effort will be the line Valenciennes-Le Cateau-Wassigny. We are confronted by a strong, well sited series of defences, and the enemy appears to have collected a certain number of reserves behind the Cambrai-St. Quentin front. I therefore do not propose to attack until the American-French attack has gone in. This latter attack *might* draw off some of the enemy's reserves from our front. I therefore would like to attack two or three days *after* the main American-French attack. If we could arrange this, there was a chance of the enemy's reserves being unavailable for either battle.
>
> After talking over the situation, I decided that the order of attack is to be as follows:—
>
> | | |
> |---|---|
> | American-French attack | Z day |
> | First Army } | |
> | Third Army (left) } | Z +2 |
> | Byng attacks Canal and crosses | Z +4 |
> | Rawlinson attacks Canal and crosses | Z +4 |

> All were quite pleased with my arrangements. Before my intervention Byng and Rawlinson were each inclined to try and get the better of each other.

All this (slightly amended) was formalized by the Generalissimo at a conference of Commanders-in-Chief at Supreme Headquarters at Bombon on 23 September:

> . . . I definitely fixed the time schedule for the general offensive from the Meuse to the North Sea, viz.:

> September 26th — A Franco-American attack between the Suippe and the Meuse.
> September 27th — An attack by the British First and Third Armies in the general direction of Cambrai.

> September 28th — An attack by the Flanders Group of
> Armies between the sea and the Lys,
> under the command of the King of the
> Belgians.
> September 29th — An attack by the British Fourth Army,
> supported by the French First Army, in
> the direction of Busigny.

So the stage was set.

"Mopping-up," after the Battle of St. Mihiel, took until 16 September; that left only ten days to the opening of the Franco-American attack in the Argonne. There is no question that, strategically, the attack was going in at the right place: thirty miles in front of the new American line lay Mézières, an important junction on a vital east–west railway. The British attacks towards Cambrai and St. Quentin threatened equally important north–south lines. The loss of these railways by the Germans—either through long-range artillery fire or by actual capture —would be a disaster, making it impossible for them to withdraw their vast four-year accumulation of war material, and many of their troops as well. But thirty miles was a long way in 1914–18 terms, and thirty miles which included the Argonne Forest presented daunting tactical problems for any army.

The main Argonne Forest lies between the River Aisne in the west and the River Aire in the east. Steeply sloping, thickly wooded, with dense undergrowth, the forest made a natural defensive position of great strength, commanding the Aire valley. Between the Aire and the Meuse lay more wooded heights, the first and most important being 1,200-foot Montfaucon facing the American centre corps. These heights, forming the watershed between the two rivers, also commanded the valleys, so that the American attack would have to be made, in effect, down a double defile. But it was more than ground that the Americans would have to overcome: the Germans, though they relied here on natural defences far more than they did on the more open northern sectors of the Western Front, had nevertheless constructed four lines of defence, of which the third, the Kriemhilde Stellung, was the most formidable. These positions, says Pershing, contained

> fortified strongpoints, dugouts, successive lines of trenches, and an un-
> limited number of concrete machine gun emplacements. A dense net-
> work of wire entanglements covered every position. With the advantage
> of commanding ground, the enemy was peculiarly well located to pour

oblique and flanking artillery fire on any assailant attempting to advance within range between the Meuse and the Argonne. It was small wonder that the enemy had rested for four years on this front without being seriously molested.

Daunting though the tactical problems might have been (it must be remarked that there is no evidence of any American officer actually being daunted; this was an army full of self-confidence), the logistical problems were infinitely more so. It would have been difficult enough to prepare an entirely fresh army for this battle in the time given; now, however, out of some 600,000 men (Americans and French) deployed on the American First Army front, at least 400,000 had to be extracted from the St. Mihiel sector and brought across—always a difficult manoeuvre.[17] This mass of incoming Americans was, of course, displacing French (and Italian) divisions—some 220,000 men had to be taken away to make room for the newcomers—so that in all there were about 820,000 men on the move in the Meuse-Argonne area. The man in control of this vast migration was Colonel George C. Marshall, of the First Army Operations Section. The qualities which distinguished the future U. S. Chief of Staff and Secretary of State were already well in evidence.

In the First Army, says Marshall's biographer,[18] some 428,000 men were brought to their new positions by truck ("lorry" to the British); "the rest walked." It was still a war in which men marched to battle, yet in this mass movement by mechanical means 1918 once more gives us a glimpse of the future style of warfare. Nor need one exclaim at the figure of more than 90,000 horses and mules involved in this feat of transportation; the German Army which entered Paris in 1940 depended chiefly on horse-drawn transport, as did the Soviet armies which entered Germany in 1945. But it is a salutary reminder of the exigencies of an artillery war that among Marshall's other problems was the assembly of nearly 3,000 guns with 40,000 tons of ammunition, which would need to be replenished at the rate of 3,000 tons a day. All in all, the deployment of the American First Army for the Battle of the Meuse-Argonne by 26 September takes on the look of a miracle.

Miracles ended there. The attack went in on a forty-mile front, equally divided between the American First Army under Pershing and General Henri Gouraud's French Fourth Army, in the early hours of 26 September.[19] German resistance on the first day was not strong, except in the Montfaucon area facing the American centre (V Corps). Nevertheless, across this tangled landscape, described by General Hunter Liggett of I Corps[20] as "a natural fortress beside which the Virginia wilderness in which Grant and Lee fought was a park," the day's advance along the whole front averaged no more than two to three miles. The Americans used 189 light tanks, all of French manufacture and a quarter of them manned by French crews; the French had over 300 tanks, twenty-nine of them heavy. But this was not tank country by any stretch of the imagination, and the Germans skilfully added to the difficulties of the Allied armour by minefields constructed of 5.9-inch shells. Once more it was the artillery which had to carry the infantry forward, especially on the French front where Gouraud now had to find the answers to that very defence in depth which he had employed so effectively in July.

On 27 September German resistance stiffened as fresh divisions were thrown into the fight. Counter-attacks in the familiar German manner were launched against both French and Americans. By 30 September the maximum depth of the Allied advance was still only eight miles. On the other hand, there were tangible gains to show for all this effort over and above the small gain of ground: some 18,000 prisoners and 200 guns. Yet it was time to call a halt. One senses a certain impatience in the American command at the slow progress of the front-line divisions. They suffered heavy losses in some places from the flanking fire of artillery and machine-guns; Pershing speaks of breakdowns of liaison between units due to the broken terrain, and lack of teamwork between infantry and artillery due to the simple fact of their being strangers to each other. For many of these divisions, it must be remembered, this was their first experience of any kind of battle. All of this was undoubtedly perplexing for the American command. According to Foch, "It tried to overcome these difficulties by increasing its forces in the front line; but this only intensified these difficulties, and resulted in a complete blocking of its rear and the bottling up of its communications."

The trouble was that there were only three roads into the battle area, and while Marshall had performed the miracle of assembly, nothing could resolve the problems of maintenance, reinforcement and supply for so many men once fighting began. There were dreadful scenes on the lines of communication: in one place a traffic block which lasted for twelve hours. On 29 September M. Clemenceau himself, visiting the First Army, and wishing to go into the newly captured town of Montfaucon, was unable to get there because of the congestion of an American divisional relief. Some units received no rations for four days; there was even talk of men starving to death in the front line. Clearly there had to be a pause to sort all this out, replace really incompetent individuals, reorganize units and bring in more experienced formations. It was a moment of considerable chagrin for the American

Army command, especially after the easy victory at St. Mihiel. The truth is, however, that too much had been asked of an army which was still in the very process of formation. As Pershing says:

> It was one thing to fight a battle with well trained, well organised and experienced troops, but quite another matter to take relatively green troops and organise, train and fight them at the same time. Some of our divisions that lacked training could not have been considered available for this operation had it not been for our belief that the morale of the enemy in general was rather low and that this was the opportunity to throw our full strength into the battle with the intention of winning the war in 1918.

So the Americans paused to draw breath—but not for long.

It is possible to speak of a plan now unfolding, but with our fresher memories of planning in the Second World War we need to be very careful to understand exactly what we mean. Planning for D-Day (6 June 1944) began in April 1943; within months the planning staff had expanded to such an extent that "the walls of Norfolk House were developing an outward bulge,"[21] and by the time it reached its peak it was "a figure of some significance in the London real estate business."[22] As we have seen, Foch's staff was minute, utterly inadequate for this sort of work; in 1918 even the national and group headquarters did not go into detail. The real, practical details of each battle were left to that now virtually unknown body of men, the corps commanders, aided by their divisional commanders and supervised by their army commanders.

The next phase of the advance on the main British front might be called the "battles of the canals." On the left, or northern flank, General Horne's First Army faced the obstacle of the Canal du Nord; on the right Rawlinson's Fourth Army faced the St. Quentin Canal—both of them integral features of the Hindenburg Line. For 27 September, the day after the Franco-American attack in the Argonne, the schedule prescribed an assault on the Canal du Nord, supported by the left wing of Byng's Third Army. The spearhead of General Horne's operation was to be the Canadian Corps, and it was on Lieutenant-General Currie and his corps staff that the burden of planning fell, with not much time to do it in.

Like the Australians, the Canadians were now very tough, resilient battle practitioners, and it was as well that they were. "Not only was there the obstacle of the canal itself; on the far side marshes extended north and south of the Arras-Cambrai road, and these the enemy could

cover by machine-gun fire from trench systems to the rear. Furthermore the high ground to the east gave the Germans full command of
the canal approaches. It was not an encouraging prospect."²³ Currie
ruled out a direct attack on this sector of the front; instead he asked
for his corps boundary to be extended southward, where the canal cutting contained no water and there were no marshes. Here he proposed
to push two divisions through on a narrow front, then fan them out to
a width of some six miles, supporting them with a third division. It was
an ambitious project, testing for any army in any war. Currie's old
corps commander, Byng, came to see him and looked over his plan.
Byng admitted that he thought it was the best possible in the circumstances, but at the same time questioned wonderingly, "Old man, do
you think you can do it?"

Currie thought he could, and he did. Once more it was artillery that
would provide the main preparatory and supporting work, and General
Horne being an artilleryman there was no doubt that this would be of
a high standard in the First Army. But even for the best of artillery the
fire and movement programme elaborated for 27 September was complex and difficult. The gunners did not fail, however; their barrage
opened at 5:20 A.M. (dawn assaults were the rule by now) and the infantry, usually hard to please in these matters, described it as "very
good." They went forward "hugging their artillery cover." Only sixteen
tanks were available; they did useful work in silencing enemy machine-
guns, five of them being put out of action by German fire. A vivid
story by a "Correspondent at the Front" of three old tanks being
sacrificed to form a bridge in the dry canal, while "over their bodies
the new strong tanks passed with giant strides," revealed only the
lively imagination of the correspondent concerned.

The Canadian Corps passed beyond all its objectives on 27 September, carrying forward with it the British 11th Division on its left. Elsewhere, and on the Third Army front, the attack was less successful,
generally stopping on the line of the second objective; nevertheless, by
the end of the next day the two armies between them had made a
breach twelve miles wide and six miles deep in the German defences. It
was noticed with some dismay that German resistance was on this occasion very stiff, not only by machine-gunners and artillerymen but
also by counter-attacking infantry. Bitter fighting on the 29th cost the
Canadians over 2,000 casualties. On 1 October, despite the expendi-
ture of 7,000 tons of shells on the Canadian Corps front alone, there
was more heavy fighting resulting in a gain of only about one mile. By
now the corps was very tired, and a pause for rest was clearly indicated. In five days' fighting it had taken over 7,000 prisoners and

205 guns; this was a fine feat, but only a small part of the picture of the changing war.

The twenty-eighth of September was the day of the Flanders Group. This consisted of the Belgian Army, twelve strong infantry divisions and a cavalry division, supported by six divisions of French infantry and a cavalry corps of three divisions, and the British Second Army of ten divisions. The Belgians had had a quiet war; they had fought stoutly in the 1914 campaign (whether they should have defended Antwerp for longer than they did is an open question) and again in the defensive battle of Flanders in April 1918. At all other times it had been King Albert's policy to nurse this remnant of his country's force, which it would be impossible to replace while Belgium remained under enemy occupation. He had accordingly taken no part in the great Third Battle of Ypres in 1917, somewhat to the disappointment of the British High Command. Now, however, with the strong backing of his allies, he was ready to play his part.

On the immediate right of the Belgians was the British 9th Division. To the old soldiers, survivors of "Third Ypres" and the Battle of the Lys, the Ypres Salient was no novelty. Brigadier-General J. L. Jack, commanding the 28th Brigade, wrote in his diary on 25 September:

> How familiar the place-names of today were 14 months ago: the Menin and Lille Gates, Bellewaarde and Westhoek Ridges, Zonnebeke Redoubt. We shall presently assault the identical positions then attacked by the 8th Division, containing the 2/West Yorks under my command. The bones of most of my officers and many of the other ranks lie between here and Zonnebeke. I hope the 28th Brigade will have better luck . . .[24]

The brigade did have better luck. The two left-hand corps of the Second Army advanced between four and a half and six miles on 28 September. Jack recorded:

> The day's success has been astonishing: an advance of over five miles (more than in four months' bloody fighting last year). No doubt the hostile shelling has been less severe than formerly, and his infantry, behind ample defences, have not put up their wonted resistance. Nevertheless, allowing for every mercy (including our smoke screens), the good leading and drive of all ranks from sunrise to sundown, through this bullet-swept wilderness, has been admirable, hustling the enemy off his feet.

This battle—the "Last Battle of Ypres"—displayed once more that ground is nothing, morale is everything. The ground over which the

Allies were advancing was the same old Salient battlefield, bare of all
vegetation, virtually all its buildings reduced to rubble, seamed with
old trenches and rusty wire, pockmarked with shell craters lip to lip.
The weather was as wet and depressing as it had been for so much of
the campaign of 1917. Yet one by one the place-names which had
caused the British Army such endless anguish in that gloomy year were
taken in one day, or possibly two. This, of course, was in part the fruit
of "Third Ypres" itself, the "greatest martyrdom" of the German
Army, which had torn its heart out, and reduced it, in Ludendorff's
words, to a "militia." For that reason, if no other, it was a pity that the
most sombre place-name of all, the one with the most emotive and
saddening connotations, Passchendaele, should have been just inside
the Belgian sector, so that today the plaques in the village square com-
memorating its liberations bear the names of the Belgian regiment
which entered it on 28 September 1918, and the Poles who did so
again in 1944. On the slope just below the village stands Tyne Cot
cemetery, where nearly 12,000 soldiers of the British Empire are
buried, and the names of some 35,000 more who have no known
graves are inscribed. These are the men who fought for Passchendaele.

On 29 September the advance was almost as great as on the previous
day, but the rain continued to fall, and the bog-like conditions which
had made the British offensive in 1917 such unmitigated hell began
rapidly to return. It was one thing to advance over such ground against
an enemy whose will to resist was no longer what it had been; it was
something quite different, as the Americans had found in the Argonne,
to maintain impetus for any length of time. While the Germans
brought up reserves the Allies floundered—and in so doing created the
occasion for yet another of those glimpses into the future which
abounded in 1918. We have seen how, at Le Hamel on 4 July, the first
air-drop of ammunition to troops in battle had taken place (see p.
71). On 2 October there was yet another portent: news came that
leading Belgian and French formations had exhausted their food
supplies, and eighty aircraft (including two British squadrons) airlifted
15,000 rations to these troops. The rations were packed in batches of
five or ten in small sacks of earth carried in the cockpits of the
aeroplanes. These were thrown out at a height of about 300 feet; the
earth cushioned the impact so that the rations were undamaged. The
total amount dropped was thirteen tons, a ludicrously small quantity
by the standards of, say, the Fourteenth Army's air supply during the
monsoon advance to the Chindwin in 1944—but everything has to
have a beginning.

The second of October brought a pause for reorganization in the
Flanders offensive; by then it had taken some 10,000 prisoners and

300 guns, of which the British Second Army's share was 4,672 prisoners and 100 guns.

So far so good: each new phase of the Allied offensive had opened with success—hard-bought in the Argonne on 26 September, also hard-bought but more spectacular aginst the Canal du Nord on 27 September, startling, in the light of past experience, in Flanders on 28 September. It was on this day that Ludendorff came to certain sombre conclusions: "The enemy had to be asked for peace and an armistice. The military position, which would all too probably get worse, demanded this." The First Quartermaster-General was clearly on a rack: peace—but what kind of peace? What sort of peace could Germany expect from such implacable enemies as Clemenceau and Lloyd George? On the other hand, there was President Wilson, with his Fourteen Points; perhaps Germany could find in these a less painful means of extracting herself from her predicament. Perhaps the war-spirit of the German nation would revive, especially if the battle-front approached the frontiers of the Fatherland. Perhaps the Allies would fall out among themselves. All these speculations paraded back and forth in his mind, while reports of retreat and confusion and loss continued to come in from the fronts. All pointed in one unmistakable direction: "We must plainly sue for peace if peace could be had." So Ludendorff reached his decision:

At six o'clock on the afternoon of the 28th of September, I went down to the Field-Marshal's room, which was one floor below mine. I explained to him my views as to a peace offer and a request for an armistice. The position could only grow worse, on account of the Balkan situation, even if we held our ground in the West. Our one task now was to act definitely and firmly, without delay. The Field-Marshal listened to me with emotion. He answered that he had intended to say the same to me in the evening, that he had considered the whole situation carefully, and thought the step necessary. . . . The Field-Marshal and I parted with a firm handshake, like men who have buried their dearest hopes, and who are resolved to hold together in the hardest hours of human life as they have held together in success. Our names were associated with the greatest victories of the world war. We now shared the conviction that it was our duty to sacrifice our names to ensure the step being taken that we had done everything humanly possible to avoid.

Even now, in this black hour, the German leaders would not admit that all was lost. They still thought in terms of holding their ground in the West. Their idea of an armistice was "a regular and orderly evacuation of the occupied territory and the resumption of hostilities on our own borders." As regards the East, where Ludendorff's crazy ambitions had already done Germany so much harm, "we did not consider any abandonment of territory." Clearly they were going to need a little more persuading; the moment was at hand, and the instrument of persuasion, once more, was General Rawlinson's Fourth Army, now about to chime in as Haig and Foch had planned.

The Fourth Army was now right up to the Siegfried Stellung at its strongest point between St. Quentin and Vendhuille. Here the carefully devised fortifications of what the British called the "Main Hindenburg System" and "Hindenburg Support System" had the additional protection of the St. Quentin Canal. This was the obstacle which faced the British IX Corps, one which, in the words of the historian of the 46th Division, "might easily have proved insuperable in the face of a determined enemy. The mere sight of it from our front line trenches inspired respect, and might well have caused fear of the outcome in the hearts of any but the stoutest soldiers."[25] Not surprisingly: the canal here ran through a cutting with almost perpendicular sides, thirty to fifty feet high; in the northern part of the IX Corps sector, in front of Bellenglise, a dam ensured a depth of six to eight feet of water;[26] to the south it was, in the words of the divisional history, "practically dry," but according to the Official History contained "8 feet of mud." Either way, wet or dry, it was thirty-five feet wide, with barbed wire on the banks and on the bottom. In short, this was a good locality to leave alone. Further north, however, in front of Bellicourt, the canal ran into a tunnel, making a "bridge" three and a half miles wide where, despite dense field fortifications, the chances of a breakthrough with tanks were clearly much greater.

This was the sector naturally chosen for the main thrust—it could almost be said that it chose itself. Once more Rawlinson entrusted the task to his most reliable troops, the Australian Corps, and once more the planning was in the hands of the meticulous Monash. His chief problem now was the sheer weariness and weakness of his Australian divisions. This was not to be wondered at: 25 September was the first day since 7 April that some part of the Western Front was not being held by Australian infantry. Already (21 September) there had been symptoms of over-strain when 119 men of the 1st Battalion had refused to attack and made their way to the rear; and there were disturbances of an entirely different character when six of seven battalions ordered to disband to provide reinforcements for others flatly refused to do so. Evidently even the fine spirit of the Australians was wearing thin: the 1st and 4th Divisions urgently needed rest; the 3rd and 5th probably had one more attack in them; the 2nd was available for support. Two weak divisions, even of such quality as these, were not going to be enough to break the Hindenburg Line.

Monash asked Rawlinson for two strong divisions to replace his 1st and 4th. What he got surprised and delighted him: the American II Corps, 27th and 30th Divisions, commanded by Major-General George W. Read. Monash tells us: "My experience of the quality of the American troops, both at the battle of Hamel and on the Chipilly spur,[27] had been eminently satisfactory. It was true that this new American Corps had no previous battle service, but measures were possible to supply them with any technical guidance which they might lack." Monash speaks here as a staff officer; he was one of the most brilliant of these, but never famous as a front-line soldier. As the Australian Official Historian pointedly remarks, "Monash often lacked knowledge of what had happened in battle." On this occasion it caused him to underrate the great difficulties that would face completely raw soldiers in the complex conditions of modern battle; such a degree of inexperience (the Australians themselves had suffered grievously from it in their early days, both at Gallipoli and in France) could not be compensated for by the brief attachment of over 200 Australian officers and N.C.O.s as technical advisers to the American units. Nor did the American habit of sending large numbers of their own officers away simultaneously on training courses help matters.

Ignoring these hazards, and the further even greater difficulty that on one part of the front the Germans still held important outposts, Monash drew up his plan with his habitual great regard for detail, but on this occasion with more than usual trust. Assuming—it was "a most dangerous assumption," says the Australian Official Historian—that the German outposts would be captured in time, he gave the Americans the "simple" task of making the first advance behind the barrage, and the Australians the more difficult one of exploitation. Rawlinson accepted this plan, but more than doubled the tank allocation: eighty-six for the Americans, seventy-six for the Australians. On 26 September Monash called together General Read and his two divisional commanders, Major-General J. F. O'Ryan (27th Division) and Major-General E. M. Lewis (30th Division) with their chiefs of staff, and the two Australian divisional commanders, Major-General J. Jellibrand (3rd Division) and Major-General Sir J. Talbot Hobbs (5th Division). "No one present," he says, "will soon forget the tense interest and confident expectancy which characterized that meeting. America, a great English-speaking democracy on one shore of the Pacific, was to co-operate with Australia, its younger sister democracy on the opposite shore, in what was the greatest and what might be the most decisive

battle of the great European War." Monash's exposition was as lucid
as ever. While the conference was in session Haig also appeared;
Monash begged him to address the officers assembled. "So I went into
the room and shook the senior officers by the hand and said a few
words of encouragement. I told them that the biggest battle of the
war had started this morning—the enemy would be attacked by 100
divisions in the next three days. . . . All seemed very much heartened
by my brief address."

There was nothing wrong with the grand strategy; the tactical situation was more dubious—a familiar circumstance in that war. For the
American 27th Division the task was going to be exceedingly difficult:
their main attack would be directed against some of the most powerful
defences in existence, which had thwarted veteran British divisions for
the past week; they were asked to make, in Monash's own words, "a
deeper penetration than we have ever made before." Finally, when the
tunnel was crossed, the Americans would have to undertake difficult
changes of direction as they fanned out to the flanks. The Australian
Official Account says: "The task thus allotted to the Americans by
Monash was at least as great as any that he had ever set for Australian
divisions, if not greater. But the whole plan was based on the premise
that the Germans' morale was progressively falling." This was, no
doubt, the case—but what mattered was the question of degree. Beneath a confident exterior Monash himself was not by any means
happy. As he says, "For the first time I had to gamble on a chance. It
was contrary to the policy which had governed all my previous battle
plans, in which *nothing* had been left to chance."

At no stage had it occurred to Monash to attack anywhere but in the
tunnel sector. "To cross the canal unaided, he held would involve great
loss of life; he would not have committed the Australian troops to the
attempt, and did not suggest the task for others."[28] Fortunately—as it
turned out—Lieutenant-General Sir Walter Braithwaite,[29] commanding
IX Corps, thought otherwise. When Monash submitted his own plan to
Rawlinson, Braithwaite also submitted one—a very bold scheme indeed for passing a division over the canal in front of Bellenglise, immediately on the right of the American 30th Division, and then passing
another division through it to capture the main defences. Rawlinson
was not dismayed by the obvious difficulties; he accepted Braithwaite's
plan as an addition to Monash's, and lived to rejoice that he had done
so. The division selected to make this seemingly impossible attack was
the 46th (North Midland) Division, Territorial Army, with the 32nd
Division "leapfrogging" for the second phase.

The 46th was the first Territorial Division to be constituted as such
in France (15 February 1915). Its regiments were Lincolns, Leices-

ters, North and South Staffordshires, and Sherwood Foresters from Nottinghamshire and Derbyshire; even in 1918, after many casualties and replacements, it still retained a good deal of its dour regional Midland character. It was not a distinguished division; like most, it had had its bad days as well as its good. In October 1915 it had attracted unfavourable notice at G.H.Q. for apparent lack of training and discipline. But in 1918, until just before this battle, it was commanded by Major-General W. Thwaites, an excellent officer who turned it, in his successor's words, "into a fighting machine in which every officer and man was imbued with a real soldier's spirit." The successor, Major-General Sir Gerald Boyd, was himself a man of special calibre. Having failed to gain entry to the Royal Military Academy, Woolwich, as an officer cadet, he joined the Army as a private soldier, and fought in the ranks of the Devonshire Regiment in the South African War. By 1914 he had won his commission and was a staff captain; now, in 1918, he was about to supervise one of the most wonderful feats of the war.

Preparations for the attack were carried out in General Boyd's division with the same scrupulous care as had been observed in the Fourth Army as a whole before the Battle of Amiens. That there was going to be an assault on the Hindenburg Line could not be disguised; there was no question of surprise as regards the main intention. But it was possible to surprise the enemy with the timing, and above all with the inclusion of the Bellenglise canal sector. This meant that there must be no hint of unusual activity on the 46th Division's front (or behind it), nothing to arouse the suspicions of the bold Luftwaffe pilots, whose scarlet-painted aeroplanes swooped across the lines through rifle and machine-gun fire "for all the world like huge red birds diving down on the look-out for their prey on the ground beneath."[30] The 46th Division told them nothing.

The steep-sided canal made a perfect tank obstacle, so the allocation of tanks to IX Corps was only twenty-four, to be used in the second phase. As ever, the main reliance would be on the guns. General Boyd's divisional artillery was reinforced for the occasion, though over 1,000 of the Fourth Army's 1,600 guns and howitzers were on the main front of attack by the Australian Corps. Everywhere there was intensive activity in the Royal Artillery brigades and batteries, as complex barrage time-tables were worked out, a precise rôle being allotted to every single gun. For full effectiveness, especially when enemy retaliation began, the artillery needed to be linked to every headquarters concerned by an intricate system of telephone cables. In the great set-piece battles of the past three years these would have been buried underground, sometimes as much as six feet deep.[31] It was on the preservation of these cable lines that command depended: "the ONLY place where it was possible to know what was going on was at the end of a wire."[32] In September 1918, however, there was no question of burying the cables; they had to lie on the surface all the time, exposed to the dangers, not only of enemy fire, but of cutting by the wheels of British transport taking quick cross-country routes by night.

> Lines were cut not once or twice, but twenty or thirty times a night, and linemen were out working practically continuously. Perhaps the most exasperating incident occurred, however, when, on the night before the battle, a cavalry unit which shall be nameless settled down for the night midway between Divisional Headquarters and an important forward communication post, and signalized its arrival by cutting out some hundred yards or so of the three twin cables which formed the main divisional route, in order to use them as a picket line for their horses. After this "Signals" felt that Fate could have no harder blows in store for them.[33]

For this operation, important and onerous though the tasks of other arms might be, it was on the Royal Engineers that the final responsibility for success or failure would fall: it was their job to devise the means of crossing the canal. There was no lack of ingenuity in the corps, whose promise had always been that if a thing was difficult they would do it at once, but if it was impossible it might take a little longer. They made wooden piers, for use either as foot-bridges or as rafts, supported by empty petrol tins or bundles of cork mats. They provided collapsible boats, mud-mats made of canvas rolls reinforced by reeds, life-lines and scaling ladders for climbing the steep canal banks. "Finally, some genius hit on the novel idea of making use of life-belts on a considerable scale. The latter idea in particular promised considerable prospects of success; the authorities at Boulogne were telegraphed for the life-belts from some of the leave-boats, and over 3,000 were collected and were sent up and issued to the storming troops."[34] All these contraptions were tested on the eve of the attack, 28 September, by men of the Staffordshire Brigade (which was to lead it) on the moat of a château. It was found that the collapsible boats could be opened and launched in twenty seconds; fully loaded men discovered that they could swim across forty yards of deep water in the life-belts without any danger of drowning; a man who could not swim was hauled across by a life-line, similarly supported and equally safe. Everyone was much encouraged; now all that remained was to see that all this equipment was in the right place at the right time, and that the Royal Engineers were at their battle stations. This was done.

Elsewhere the portents were less pleasing. At 5:30 A.M. on 27 September, a wet, misty morning, the 106th Regiment of the American

27th Division had attempted to clear the outposts of the Hindenburg Line, and in so doing performed the preliminaries of the birth of an enduring legend. The task of the 106th Regiment was to advance some 1,000–1,500 yards on a front of rather more than two miles and capture three obstinately held strongpoints. The regiment, supported by twelve tanks of the 4th (British) Battalion, advanced behind a creeping barrage whose 15 per cent ingredient of smoke-shell did nothing for visibility. The 106th took some 2,000 men into action in its three battalions, a rather low figure by American standards, but worse still was the poverty of officers: twelve companies could only muster eighteen officers between them. The Australian Official History comments: "An Australian brigade at that time, though reduced to 1,200 rifles, might have undertaken the task, but would have put in at least 40 company officers, and many N.C.O.s with equal experience, and would have required all its skill and 'bluff' to succeed."

What really happened on that unhappy day will always remain obscure. Early reports indicated that one by one the strongpoints were being taken by the American infantry, and some 250 prisoners dribbling in seemed to prove that this was so. Then there were less optimistic signs; it began to look as though the strongpoints, even if they had been captured earlier, were now lost again. Exact information was non-existent; the idea grew that the Americans had gone forward too fast, leaving nests of Germans behind them, who had now attacked them in the rear. Once promulgated, this notion took a firm grip and coloured all interpretations of the American experience, not only on the day but later. Meanwhile conflicting information continued to puzzle the local commanders. By the morning of the 28th, however, it was perfectly clear that the 106th had failed, with heavy loss. The results of this were far-reaching. It was not merely that the Germans would still need to be dislodged from their outposts; far worse was the persisting belief that Americans in considerable numbers were still out on the battlefield, making it impossible to provide a creeping barrage for the main attack next day. Haig found Monash "in a state of despair" at this realization, and tried to encourage him by telling him that it was "not a serious matter." He then went on and met General Read, whom he considered "a good honest fellow, but all this class of warfare is quite new to him, and he was genuinely very anxious. I did my best to cheer him up, and told him that the reality was much simpler than his imagination pictured it to his mind." The Australian Official Historian thought these remarks of Haig's showed it "doubtful if he himself understood the facts or their implications." The full implications probably *were* only perceptible at "ground level"; at his higher altitude, Haig was feeling well pleased that day, as news of the

Second Army's successes came in, and Byng reported more gains on the Third Army front where he considered the enemy "shows signs of 'cracking.'"

Monash and Rawlinson believed and continued to believe the story of the American charge, the failure to "mop up," and the Germans reappearing to take them in the rear. Most British historians have followed this version of events both for 27 September and for the main attack on 29 September. Dr. C. E. W. Bean, the Australian Official Historian, however, having examined with great care the American and German records of the battle, begs to differ.[35] His belief is that on both days (and 29 September was a morning of dense fog, far worse than the 27th) the Americans quickly fell into confusion, often losing direction and contact with each other. On the 27th, as their few officers fell —seventeen out of the eighteen with the companies became casualties —the leaderless troops simply did not know what to do. Indeed, they were not always even able to recognize the dangers that threatened them; a number of Americans were found at one stage sitting quietly in the bottom of a trench, oblivious of the fact that the Germans were bombing their way up it. The inexperienced Americans thought the explosions were being caused by shells passing overhead. Many other parties of Americans came to grief in the face of German counterattacks, not from behind, as the legend insisted, but from in front, in the normal German manner. The wild charge was a myth; those who reached their objectives were quickly killed there. One German regimental history said: "The Americans made a middling impression on our troops; they appear very unskilled in attack; in close fighting they mostly were very helpless and lacking in dash." Certainly these New Yorkers of the 27th Division were not the same sort of soldiers as the tough Marines and regulars of the 1st and 2nd Divisions, but the German verdict is unfair to men fighting at a very grave disadvantage. Courage they did not lack; their casualties that day were 1,540, virtually all in the 106th Regiment, which may not have known how best to fight, but did not easily learn how to surrender either.

For the 27th Division 29 September was 27 September again, writ large. Monash, as soon as he realized that his plan had fallen to pieces, asked Rawlinson for a day's delay to clear up the mess, but the Army Commander, aware of the actions of other armies, including the French First Army on his right, could not permit this. On General O'Ryan, therefore, fell the agonizing decision as to whether to put down a close barrage in the normal way on the 29th, and risk killing Americans out in front, or to launch his division's main attack some 1,000 yards behind the protective screen and hope to catch it up. He concluded that to risk putting the barrage down on fellow Americans

'. . . a perfect tank obstacle': the entrance to the St Quentin Canal tunnel at Bellicourt. The sheer 30'-50' sides of the canal cutting were impassable to tanks, which had to pass over the tunnel. Bellicourt was captured by the American 30th Division, supported by the 5th Australian Division

Men of destiny. *Left:* Major-General Sir Gerald Boyd, commanding the 46th (North Midland) Division, 'a man of special calibre' who served four years in the ranks before obtaining his commission. His division captured 4,200 of the 5,300 prisoners taken on 29 September.

Right: Lieutenant-General Sir Walter Braithwaite, commanding IX Corps, who submitted the plan for storming the Hindenburg Line at Bellenglise

'. . . some genius hit on the idea of making use of life-belts': North and South Staffordshires of the triumphant 46th Division, some still wearing their life-belts, some with captured German helmets, lining the steep sides of the St Quentin Canal and being addressed by their Brigadier, J. V. Campbell V.C., after their wonderful feat of arms

'The 46th Division had done its share': a touch of pride and panoply amid the ruins, as the band of the 137th (Staffordshire) Brigade celebrates the victory of Bellenglise

'An advance of four or five miles a day was good, eight or ten very good': a scene on the roads in October, infantry being brought forward in lorries, gunners pulling an 18-pounder out of a ditch

'They surrender in hordes, whenever the enemy attacks' (Prince Rupprecht): these Germans are giving themselves up to the advancing Australians

'The role of the five British armies in the final victory is unmistakeable . . .': the situation map which hung in Haig's office in his Advanced Headquarters train, as it stood on 25 September, clearly showing the density of German divisions facing the British front

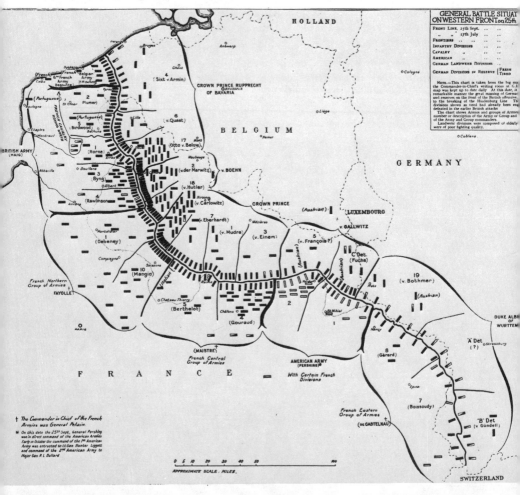

would be "repulsive to the mass of the officers and men of the division and destructive of morale." So once more the 27th would go into battle with a handicap.

The result was predictable: in the murk of a dense autumn fog, thickened by smoke-shells and the smoke of bursting high-explosive, the three regiments of the 27th Division (105th, 107th and 108th) were soon in the same sort of difficulties as had afflicted the 106th two days earlier. Advancing Australians of the 3rd Division, expecting to go a considerable distance before passing through the Americans, were startled to find themselves in a battle almost at once. Their strict orders were not to become involved in the American fighting, but to press forward through the Hindenburg Line as fast as possible. Local commanders soon realized that this was out of the question. So mixed groups of Australians and Americans, separated from each other, and lost to the sight of their higher commanders in the fog, fought it out the hard way all day long with heavy casualties—another 3,500 in the 27th Division, over 1,000 in the Australian 3rd.

Progress was much less than anticipated; in this sector it was once again the outposts of the Hindenburg Line, not the Line itself, that occupied the Fourth Army. The tanks, from which much had been expected, proved disappointing: "September 29th was perhaps the most trying day the tanks had experienced during all the battles in which they took part with the Fourth Army."[36] Their story makes depressing reading: eight destroyed on an old British minefield; seven approaching to within 100 yards of Gillemont Farm, then all being put out of action as they emerged from the fog; ten out of twelve "put out of action by direct hits" or ditched in another place; four more "put out of action almost at once," four Mark Vs and eight Whippets on the right losing all the Mark Vs and five of the Whippets "within fifteen minutes of starting," others forming "an excellent target for the anti-tank guns" when the fog began to clear, and so on. Altogether, out of 141 tanks committed to the battle on 29 September, seventy-five—more than 50 per cent—became casualties.

So it was demonstrated once more (see pp. 90–92) that the tanks of 1918 were not war-winners, despite the mendacious alibi for defeat offered to the Reichstag party leaders by the High Command emissary, Major von dem Bussche, three days later. "The enemy," he told them,

has made use of tanks in unexpectedly large numbers.[37] In cases where they have suddenly emerged in huge masses[38] from smoke clouds, our men were completely unnerved. Tanks broke through our foremost lines, making a way for their infantry, reaching our rear,[39] and causing local panics, which entirely upset our battle control. When we were able to locate them our anti-tank guns[40] and our artillery speedily put an end to them. But the mischief had already been done, *and solely owing to the success of the tanks we have suffered enormous losses in prisoners* [my italics][41], and this has unexpectedly reduced our strength and caused a more speedy wastage of our reserves than we had anticipated.[42]

The truth of 29 September, displayed all along the front of the Australian Corps, was precisely opposite. The Australians and Americans and their British tank crews made the disagreeable discovery that the Germans were now taking the measure of tanks, and had devised various methods of dealing with them. Once more it is Dr. Bean who brings sanity and clarity into the picture; it is he who describes the "tank forts,"

> six or more in each divisional sector, each fort containing at least one or two field guns, several heavy and light machine guns, anti-tank rifles, and an infantry escort. The infantry were also supported by attached sections of field batteries and by "close fighting batteries"[43]—methods in which the Germans were far more practised and skilful than most British or Dominion forces and to which they resorted more than ever after the "tank battle" of August 8th.

Some will no doubt feel that they recognize, in that passage, the lineaments of the flexible, adaptable opponents they met in the *Afrika Korps* and elsewhere in the Second World War.

The American 30th Division, on 29 September, did not share all the tribulations of the unlucky 27th. With the advantage of a clean start-line, the infantry was at least able to make its initial advance close to the barrage, and early progress was good. But then, in the fog shroud, confusion set in; it was not to be wondered at. Even in proper daylight, the zig-zagging belts of wire and the intricacies of the multiple trench system would have tried any troops; the 30th Division, in the murk, split into small parties and lost direction, and soon the advance slowed up. The Australian 5th Division then arrived, to find itself, like the 3rd, engaged in battle considerably sooner than it expected. For the rest of the day Australians and Americans tried to make more progress against stiff opposition—"a very severe day's fighting"—ending well short of their final objective, but considerably ahead of their comrades on the left, and with their right in contact with the British IX Corps. The 30th Division had 1,881 casualties; by 2 October the Australian 5th had lost 1,500 officers and men.

Measured by results on the main battle-front, 29 September was not a good day. Fortunately, there was another criterion. Led by the 137th Infantry Brigade (Brigadier J. V. Campbell, V.C.; ⅕th South Staffordshires, ⅙th South Staffordshires, ⅙th North Staffordshires), the 46th Division launched its attack across the St. Quentin Canal at 5:50 A.M. The fog which had been so unkind to the Americans was in general a great aid to the 46th Division, although, as we shall see, the back areas did not find it a blessing. Keeping well up to their barrage, the North Midlanders quickly overran the German forward position. The divisional history describes their practised technique: "In small parties and *protected by the fog,* they worked their way up to within a short distance of the enemy trenches, then, rising with a shout, dashed in with the bayonet, the enemy giving way in all directions and many of them making good their escape through the fog, in spite of considerable casualties inflicted by the artillery as they retired" [my italics].[44]

Soon the Staffordshire men reached the canal, and the time came to put to the test of battle all the devices prepared by the engineers. This was the moment of truth, entailing an inevitable delay which might be critical:

> It was in such a situation as this that *the fog proved so invaluable*. The farther bank of the Canal was strongly defended by the enemy with rifle fire and light machine guns fired from concrete emplacements, but at this period of the day it was impossible to see more than a few yards, and the enemy could not tell with any certainty where our troops were until they were right upon them, when the latter lost no time in charging, and quickly silenced the enemy machine guns by the destruction of the guns' crews. So quickly indeed was progress made, that comparatively few casualties were suffered in this very difficult operation. This was again in great measure due to the splendid leading of both officers and N.C.O.s. Any hesitation at this juncture would have been fatal and might have resulted in the total failure of the attack. It was absolutely essential for success that the troops should keep up with the barrage and *make the utmost use of the fog* [my italics].[45]

By 8:30 A.M., exactly according to the time-table laid down, the 137th Brigade had succeeded in clearing its way to the canal, crossing it, and storming its way through a fortified line which the Germans had done everything in their power to make impregnable—indeed they believed they had succeeded in doing so. The Staffordshires, waiting for the supporting brigades to pass through them, had every right to look as pleased with themselves as they do in the wonderful photographs which show them massed on the canal banks, many still wearing the life-belts which had carried them triumphantly across. They had taken 2,000 prisoners (considerably more than their own numbers) and their casualties, including those suffered two nights earlier in repelling a German counter-attack, amounted to less than 600 officers and men.

Also exactly on schedule, the 138th and 139th Brigades came up and passed through, and equally successfully attacked the next objectives. Resistance stiffened, however, and as the fog began to disperse both infantry and supporting tanks—coming down from Bellicourt where they had crossed the canal by the tunnel—were exposed to heavy artillery and machine-gun fire. The advance continued, nevertheless; meanwhile, in the rear, the fog which had so helped the assaulting battalions was having a very different effect. All landmarks were blotted out, with the result that "the whole region immediately behind the old front line [was] soon filled with columns of prisoners, returning wounded, stragglers, reinforcements and a medley of orderlies and odds and ends of transport of every description, wandering about in all directions, and with little hope of finding their way anywhere until the mist cleared."[46] For the wounded this situation was particularly harrowing: stretcher-bearers constantly lost themselves in the fog, walking wounded were unable to find the first-aid posts and dressing stations. But once again it was in the sensitive area of communications that the worst damage was done. A complete system of visual communication was rendered useless; lines were continually cut, and in the fog it was extremely difficult to find the two ends for joining; orderlies vanished in the gloom and were seen no more. In fact it was a miracle that senior officers managed to retain any control whatever; such were the difficulties of generalship in that war, which critics rarely acknowledge.

Generalship, indeed, found few opportunities of expressing itself on the field of battle; often it expressed itself only in the training of troops beforehand, and in careful preparation for the event. Both of these now had their reward: at 1 P.M. General Boyd rode out from his headquarters to congratulate his brigadiers and their admirable soldiers.

> The mist by then had completely cleared and the sight was one for which every commander worth the name had lived during the long years of the war. As far as the eye could see, our troops were pushing forward; batteries were crossing the Canal and coming into action; Engineers everywhere at work; large bodies of prisoners were coming in from all sides; and the men of the 32nd Division were advancing fast. The enemy were shelling the line of the Canal and Bellenglise, but no one seemed to mind.
>
> It was indeed a break-through.
>
> Thus the battle ended early in the afternoon with the complete attainment of all objectives, and, at 5.30 p.m., the advanced troops of the

32nd Division passed through our front line in pursuit of the retreating enemy.[47]

There are really no words for what the 46th Division had achieved. Modestly the divisional history says: "The breaking of the Hindenburg Line marked a definite stage in the history of the war, for it opened the way to a war of movement which could only end in one way. The 46th Division had done its share." It had done much more: out of 5,300 prisoners taken by the Fourth Army on 29 September, 4,200 were taken by the 46th Division; it also captured seventy guns, and made possible the deepest penetration on the whole army front—some 6,000 yards. And the price of this scarcely believable triumph was less than 800 casualties.

Piece by piece the higher commands put together the jigsaw picture of the day's events. At Fourth Army Headquarters, conscious of the setback on the Australian Corps front, which had also prevented any significant gain by the British III Corps on the left, full realization of what had been achieved was perhaps a little slow in coming: "Such high hopes had been held of a sweeping and decisive victory on September 29th, that the check received at the northern half of the tunnel defences was for the moment the cause of some disappointment. It was soon realized, however, that, although we had not achieved all that was desired and expected, we had, nevertheless, inflicted a crushing defeat on the enemy."

This was indeed the case, and no one expresses it better than Haig's biographer, Duff Cooper: "When the month of September was ended and the Hindenburg Line had fallen, the war in fact was finished, although for six more weeks the fighting continued while the facts were slowly being realized by the soldiers and statesmen on either side."

Chapter VII: Notes

1. (p. 119) In his *War Memoirs,* having "perused very carefully all the minutes of the War Cabinet," Lloyd George concludes that "Sir Henry Wilson acted entirely on his own initiative on this occasion. . . . I cannot account for Sir Henry Wilson's letter to Haig. There was a streak of mischief—not to say malice—in his nature which often made trouble and sought to make trouble. On the other hand he was very anxious at this date to ingratiate himself with the Commander-in-Chief, who distrusted him through and through. . . . You can never track down the motive in so labyrinthine a character as that of Sir Henry Wilson." (Odhams, 1936, ii, p. 2030).

All of which prompts once more the question, why was he so anxious to appoint such a man to the post of Chief of the Imperial General Staff? In this particular case we do not need to look for labyrinthine motives; Wilson was merely reporting what he knew to be the case, even if no formal discussion of manpower or casualties occurred to be recorded in the Cabinet Minutes. Asides and private conversations would have given Wilson justification for concern, but the telegram was nevertheless quite improper. As he said in a letter to Haig, it "was only intended to convey a sort of distant warning and nothing more. All so easy to explain in talking, all so difficult to explain in writing."

2. (p. 120) A scathing retort; see Duff Cooper, *Haig*, Faber, 1935, ii, p. 361.
3. (p. 121) H. W. Wilson and J. A. Hammerton: *The Great War*, Amalgamated Press, 1919, vol. xii, p. 447.
4. (p. 121) Alberich was the malicious dwarf of the Nibelung Saga; it was on this front that the Germans made their main withdrawal before Nivelle's offensive in 1917, doing much malicious damage in the process. Some historians have been misled into thinking that the name attaches to the withdrawal operation; in fact it attaches only to the sector of the defences in question.
5. (p. 121) Sir Frederick Maurice: *The Last Four Months*, Cassell, 1919, p. 137.
6. (p. 122) Major-Gen. Sir Archibald Montgomery: *The Story of the Fourth Army in the Battles of the Hundred Days, August 8th to November 11th, 1918*, Hodder and Stoughton, 1920, p. 149.
7. (p. 123) *Douglas Haig: The Educated Soldier*, Hutchinson, 1963, pp. 464–65.
8. (p. 124) The count was still incomplete.
9. (p. 125) But, as Duff Cooper pertinently asks, "Would they have preferred him to have been pessimistic in the past? A general who goes into battle without the confidence of victory is not fit to command" (op. cit.).
10. (p. 126) General Byng's memory failed him; it was not the 6th Division but the 62nd.
11. (p. 126) At the Battle of Vionville—Mars-la-Tour on 16 August 1870 the Brandenburg *III Corps* and the Hanoverian *X Corps* successfully fought a whole French Army virtually unaided. British officers of Byng's and Repington's generation were steeped in the history of the Franco-Prussian War and many of them knew all its battlefields intimately.
12. (p. 129) III Corps (Lieut.-Gen. Sir R. Butler), a newly reconstituted IX Corps (Lieut.-Gen. Sir W. Braithwaite) and the Australian Corps (Lieut.-Gen. Sir J. Monash).
13. (p. 130) Figures may "speak for themselves," but not always with one voice. Readers may glimpse the historian's difficulties from the following: the British Official History firmly follows the Australian Official Account with the statistics quoted; the figure of 6,800 infantry engaged is from the Australian Account. But *The Story of the Fourth Army*, written by Major-Gen. Sir Archibald Montgomery, the Army's Chief of Staff, with full access to all its documents, says that the Australians captured 87 guns, that their total of infantry engaged was 5,902, that they took 1,700 prisoners, and that their casualties were 1,022.
14. (p. 131) See Note 1; the Government's preoccupation with manpower is obvious.
15. (p. 131) Lieut.-Gen. Sir John Du Cane, British liaison officer at Foch's H.Q.
16. (p. 131) Ludendorff: *My War Memories*, Hutchinson, 1919, ii, pp. 714–15.
17. (p. 135) Both Foch and Pétain doubted whether it was feasible.
18. (p. 135) Forrest C. Pogue: *George C. Marshall: Education of a General 1880–1939*, MacGibbon and Kee, 1964.
19. (p. 135) Pershing and other American sources say the First Army attacked at 5:30 A.M. and the French half an hour later. Foch and the British Official Historian say the French attacked at 5:25 and the Americans five minutes later.
20. (p. 135) Later Commander of the First Army.
21. (p. 137) Lieut.-Gen. Sir Frederick Morgan: *Overture to Overlord*, Hodder and Stoughton, 1950, p. 256.
22. (p. 137) Ibid.

23. (p. 138) Nicholson, *Canadian Expeditionary Force 1914–1919*, p. 441.
24. (p. 139) *General Jack's Diary*, ed. John Terraine, Eyre and Spottiswoode, 1964, pp. 269 and 273–74.
25. (p. 142) Major R. E. Priestley: *Breaking the Hindenburg Line: The Story of the 46th (North Midland) Division*, T. Fisher Unwin, 1919, p. 31.
26. (p. 142) The Official History says seven to ten feet.
27. (p. 143) See pp. 67–72 and 95–96.
28. (p. 144) Australian Official History, vol. vi, p. 945.
29. (p. 144) General Braithwaite had been chief of staff to General Sir Ian Hamilton in the Gallipoli campaign in 1915; returning to France he commanded first the 62nd Division, then XXII and now IX Corps.
30. (p. 145) Priestley, op. cit., p. 37.
31. (p. 145) For example, between 1 April and 30 June 1916 the Canadian Corps alone buried 420 miles of cable six feet deep.
32. (p. 146) General Sir Alan Bourne to the author, 24 June 1966.
33. (p. 146) Priestley, op. cit., p. 39.
34. (p. 146) Ibid., p. 42.
35. (p. 148) Vol. vi of the Australian Official Account came out in 1942. The comparable volume of the British Official History is dated 1947, but according to Sir James Edmonds the Australian version appeared "in the interval between the compilation of the present volume and its being sent to press." This affords us an interesting glimpse of the stately tempo of official history, and explains why the British text follows the "orthodox version." Montgomery's: *The Story of the Fourth Army* came out immediately after the war while legend was still fresh, and General Monash's *The Australian Victories in France in 1918* appeared in 1936.
36. (p. 149) Montgomery, op. cit., p. 169.
37. (p. 149) Quite untrue: there were no "large numbers" after 8 August.
38. (p. 149) On 29 September the tanks were used in small groups—twelve, eight, four, often in pairs—in close support of the infantry.
39. (p. 149) Unfortunately no such thing occurred; the armoured cars of the 17th Battalion attempted a dash down the Hargicourt-Bony road into Bony, supported by some Whippets, under the impression that the Germans had gone. They had not: "four armoured cars and four whippet tanks were put out of action by anti-tank gun fire. The remainder of the whippets and armoured cars were, therefore, withdrawn to a position of safety. . . ." (Montgomery, op. cit., p. 167.)
40. (p. 150) 77-mm field guns on low wheels and using armour-piercing shells with delayed-action fuses to burst inside the tank.
41. (p. 150) The overwhelming number of prisoners on 29 September were taken in the sector where tanks did not operate.
42. (p. 150) Quoted by Sir Frederick Maurice, op. cit., p. 171.
43. (p. 150) *Nahkampfbatterien*, sometimes consisting of mountain artillery, sometimes of captured field guns.
44. (p. 151) Priestley, op. cit., p. 53.
45. (p. 151) Ibid., p. 55.
46. (p. 152) Ibid., pp. 61–62.
47. (p. 153) Ibid., p. 73.

VIII

"IF PEACE COULD BE HAD"

"... we must plainly sue for peace, if peace could be had." (Ludendorff)

It took nine days to break the Hindenburg Line; it was not until 5 October that Haig's four armies (the Fifth joined in the offensive on 1 October) forced their way through the final system. The Germans still clung obstinately to parts of the great fortification and to the town of Cambrai, to cover deep withdrawals both to north and south, but on each British Army front there was a clear breakthrough. The Australians (2nd Division) won their final victory at Montbréhain, the 46th Division distinguished itself again at Ramicourt; in the Third Army it was the New Zealanders and 62nd Division, in the First Army the Canadians were again in the lead. The net result of all their efforts was 36,000 prisoners and 380 guns. When have British armies done better?

So it was against the ominous back-drop of the crumbling of their last defensive position (the "Hermann Line" to the east really only existed on paper) that the German leaders, High Command and Government, now truly embarked on the quest that should have started on 12 August: the quest for peace, since the arbitrament of war had failed. The twenty-ninth of September at Spa was a day of conferences, all of them depressing. First, Hindenburg and Ludendorff had a meeting with von Hintze. The Foreign Secretary had little to say about foreign affairs—beyond admitting that no action had been taken on the decision of the Imperial Conference of 14 August to make approaches to the Queen of the Netherlands (see p. 103), nor, indeed, in any other direction. "Nothing positive had thus been done," says Ludendorff, glumly. As regards domestic matters, however, von Hintze had a great deal to say, but all to be summed up in two seismic sentences:

"The domestic situation was such that a complete change of system, and the formation of a Parliamentary Ministry in Berlin, was essential. He even spoke of the possibility of a revolution."[1]

This came as a profound shock to the two soldiers. As Ludendorff says, "I was unable to form any view of this, as I was not *au courant* of affairs in Berlin." All the evidence of the following days shows that if the First Quartermaster-General was not *au courant,* the Field-Marshal was even less so. This degree of ignorance, such insulation from the condition of the nation on the part of the two men who were not merely its military leaders, but who for the last year had virtually been its political chiefs too, is extraordinary. It is also a comment on the nature of German politics, whose weakness was now to be terribly revealed. Further, and more immediately, to the point, von Hintze's revelations indicated a most serious complication in the search for a peace formula.

Spa, during these last weeks of the war, became in effect the last citadel of the Empire. And it was here, in that citadel, at the Château de la Fraineuse where he was lodged, that the Emperor on that very day learned the extent of the dangers threatening him.[2] When they had digested von Hintze's information, Ludendorff and Hindenburg, in their turn, proffered an unpalatable dish: their review of the military situation. All three then agreed that the only remedy was to approach President Woodrow Wilson immediately with a proposal for an armistice and peace. It was noted hopefully that the Swiss Ambassador in Washington had praised the President's high ideals to the German Government. And now all that remained was to inform the Kaiser that his army was beaten, his régime was tottering, and his Empire must sue for peace.

In the last weeks of his reign all the facets of Wilhelm II's curious character were well displayed. Sometimes behaving with regal dignity, sometimes ranting,[3] sometimes quite supine, as though what was happening was no concern of his, sometimes blustering, he never at any time seems to have been in touch with reality, let alone in control of it. The Field-Marshal whom he trusted and admired, the First Quartermaster-General whose "brilliance" had been a main prop of the Empire, and the Foreign Secretary who was also an admiral in his fleet, arrived at the château just before noon. They told their dismal story, and they drew the moral: what was required, they said, was "revolution from above." The Kaiser must decree a parliamentary constitution. The twenty-ninth of September was one of Wilhelm's days of quiet dignity; there were no reproaches, no ravings—indeed, he took his decisions with unusual calm and despatch. He accepted the need for an immediate armistice, and then, with a little more hesitation, screwed himself up to sign "the most difficult document of his career," the proclamation of parliamentary government. But in renouncing the rôle of "All-Highest," something seemed to snap inside him: "The same day he had faced defeat at home and abroad; by the evening he appeared a broken and suddenly aged man."[4]

The confused events of the next few days reflected the confusion of the disintegrating Empire. The first result of the Kaiser's decisions was the resignation of the Chancellor, von Hertling. For two days Germany had no Chancellor, and the search for one was conducted chiefly by the Vice-Chancellor, von Payer. "It was," says Ludendorff, "a curious proceeding, in which the Sovereign abandoned all initiative." This was one of Wilhelm's supine periods. The news from the battle-front, of course, was all bad; the thunder of Haig's guns was the accompaniment of Germany's doom. On 30 September Hindenburg warned the Army Group Commanders: "Reinforcement by O.H.L. reserves can no longer be reckoned on. Nevertheless an enemy break-through must in all circumstances be prevented. . . . The important thing is to gain time and inflict heavy losses on the enemy. . . ."[5]

A good deal of the confusion which surrounds this period is due to the veil of lies with which Ludendorff has surrounded it in his memoirs. "I am unable to understand," he wrote, "how the idea ever arose that I had said that the front would break if we did not have an armistice within twenty-four hours." Between 29 September and 2 October, he adds, "there was no particular military event that could have led to any modification of my views." The truth is quite different. On the evening of the 29th Ludendorff sent Major von dem Bussche to Berlin to explain the need for an armistice to members of the Government and the Reichstag (see pp. 149–50). As the hours went by, however, and Germany remained without a chief executive, the Supreme Command became more and more agitated. With good reason: what Ludendorff was pleased to call "no particular military event" was in fact the progressive crumbling of the whole Siegfried system—in other words, catastrophe. And the effect it produced was a telegram to von dem Bussche, for the attention of the Vice-Chancellor, dated 1:30 P.M., 1 October, stressing the urgency of the armistice démarche:

> Provided that a guarantee can be given between 7 and 8 o'clock this evening that Prince Max of Baden is forming the Government, then I agree to postponement until tomorrow morning.
>
> Should there, however, be any doubt about the formation of the Government, then I must insist that the declaration be made known to the foreign powers tonight.

The origin of the telegram is "Main Headquarters" (Spa), and it is signed "von Hindenburg." But Ludendorff informs us that Hindenburg had left for Berlin with the Kaiser the night before; "I was unfortunately indispensable at Spa, owing to the position in the field." So the author of the telegram was clearly Ludendorff himself (their signatures were normally interchangeable), and its tenor was such that it could have only one meaning. It was, says Sir Frederick Maurice, "naturally assumed in Berlin to be a cry of despair, and when we consider the events which led up to it this seems to be the only possible interpretation."

The second of October was a day heavy with significance in Berlin. At a Crown Council the Kaiser and Hindenburg met Prince Max of Baden; it was upon this second cousin of the Kaiser, "the one prominent royalist liberal in the empire,"[6] that the vacant chancellorship was now being pressed. Prince Max was also a Prussian major-general and the heir to a ducal throne, neither being particularly useful qualifications in a quasi-revolutionary situation. On the other hand his known democratic tendencies and belief in the need for an early peace made him acceptable to most Social Democrats. Even he, however, was shocked when he discovered, at this meeting, how early the peace might have to be. He wanted at least a fortnight in which to prepare the ground for armistice proposals, pointing out that the headlong approach demanded by the High Command must have the appearance of capitulation; "in that case Wilson . . . will demand the German Republic." But Hindenburg (schooled by Ludendorff's panic) was adamant, and the Kaiser, with characteristic fecklessness, gave him rough support. He told Prince Max: "The Supreme Command considers it necessary, and you have not been brought here to make difficulties for the Supreme Command."[7]

How far Hindenburg, never afflicted by too much imagination, shared Ludendorff's alarms will never be certain. It is definite, however, that on 2 October he kept up the demand for an immediate end to the fighting despite every argument that Prince Max could put forward. At last the latter, in desperation, asked the simple and searching question: why, if the High Command considered the situation so desperate, did it not simply surrender to the Allies in the open field? Hindenburg was nonplussed; he was not a ready debater, and he sorely missed the quick wits and plausible tongue of the First Quartermaster-General. He promised an answer in writing the next day, and went off to consult Ludendorff on the telephone.

Meanwhile equally high drama was taking place in another part of Berlin. In the Reichstag building Major von dem Bussche was unfold-

ing the grim truths of the military situation to the party leaders. These
were men who, like all the rest of Germany including the Kaiser himself,
had been fed for years on propaganda; few of them had ever doubted
—ever even permitted themselves to doubt—Germany's ultimate victory. Even in the dark days since 18 July and 8 August they had
mostly clung to any straw of optimism, any favourable interpretation
of events, that had come their way. Their emotions may be imagined
when they heard von dem Bussche say:

> We can carry on the war for a substantial further period, we can
> cause the enemy heavy loss, we can lay waste his country as we retire,
> but *we cannot win the war* [my italics].
> Realizing this fact . . . the Field-Marshal and General Ludendorff
> have resolved to propose to His Majesty that we bring the fighting to a
> close, in order to avoid further sacrifices on the part of the German
> people and their allies . . .
> . . . we must make up our minds to abandon the further prosecution
> of the war as hopeless . . .
> . . . each new day brings the enemy nearer to his goal, and makes
> him the less ready to conclude a reasonable peace with us.
> We must accordingly lose no time. Every twenty-four hours that pass
> may make our position worse, and give the enemy a clearer view of our
> present weakness.
> That might have the most disastrous consequences both for the pros-
> pects of peace and for the military position. . . .[8]

His listeners, says Sir John Wheeler-Bennett, "were dumbfounded, utterly crushed. Ebert[9] went white as death and could not utter a word;
Stresemann[10] looked as though someone had struck him. 'We have been
lied to and betrayed,' cried Heydebrand,[11] and the Prussian Minister,
von Waldow, staggered to his feet, muttering 'There's only one thing
left now—to put a bullet in one's head.' "[12]
The extreme Left, on the other hand, the Independent Socialists,
were jubilant. One of them rushed up to a colleague, beaming, and cry-
ing out "Now we've got them!"[13] The defeat of the Empire on the battlefield was a clear signal to its enemies within; they sensed imminent
collapse, and from this moment onwards the future of the House of
Hohenzollern was more and more in jeopardy. The German Empire
faced not merely defeat but a constitutional crisis which could all too
easily follow the pattern laid down in Russia the previous year.
On 3 October at least one thing was settled, more or less satisfactorily: Prince Max accepted the chancellorship. Later he wrote the
epitaph of his brief tenure of office: "I thought I should have arrived
five minutes before the hour, but I arrived five minutes after it." On

the day of his arrival, however, whether early or late, two urgent tasks awaited him. The first was to form a government—the first government in German history that would be responsible to the elected representatives of the nation. Not unnaturally it included representatives of the strongest party in the Reichstag, the Social Democrats, one of them being the party leader, Philipp Scheidemann.

The next task awaiting Prince Max was to settle the question of the armistice. At the first meeting of the new Cabinet Hindenburg presented the formal request of the High Command, concocted after his telephone conversation with Ludendorff. It ran as follows:

> G.H.Q. holds to the demand made by it on Monday, the 29th September of this year, for an immediate offer of peace to the enemy.
>
> As a result of the collapse of the Macedonian front, and of the weakening of our reserves in the West which this has necessitated, and *in view of the impossibility of making good the very heavy losses of the last few days* [my italics], there appears to be now no possibility, to the best of human judgment, of winning peace from our enemies by force of arms.
>
> The enemy, on the other hand, is continually throwing new and fresh reserves into the fight.[14]
>
> The German Army still holds firmly together, and beats off all the enemy's attacks victoriously, but the position grows more acute day by day, and may at any time compel us to take very serious measures.
>
> In these circumstances the only right course is to bring the war to a close, in order to spare the German people and their allies useless sacrifices. Every day wasted costs the lives of thousands of brave German soldiers.[15]

Once more the document bore the signature, "von Hindenburg," but, as Sir John Wheeler-Bennett remarks, it also bore "signs of joint authorship," or, as Ludendorff blandly expressed it, it "set out again . . . in my opinion with complete accuracy, the views of G.H.Q." It did indeed. And once more there was fierce discussion among Hindenburg's barely credulous hearers. The Field-Marshal himself, no doubt finding his rôle increasingly distasteful, wavered at one point, and spoke of "fighting to the last man" if the Allies insisted on humiliating terms. Count Roedern, the new Finance Minister, tartly pointed out that while such deeds were possible for single battalions, they could hardly be expected of a nation of sixty-five millions.

It was at this stage that a further very confusing factor became apparent. The High Command, from the first, had invoked President Wilson's Fourteen Points[16] as the basis of peace negotiations, but now, as Wheeler-Bennett says, "it became more and more evident that the

Chancellor had read the Fourteen Points while the Supreme Command had not." In Prince Max's words: "The Supreme Command had probably no clear idea at first as to the fateful conditions to which the Fourteen Points must in any case commit Germany. They probably saw in Wilson's programme a mere collection of phrases, which a skilful diplomacy would be able to interpret at the conference table in a sense favourable to Germany."[17]

The truth was that the Fourteen Points, fatally confused themselves in many important respects, were nevertheless perfectly explicit in others. Prince Max put his finger on the most vital of these. Was the High Command aware, he asked, that what they proposed might lead to the loss, not merely of Germany's overseas colonies, but of what they all considered to be German soil—Alsace-Lorraine, and the Polish districts of East Prussia?

> I received from them the evasive reply: "The Supreme Command is ready to consider the cession of some small French-speaking parts of Alsace-Lorraine, if that is unavoidable. *The cession of German territory on the eastern frontier is for them out of the question* [my italics]." At the last moment the Supreme Command tried to give expression to this mental reservation of theirs, in the wording which they proposed for our Note: "The German Government agrees that Wilson's Fourteen Points shall serve as the basis of conversations." But the Ministers were —from their point of view rightly—of the opinion that no formulation should be used which would make Wilson suspicious and might provoke inconvenient questions.[18]

And so, with grave misgivings and heavy hearts, Prince Max and his Government drew up the Note to President Wilson which was forwarded to him via Switzerland next day. It ran:

> The German Government requests the President of the United States of America to take in hand the restoration of peace, acquaint all belligerent States with this request, and invite them to send plenipotentiaries for the purpose of opening negotiations. It accepts the programme set forth by the President of the United States in his message to Congress of January 8, 1918, and in his later pronouncements, especially his speech of September 27,[19] as a basis for peace negotiations.
>
> With a view to avoiding further bloodshed, the German Government requests the immediate conclusion of an armistice on land and water and in the air.

Ludendorff, the prime mover of the whole démarche, had the effrontery to say, "I regarded the Note as somewhat weak in tone, and proposed a more manly wording, but no attention was paid to my demands."

The German Note was accompanied on the same day by one of identical import from the Empire of Austria-Hungary. So the die was cast. Little did either empire guess at the awakening that was in store.

October came, and found the American 2nd Division on detached duty. It had been sent to help the French Fourth Army take an evil locality in Champagne known as Blanc Mont which had resisted repeated attacks by crack French divisions. The Marines and regular infantry of the 2nd Division had by now acquired a store of warlike worldly wisdom. They looked at the men around them—Chasseurs Alpins, colonials—they heard the guns, and they concluded: "Somethin' distressin' is just bound to happen." In such a landscape this was a fair prediction:

> The rich top-soil that formerly made the Champagne one of the fat provinces of France was gone, blown away and buried under by four years of incessant shell-fire. Areas that had been forested showed only blackened, branchless stumps, upthrust through the churned earth. What was left was naked, leprous chalk. It was a wilderness of craters, large and small, wherein no yard of earth lay untouched. Interminable mazes of trench work threaded this waste, discernible from a distance by the belts of rusty wire entanglements that stood before them. Of the great national highways that had once marched across the Champagne between rows of stately poplars, no vestige remained.[20]

"I don't like this place," declared a Marine officer. "It looks like it was just built for calamities to happen in." For his regiment, the 5th Marines, the calamity came on 3 October. The area was well-suited to German defensive tactics, and the defenders held on with unusual resolution. The American 2nd Division, according to General Gouraud's report, advanced some three to four miles during the day, taking "numerous prisoners, cannon, machine guns, and material of all kinds." But the cost was high: one battalion of the 5th Marines found itself committed to an advance across the open without artillery support—a horrible situation when the German guns found their range:

> All along the extended line the saffron shrapnel flowered, flinging death and mutilation down. Singing balls and jagged bits of steel spattered on the hard ground like sheets of hail; the line writhed and staggered, steadied and went on, closing toward the centre as the shells bit into it. High-explosive shells came with the shrapnel, and where they fell geysers of torn earth and black smoke roared up to mingle with the

devilish yellow in the air. A foul murky cloud of dust and smoke formed and went with the thinning companies, a cloud lit with red flashes and full of howling death.

The silent ridge to the left awoke with machine guns and rifles, and sibilant rushing flights of nickel-coated missiles from Maxim and Mauser struck down where the shells spared. An increasing trail of crumpled brown figures lay behind the battalion as it went. The raw smell of blood was in men's nostrils.[21]

The Marines were hard men, and they died hard; they reached their objective, and held it against counter-attack. But the battalion, which had started out about 1,000 strong, numbered little more than 100 at the end of the fight.

On the American First Army front—as with the French Fourth Army—the going was also difficult. Pershing's offensive resumed on 4 October, "meeting desperate resistance by the enemy." How desperate may be judged by the progress made—on the right, just over a mile in three days. Pershing's narrative speaks of "vicious counter-attacks," "no headway," "very severe hostile fire," fighting "characterised by the stubborn nature of the German resistance." It was I Corps on the left, under General Liggett, that did best, with a gain of three miles in two days.

To the north, on the night of 5 October, the American II Corps, withdrawn from battle after its experiences on 29 September, now returned to the line, relieving a famous formation. The last exploit of the Australian Corps had been seen that day, the taking of Montbréhain by the 2nd Division—"one of the most brilliant actions of Australian infantry in the First World War" according to Dr. Bean (who nevertheless doubts whether it was wisely undertaken, since it was not part of any general attack for important objectives). The 2nd Division then joined the other four divisions of the corps, taking their well-earned rest in camps far from the line of battle. Their proud commander tells the story of what they had achieved in 1918:

From March 27th, when Australian troops were for the first time interposed to arrest the German advance, until October 5th, when they were finally withdrawn from the line,[22] the total captures made by them were:

| Prisoners | 29,144 |
| Guns | 338 |

. . . During the advance, from August 8th to October 5th, the Australian Corps recaptured and released no less than 116 towns and villages. Every one of these was defended more or less stoutly. . . .

The total number of separate enemy divisions engaged was thirty-nine. Of these, twenty were engaged once only, twelve were engaged twice, six three times, and one four times. Each time "engaged" represents a separate and distinct period of line duty for the enemy division referred to.

Up to the time of the Armistice we had definitely ascertained that at least six of these thirty-nine enemy divisions had been entirely disbanded as the result of the battering which they had received. . . .

For the last sixty days of this period the Corps maintained an unchecked advance of thirty-seven miles against the powerful and determined opposition of a still formidable enemy, who employed all the mechanical and scientific resources at his disposal.

Such a result alone, considered in the abstract and quite apart from any comparison with the performances of other forces, is a testimony, on the one hand, to the pre-eminent fighting qualities of the Australian soldier considered individually, and, on the other hand, to the collective capacity and efficiency of the military effort made by the Corps. I doubt whether there is any parallel for such a performance in the whole range of military history.

General Monash's pride is pardonable; he commanded a *corps d'élite* and he knew it. But it was a *corps d'élite* of a special kind. Such formations existed in other armies: the French called their XX Corps the "Iron Corps," while particular divisions, notably Bretons, Chasseurs Alpins from the Haute Savoie and Moroccans, were regarded virtually as "Guard" formations; the Germans, of course, had Guard Corps, and the Prussian Guards were never anything less than formidable opponents; the Guards Division in the British Army set standards of performance which were admired even by the Australians. And we have seen (p. 23) how at the beginning of 1918 the Germans were compelled to sort their Army into "Storm Troops" and "trench divisions." But in the Australian Corps, as Monash says, an "outstanding feature was the uniformity of standard achieved by all the five divisions, as well as the wonderful comradeship which they displayed towards each other." In other words, they were *all* "Guards," *all* "Storm Troops," which is something else again.

There is one last observation to be made about the Australian Army Corps: we have seen its achievement—what was the cost? Between 8 August and 5 October the Australian casualties were:

Killed	3,566
Died of wounds	1,432
Wounded	16,166
Missing	79
Total	21,243

In that war of "bloodbaths," of "murderous offensives," with its ever-haunting images of swathes of still khaki figures lying in front of the enemy wire, and all the names on the Menin Gate at Ypres or the Thiepval Memorial, this figure of 5,000 dead in sixty days of incessant attack seems all wrong, misplaced, incongruous. Yet there it stands, a reminder for ever that even on the bloodiest fields good training, high morale and sound leadership can procure victory at a price that does not make a mockery of the word.

The day the Australian Corps left the line found Haig in a thoughtful mood. The Chief of Staff (Lawrence) reported that the Army Commanders were "anxious to attack." Haig agreed, but with certain reservations: "I ordered instructions to be issued accordingly, but the date will depend on the Fourth Army having sufficient ammunition brought up. . . . I had a talk with Lawrence and asked him to see Rawlinson tomorrow and say I insist on more thoroughness. Troops must not be sent forward to attack until everything is quite ready, and all requirements are on the spot. Then they will hold the ground which they capture."[23]

Reference has frequently been made in this narrative to "an artillery war"—which manifested itself from the early days of 1914, when the Germans startled their enemies by producing 150-mm (5.9-inch) howitzers on the battlefield, and massive 420-mm and 305-mm siege howitzers against the Belgian forts, to the moment when the last gun fell silent on 11 November 1918. Some statistics are here appropriate to show what the phrase "artillery war" means:

> In August 1914 the B.E.F. contained 486 guns and howitzers; in September-October 1918 this figure had risen to 6,700–6,800.
>
> The attack on the Hindenburg Line saw the maximum British expenditure of artillery ammunition in twenty-four hours, noon 28 September to noon 29 September: 943,847 rounds.
>
> In the later part of 1918, the French 75-mm field guns alone were firing off 280,000 rounds a day.
>
> For the Fourth Army's attack on 8 October, 600 lorry-loads of ammunition were brought up in forty-eight hours for the use of XIII Corps alone.
>
> On 9 October Lieutenant-General Sir Noel Birch, Artillery Adviser at G.H.Q., told Colonel Repington "that they were now throwing 12,000 tons of shells in twenty-four hours."

It is practically impossible to form visual images which correspond to figures like these, but it is quite clear that Haig's anxiety about ammunition supplies was not misdirected. Indeed, this was now to become an increasing preoccupation for the rest of the war, as the Allies picked their way forward across devastated zones where roads, railways and bridges had largely been destroyed. For the Royal Engineers and the Supply Services, the days of victory were days of unending toil.

The offensive resumed on 8 October on the fronts of the French First Army and the British Fourth and Third. This day's fighting, because of the prize that was gained next day, is called the Battle of Cambrai. It was not an easy day; the German rearguards fought hard, the machine-gunners once more "the hard core of the resistance," backed by vigorous artillery. Counter-attacks were frequent, and provided some unpleasant surprises. It was the Third Army which suffered chiefly from these, and in particular the 2nd and 63rd Divisions near the left of the line. A strong German counter-attack fell upon these two divisions at about 8:30 A.M., supported, for once, by tanks. Five of these made their appearance on the front of the 2nd Division, four against the 63rd; all of them were captured British Mark IVs, so that it was not until they had come to close quarters and began doing damage that they were recognized as hostile. By ten o'clock most of the 2nd Division had been pushed back to its first objective, but in the tank versus tank action which took place when the British 12th Battalion's few machines appeared, three of the five German tanks were knocked out. A trench mortar company captured another, and the fifth retired. But their efforts had considerably spoilt the efforts both of the 2nd Division and of its left-hand neighbour, the 3rd.

On the 63rd Division front the story was somewhat different. Here four tanks of the 12th Battalion were surprised by the German attack. The commander of "L 16," Captain Rowe, quickly recovered and fired a 6-pounder shot into one of the Germans, disabling it; but his own tank was immediately put out of action, and Captain Rowe was wounded. He got his crew out (the driver was killed) and went over to "L 19":

> "L 19" had already five men wounded, had been on fire, and having no gunners left, could not use its 6-pounders. Its commander, Second Lieutenant Worsap, however, nothing daunted, immediately engaged the enemy with his Lewis guns until the tank received a direct hit which set it on fire a second time. There was nothing now to be done but to evacuate the machine, and as the German counter-attack seemed to be succeeding, Mr. Worsap blew up the wreck of his tank.
>
> "L 12," the third tank, a male,[24] was hit and finally disabled before its commander and crew had discovered that the strange tanks did not belong to "C" Company. There remained "L 8" under Lieutenant Martell, but this tank had a leaky radiator and was almost out of water. It, too, had been hit, and three of its Lewis guns put out of action. Lieutenant Martell, however, sent his crew back, and he and an artillery officer

managed to get up to a captured German field gun, which the two turned round and used against the enemy's tanks, almost immediately obtaining a direct hit on one of them.[25]

At this juncture another British tank appeared, and the two surviving German machines turned round and vanished. The 63rd[26] Division resumed its advance, retook the ground it had lost and pushed on to its final objective. XVII Corps, to which it belonged, took over 1,200 prisoners on 8 October; 1,189 of them were accounted for by the 63rd Division, at a cost of 703 casualties.

This was not the only good performance of the day: in the Third Army IV Corps also did well, with 1,401 prisoners and an advance of some 5,000 yards. In the Fourth Army the star performance was by the American 30th Division, which took over 1,500 prisoners and thirty guns from the four German divisions which it encountered that day. The Fourth Army as a whole was well pleased with its haul: over 4,000 prisoners and fifty-six guns.

Only the Royal Tank Corps had occasion for regrets. It was now becoming very weary—machines as "fatigued" as men—and very thin on the ground. Further, as we have seen, the Germans were now no longer over-awed by tanks. It is indicative of this change that when, for example, twelve Mark Vs came up to help IX Corps at about 9 A.M., the local commanders thought it best not to put them into battle in full daylight, but to save them for the half-light of the next dawn.[27] On the American II Corps front, the American 301st Tank Battalion took twenty Mark Vs into action, and ten of them became casualties. Out of nineteen Mark Vs with XIII Corps, only seven survived the day. Critics of the way tanks were used in the First World War usually prefer to ignore their losses; the corps's first historian, however, with a more intimate view of matters, is quite explicit. Between 8 August and 10 October, he tells us, "no less than 819 machines had been handed over to salvage by the Tank Battalions, and these Battalions themselves had lost in personnel 550 officers and 2,557 other ranks, out of a fighting state of some 9,500."[28] It is merely silly to criticize the generals for using tanks in "penny packets" when only "penny packets" existed. As for the alternative criticism that, this being so, they should not been used at all, the answer would seem to be (this being widely understood to be the decisive offensive) what should they have been saved for? The victory parade? Or the Battle of France in 1940?

All setbacks notwithstanding, 8 October was a successful day—how successful only became apparent on the morrow. Preparations were made in both British armies (and in the First Army also) to renew the attack next day, but all along the line it was found that the enemy was now only resisting with rearguards. The Third Army reported that "the Germans appear to have vanished"; its patrols entered Cambrai from the south to link up with Canadians of the First Army coming in from the north. They found the town deserted, pillaged and on fire. Haig went up to the Third Army's front of attack, noted the strength of the defences that had been overcome, and remarked wonderingly: "It was only yesterday that the enemy was driven from this great fortress, and yet I was able to walk about today, 24 hours later, almost out of hearing of his guns."[29]

It looked at last as though the time had come for pursuit, and with luck this might be converted into rout. As the Allied armies passed beyond the Hindenburg Line, they came into country which bore little trace of the devastation of war. It was the characteristic landscape of northern France, vast open fields, unhedged, rolling away to distant horizons, sprinkled with compact, undamaged villages, large farms, and woods which actually contained trees, not splintered stumps. In theory this was good cavalry or tank country; but, as we have seen, the tanks for an armoured rush were simply not there, and as for cavalry, as an American said, "you can't have a cavalry charge until you have captured the enemy's last machine gun."[30] The weather, during these last weeks of the war, was continuously bad, which also helped to make progress slow. Behind every Allied army lay the desert region of the old battlefields, almost devoid of communications, while in front the Germans carried out systematic demolitions as they retired. The Official History and others nevertheless use the word "pursuit" in describing this phase of the war. It is important to recognize exactly what this means: "An advance of four or five miles a day was good, eight or ten very good. The popular conception of a victorious army sweeping forward with horses at the gallop and men at the double was not to be seen on the Western Front in the autumn of 1918."[31]

However, *some* galloping was attempted, and occasionally, against all the odds, it was successful. Haig, himself a cavalryman, had clung to his three cavalry divisions (the French had five) against all pressures; he had always believed that the day would come when horsemen, free at last of trenches and barbed wire, would supply the means of clinching victory. As his armies prepared for the assault on the Hindenburg Line, he felt that this day might be at hand, and on 24 September he wrote to the C.I.G.S., asking: ". . . whether you have been able to collect and will send me some Yeomanry, cyclists, motor machine guns, motor lorries, etc. In fact anything to add to our mobility. The resources of the French and of ourselves here are being strained to the utmost for the forthcoming effort. Anything you can spare should be sent to us *at once*."

Now the Hindenburg Line lay behind him. The Cavalry Corps was massed on Rawlinson's front, and its commander, General Kavanagh, was given discretion for deciding "when and where his command can push forward beyond the infantry." Haig envisaged it thrusting through to play havoc in the enemy's rear, and harassing his flanks; on 7 October he was talking to Major-General Salmond, commanding the R.A.F. in France: "In reply to my question as to whether he was ready to support the Cavalry Corps with large numbers of low-flying machines, in the event of the enemy breaking . . . he replied that all were quite ready to act, and he could concentrate 300 machines practically at once."[32]

Reality did not match this vision. During the next three days cavalry units repeatedly tried to carry out the aggressive rôle assigned to them, and repeatedly they had to be withdrawn until the infantry and artillery could deal with the German rearguards, or the presence of Whippet tanks could cause these to make off. Only once, on 9 October, was there a successful mounted action, when the 3rd Cavalry Division gave valuable support to the 66th Division approaching Le Cateau. The most spectacular performance was by the Canadian Cavalry Brigade on the left. Machine-gunners in the village of Clary and the Bois de Gattigny had held up the 66th Division, and opened fire on the Canadians when they appeared:

A spirited charge over 1,500 yards of open ground by Lord Strathcona's Horse cleared out the enemy rearguard near Clary. Then, in the face of scattered shelling and machine-gun fire from Montigny on their left, the Strathconas worked their way around the edge of the Bois du Mont-aux-Villes—a northern extension of the Bois de Gattigny.

Meanwhile the Fort Garry Horse, supported by the attached R.C.H.A. battery, had attacked the Gattigny Wood. While one troop of the regiment successfully charged the machine-guns in the southern half of the wood—though losing more than half its men in this attempt—a squadron galloped through a gap between the northern and southern halves of the wood to take the same objective in flank. With the assistance of infantry of the South African Brigade (of the 66th Division) in mopping up, the Bois de Gattigny was cleared shortly after 11.00 a.m. The encounter had yielded approximately 200 prisoners, a 5.9-inch howitzer and about 40 machine-guns.[33]

The Canadians pressed their advance to the outskirts of Le Cateau. On their right the 6th Cavalry Brigade, 3rd Dragoon Guards and Royal Dragoons leading, captured the village of Honnechy in fine style and linked up with the Canadians. As evening approached the 7th Cavalry Brigade took over from both, and two armoured cars attached to it actually entered Le Cateau, but as the Germans were still there in strength they had to retire. By the end of the day the 3rd Cavalry Division had taken over 500 prisoners (400 to the Canadians), ten guns and sixty machine-guns. There can be little doubt that the moral effect this produced was much greater than the material; this was normally the case.[34] One German regimental history gives a detailed but fanciful account of being charged by wave after wave of cavalry: "There must have been fifteen or twenty of them, and wave after wave collapsed under infantry, machine-gun and artillery fire."[35] This was the 6th Brigade's attack, and its casualties were

	Officers	Other Ranks
Killed	2	14
Wounded	11	134

with 255 horses disabled. The Canadian Brigade lost 168 men killed, wounded or missing, and 171 horses. It had been a good day's work. Nevertheless, as the Official History says, ". . . the cavalry had done nothing that the infantry, with artillery support and cyclists, could not have done for itself at less cost; and the supply of the large force of horses with water and forage had gravely interfered with the sending up of ammunition and the rations for the other arms, and with the allotment of the limited water facilities."

On 10 October the Cavalry Corps was withdrawn. It was the same story all along the Allied line; the truth was, as Brigadier Barclay has wisely written, that "Foch was caught by a hiatus in the mobile arm: horsed cavalry had become obsolete and the blitzkrieg tank had not yet been developed."[36] The moral is quite simple—that it can be a grave disadvantage to operate at a turning point of technology; and the First World War was full of them.

The day (8 October) that the British forces encircled Cambrai was also the day that America replied to the German Armistice Note. We have seen (pp. 162–63) how the new German Government rephrased the equivocations of the High Command in an attempt to lull President Wilson's suspicions and avoid what Prince Max called "inconvenient questions." To their chagrin, he and his colleagues now found that they had "underrated the alertness of our opponents." The American Note most "inconveniently" demanded clarifications:

Before making a reply to the request of the Imperial German Government, and in order that the reply shall be as candid and straightforward as the momentous interests involved require, the President of the

United States deems it necessary to assure himself of the exact meaning of the Note of the Imperial Chancellor.

Does the Imperial Chancellor mean that the Imperial German Government accepts the terms laid down by the President in his address to the Congress of the United States on January 8 last and in subsequent addresses, and that its object in entering into discussions would be only to agree upon the practical details of their application?

The President feels bound to say, with regard to the suggestion of an armistice, that he would not feel at liberty to propose a cessation of arms to the Governments with which the Government of the United States is associated against the Central Powers so long as the Armies of those Powers are upon their soil.

The good faith of any discussion would manifestly depend upon the consent of the Central Powers immediately to withdraw their forces everywhere from invaded territory.

The President also feels justified in asking whether the Imperial Chancellor is speaking merely for the constituted authorities of the Empire who have so far conducted the war.

He deems the answer to these questions vital from every point of view.

The content of this reply to the Germans was unexceptionable; the manner of its drafting and presentation was not. And it was here, right from the very beginning of peace proceedings, that the fatal weaknesses in the Allied political position appeared which would dog the peace-making to the very end. President Wilson was proposing to speak for his Allies—but what did they wish to say? When the German appeal for an armistice arrived, the leaders of France, Italy and Britain were conferring in Paris. Lloyd George tells us: "For the first days of this Conference we were without any official notification about the Peace Notes. President Wilson was sitting on them, despite the request in the German Note that he should 'acquaint all belligerent States with this request.' He decided to frame and dispatch his own reply without any consultation with his associates in the common enterprise."[37]

A fatal flaw in Woodrow Wilson's character was now making itself daily more apparent. The President of the United States is, by virtue of the constitutional powers invested in him, in many respects the most powerful man in the world, especially in wartime, when his joint office of Chief Executive and Commander-in-Chief finds full expression. Yet even the President's powers do have limitations: in a coalition war, consultation with one's allies is essential; in a democracy, accommodation with one's political opponents on vital issues (like war and peace) is equally so. Wilson neglected both these considerations. His motives may perhaps be best summed up as the arrogance of the high-

Scenes of destiny. *Above:* 'utter and wanton destruction': part of the Grande Place of Douai, entered by the British First Army, 17 October. *Below:* 'the ancient glories of Bruges were found unscathed'. King Albert of the Belgians takes the salute in the Grande Place at Bruges on 25 October

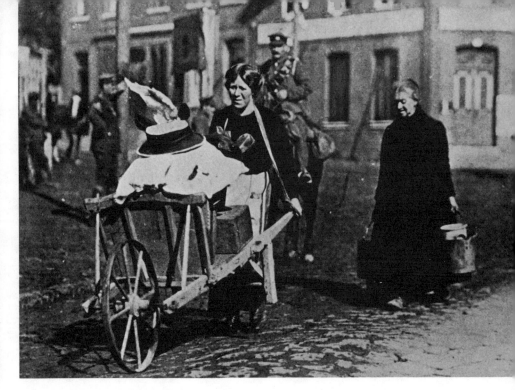

'All civilians had been evacuated . . .': French women with their few portable belongings returning to their homes in Maretz

'. . . the Belgian coast was clear of the enemy': Belgian civilians whose homes had been destroyed moved quickly into old German dug-outs and fortifications. The Wilhelm II Battery at Knocke was still inhabited well into the 1920s

'We have taken one quarter of the enemy's guns': these are guns captured by the Canadians in the advance on Cambrai. The total taken by the British, 18 July to 11 November, was 2,840

'550 guns had been taken by King Albert's Group': among them was the Wilhelm II Battery at Knocke, naval 305-mm guns, used to fire on the harbour and shipping at Dunkirk. They were wrecked in their emplacements by the departing Germans

'. . . an artillery war': the sound of gunfire never entirely ceased on the Western Front throughout the war. This 60-pounder is taking its part in the dawn barrage on the Canal du Nord, 27 September. Field artillery is moving up on the right

'. . . they found the town deserted, pillaged and on fire'. Canadian patrols entering Cambrai on 9 October

minded man—a virtually invincible and frequently disastrous condi-tion. What made it especially remarkable, and especially dangerous, in October 1918, was the fact that a Congressional election campaign was in progress, and, as the year was to reveal again, the heated atmos-phere of an election is unsuited to the cool calculations of lasting peace.[38]

When the Allied leaders considered Wilson's reply to Germany on 9 October, reactions were mixed. M. Clemenceau (whose reservations were to be powerfully expressed at the Peace Conference next year) thought the American Note excellent. He did not recommend any questioning or delay; he was content with the stipulation that occupied territory in France, Belgium, Luxemburg and Italy should be evac-uated forthwith. Lloyd George, however, could not agree:

> I pointed out that the speech in which Prince Max of Baden had defended and explained the German Peace Note to the Reichstag on October 5th was the speech of the Chief Minister of a defeated Empire. Had either Clemenceau or I made such a speech, the world would say that we were defeated. In Prince Max's place I would accept President Wilson's proposals without alteration. The Prince would no doubt read-ily accept the Fourteen Points; but there were matters in them of which I would like to know a little more—for example, the Freedom of the Seas in war-time. This was quite unacceptable to the British nation. Prince Max would also no doubt readily accept the evacuation of occu-pied territories as a condition of the armistice. In fact, the Germans were even now evacuating their territory, and it was only Marshal Foch who was delaying them and knocking them about in the process. A difficulty arose regarding the first point in the President's letter, because of the uncertainty of interpretation of the Fourteen Points; there was vagueness, for instance, about Alsace-Lorraine.[39] His second point, however, dealing with the Armistice, was more serious, for if the Ger-mans accepted this view, they could say they had accepted President Wilson's proposal, and if we had said nothing they could maintain that nobody had protested against it, and that they were entitled to regard it as the sum of the Allied conditions for an Armistice.[40]

It was clear that "moments of truth" were at hand: the Fourteen Points had been well enough as a test of Germany's intentions at the beginning of the year, when the collapse of Russia once more seemed to put winning cards into her hand. But as practical peace terms, now that Germany was probably defeated, they were far less alluring. The question of freedom of the seas had almost brought America into the war on Germany's side in 1915, so much did American opinion resent the British Admiralty's claim to the right to search neutral shipping for contraband of war. For an island nation, however, depending upon sea-borne trade and relying heavily on seapower both as a defensive and as an offensive weapon, this right was a fundamental of survival. Here, evidently, was a large arena of discussion between the two Allies. And for France and Belgium (and, indeed, Italy) there would be matters concerning the reparation for material damage inflicted by enemy occupation on which the Fourteen Points said nothing. And for all the Allies there was something else as well, hinted at, but not as yet even discussed, let alone clarified in Allied counsels, in the American Note. Lloyd George says:

> . . . we were really still dealing with the old military Imperialist clique. . . . The democratisation of the German Government was at this stage no more than a dummy façade, imposed as an emergency war measure by the Emperor to meet Allied criticism. Its composition had in the main been determined by the reactionary retiring Chancellor, Hertling, and the new Chancellor, Prince Max, was selected by a Council of War and not nominated by a democratic body. The terms and the dispatch of the appeal for an armistice had been dictated by the same Council of War. The hands might be sketchily gloved in a democratic pelt, but the voice was the voice of Ludendorff. . . .
> As for Wilson's Fourteen Points, they might be, and in the main were, in harmony with our desired terms, but they were in places phrased in the language of vague idealism which, in the absence of practical application, made them capable of more than one interpretation. It was not sufficient for Germany to express readiness to negotiate on the basis of the Fourteen Points, unless we were in a position to insist on her accepting our exegesis of the sacred text.[41]

We have seen how wide of the mark this interpretation of the situation in Germany, and of the currents flowing there, was; yet this was what the European Allies were thinking, and it was with these thoughts in mind that they addressed a response to President Wilson, having studied his reply to Germany. They expressed admiration for the lofty sentiments which inspired that reply, and warmly agreed that the evacuation of all invaded territory must be the preliminary condition for any discussion of an armistice. But this was not, in their opinion, sufficient for the actual conclusion of the armistice itself. They told the President:

> It would not prevent the enemy from taking advantage of a suspension of hostilities to place himself, at the expiration of an armistice not followed by peace, in a better military situation than at the moment of the interruption of hostilities. They might be enabled to withdraw from a

critical situation, to save their stores, to reform their units, to shorten their front, to retire without loss of men upon new positions which they would have time to select and fortify.

The conditions of an armistice can only be fixed after consultation with the military experts and in accordance with the military situation at the actual moment when negotiations are entered on. These considerations have been strongly urged by the military experts of the Allied Powers, and particularly by Marshal Foch. . . .

The three European Ministers commended these thoughts to President Wilson "for his fullest attention."

The reference to "consultation with the military experts" points to yet another flaw in Wilson's method of conducting business: it seems inconceivable that he could have framed a reply to a request from an enemy power for an armistice without consulting the military—who must include the Generalissimo under whom his own forces were fighting. Yet this was the case. The Europeans, on the other hand, had taken military advice; at their meeting on 8 October they had before them a note from Foch, setting out what he considered to be the essential terms. There could be, he said, "no question of ceasing hostilities" without certain prerequisites. The first of these was the liberation of invaded territories and the return of populations removed from them; among these territories he firmly listed Alsace-Lorraine. Secondly, he demanded bridgeheads over the Rhine, in case negotiations broke down. Thirdly, he demanded Allied occupation of the whole left bank of the Rhine as security for reparations. In addition he insisted that all war material which the Germans could not remove should be left intact; that German units which were not evacuated within a prescribed time should become prisoners of war; that all railway material should be left in place, and all French and Belgian material "immediately restored"; that all military installations (camps, barracks, arsenals, etc.) should be left intact; that the same should apply to "industrial establishments and factories of every kind."

When these terms were read out both Lloyd George and the Italian Foreign Minister, Baron Sonnino, thought them too severe; Mr. Bonar Law, the Conservative leader, who was also present, said that they "amounted virtually to unconditional capitulation." And now an ominous phrase began to make itself heard: Two days later Foch showed his proposed armistice terms to Haig, who remarked "that the only difference between his conditions and a 'general unconditional surrender' is that the German Army is allowed to march back with its rifles, and officers with their swords." Similar thoughts had already occurred to some in Germany; the German Government was dismayed at the tone of Wilson's reply, which it received on 9 October. The Minister of

War, Scheuch, pointed out the significance of the demand for immediate evacuation of occupied territory: ". . . the evacuation, apart from the danger of a disorderly return of the troops to the Homeland, is the signing and sealing of our inability to defend ourselves; it is 'unconditional surrender.' "

So, indeed, it was; and it was precisely this that the Republican Party in the United States was now campaigning for—"unconditional surrender," *as opposed to* Wilson's Fourteen Points. At the hustings it was a phrase with magical appeal; it had been enshrined in the American folk memory ever since that day in 1862 when Brigadier-General U. S. Grant, commanding the Union Army in Tennessee, addressed his famous answer to General S. B. Buckner, commanding the Confederate garrison of Fort Donelson:

Sir: Yours of this date, proposing armistice and appointment of commissioners to settle terms of capitulation is just received. No terms except unconditional and immediate surrender can be accepted. I propose to move immediately upon your works.

I am, sir, very respectfully,

Your obedient servant . . .

Grant's phrase was liable to come readily into American minds and trip easily off American tongues. In the limited context of the capture of Fort Donelson, it was unobjectionable; in the totally different context of the Casablanca Conference in January 1943, it was entirely mischievous; in October 1918 the mischief was that the victorious powers moved steadily towards a demand for unconditional surrender without recognizing or admitting that they were doing so—and that was a fault which would overshadow both the peace negotiations and the settlement that followed from them.

Meanwhile the Germans themselves, without any particular malicious intent, but just because that was the kind of war it was, were fanning the flames of anger and vengeance. On 4 October the Japanese liner *Hiramo Maru* was torpedoed off the Irish coast and sank with a loss of 292 lives. On 10 October, with President Wilson's Note still fresh on the German Government's agenda (though a mere U-boat captain was not to know this),[42] the mail packet *Leinster* was twice torpedoed in the Irish Channel, and 527 more lives were lost. There was, says Lloyd George, "a howl of indignation" which effectively drowned any charitable feelings towards the defeated enemy—and for good measure British opinion was simultaneously inflamed by German intransigence over the emotive issue of the treatment of prisoners of war.

It was against this distressing and discouraging background that the Germans framed their reply to President Wilson's questions, and that this reply was received by the Allies. The German Government announced that it accepted the Fourteen Points

. . . as the basis of a lasting peace of Right.

The purpose, therefore, of the discussions to be initiated would be solely to agree about practical details of the application of those Points. The German Government assumes that the Governments of the Powers which are allied with the United States place themselves also upon the basis of the pronouncements of President Wilson.

The German Government, in agreement with the Austro-Hungarian Government, declares itself ready for the bringing about of an armistice in compliance with the proposals of the President. It submits that the President should arrange for the meeting of a mixed Commission, whose business it would be to arrive at the agreements necessary for the evacuation.

The present German Government, which bears the responsibility for the peace step, is formed by negotiations and in agreement with the great majority of the Reichstag. Sustained in all his actions by the will of this majority, the Imperial Chancellor speaks in the name of the German Government and the German people.

So the German Note met Wilson's queries at every point: the Fourteen Points were explicitly accepted as terms, not as debating theses; evacuation of occupied territory was agreed in principle, with a practical proposal for carrying it out; and the new Government referred its authority to the Reichstag and the people, not the Emperor. It was a conciliatory response, and in better times might have been seen to be such and treated accordingly; unfortunately, however, the chastened mood and accommodating gestures of the German Government had been overtaken by events—and by three torpedoes. Wilson lost no time in replying; his second Note (14 October) revealed some significant shifts in American thinking. First, the President fully accepted the suggestion of the Allied ministers that the actual armistice conditions should be left to the military advisers, and must "provide absolutely satisfactory safeguards and guarantees of the maintenance of the present military supremacy of the Armies of the United States and of the Allies in the field." He continued:

The President feels that it is also his duty to add that neither the Government of the United States nor, he is quite sure, the Governments with which the Government of the United States is associated as a belligerent will consent to consider an armistice so long as the armed forces of Germany continue the illegal and inhuman practices which they still persist in. At the very time that the German Government approaches the Government of the United States with proposals of peace, its submarines are engaged in sinking passenger ships at sea—and not the ships alone but the very boats in which their passengers and crews seek to make their way to safety; and in their present enforced withdrawal from Flanders the German Armies are pursuing a course of wanton destruction which has always been regarded as in direct violation of the rules and practices of civilised warfare. Cities and villages, if not destroyed, are being stripped not only of all they contain but often of their very inhabitants. The nations associated against Germany cannot be expected to agree to a cessation of arms while acts of inhumanity, spoliation and desolation are being continued which they justly look upon with horror and with burning hearts.

These were strong words; one cannot help feeling that they were addressed as much to the American voters as to the German Government. But there was more—and again one has the sense of more than one target being aimed at. Wilson reminded the Germans that one of the terms which they professed to accept was "the destruction of every arbitrary power anywhere that can separately, secretly and of its single choice, disturb the peace of the world; or, if it cannot be destroyed at present, at least its reduction to virtual impotence." Now this was not one of the Fourteen Points; it was an addendum which, in Wheeler-Bennett's words, "had become annexed in the nature of a supplement" to the Fourteen Points in a speech at Mount Vernon on the Fourth of July.[43] The "arbitrary power" here referred to was clearly the German Empire. The speech had thus marked a departure from previous policy which had not been sufficiently appreciated, especially in Germany. It contradicted flatly the President's statement of 27 August 1917: "Punitive damages, the dismemberment of empires . . . we deem inexpedient, and in the end worse than futile, no proper basis for a peace of any kind, least of all for an enduring peace." Equally it contradicted what he had said in his message to Congress on 4 December 1917: "We do not intend to inflict any wrong on the German Empire nor to interfere in any way in its internal affairs." As Sir John Wheeler-Bennett says: "It was gradually becoming clear that the Allies aimed not only at the capitulation of the German army in the field but at the abdication of the Emperor and the creation of a Government based upon accepted democratic institutions."[44]

This was a large matter to raise so abruptly, and at such a time. The next question was what the Germans would make of it—and that was something which, once more, would be decided by the armies locked in combat on the Western Front.

On 9 October Haig received a telegram from the Prime Minister, which (slightly amended) said:

I have just heard from Marshal Foch of the brilliant victory won by the First, Third and Fourth Armies and I wish to express to yourself, Generals Horne, Byng and Rawlinson and all the officers and men under your command my sincerest congratulations on the great and significant success which the British Armies, with their American brothers in arms have gained during the past two days. The courage and tenacity with which the troops of the Empire, after withstanding the terrific enemy onslaught of the spring of this year, have again resumed the offensive with such decisive results is the greatest chapter in our military history. The smashing of the great defensive system erected by the enemy in the west and claimed by him to be impregnable is a feat of which we are all justly proud and for which the Empire will always be grateful.

Haig was not altogether pleased. There was, first of all, the matter of the "slight amendment," of which he told his wife two days later: "as the message originally reached me, no mention at all was made of Horne and the First Army, when the Canadian Corps actually were in Cambrai, and have had such hard fighting for Monchy-le-Preux, the Drocourt-Quéant line etc." Indeed, said Haig, of all the congratulations that he had recently received, "the Prime Minister's shows the least understanding of the great efforts made by the *whole* of the British Army. He speaks of the 'success' of the last '*two* days.' In the papers I see some friend of his has altered the word to '*few* days.'" It is extraordinary, even by Lloyd George's curious standards, that the great decisive British victories of August and September, which had caused the Germans to sue for peace, should apparently have passed unnoticed in Downing Street. But, as Duff Cooper points out, there was something even worse about this message:

The suggestion that the Prime Minister of Great Britain relied exclusively upon the French Generalissimo for his information regarding the movements of the British Army was, to say the least of it, infelicitous and, in view of Mr. Lloyd George's long experience in the use of words, it could hardly have been unintentional. He wished to make it plain that Foch, not Haig, was winning the war, and that Haig, like other subordinate army commanders and his American brothers in arms, was only to be congratulated when Foch was kind enough to say he had done well.[45]

Meanwhile "the greatest chapter in our military history" continued to unfold. The last weeks of the war, on the British and American fronts,[46] were a period of virtually unbroken activity, the Americans inching their way painfully through the entanglements of the Argonne, sometimes supported by the French Fourth Army, sometimes not; the British endeavouring to pursue the enemy, and fighting him when they caught up with him, expecting very little help from the French First Army on their right, and generally receiving just that. The French Army had now practically reached the end of its tether, which was not to be wondered at; Foch tells us that between 1 July and 15 September French casualties had amounted to no less than 7,000 officers and 272,000 other ranks[47]—and this on top of some 245,000 in the defensive battles earlier in the year. French and British alike had great difficulty in finding replacements for their losses (even the Americans were now having problems, especially their II Corps); units were weak and the men in them very, very tired. "Those last months hang cloudily in my mind," wrote a British officer who had come out in 1915. "Probably I was more fatigued than I knew."[48]

The new style of war—which would have seemed entirely normal to the highly trained Expeditionary Force of 1914—was unfamiliar and often disconcerting to the Army of 1918. The Official History tells us why: "The years of trench warfare, the necessary issue of lengthy orders entering into meticulous detail, and the rehearsal of attacks over a marked-out practice course with fairly well-defined objectives, had produced an army which was prepared to stand enormous losses uncomplainingly, but was practically devoid of real tactical sense." Great responsibilities now devolved on junior officers, most of them mere boys with very little training (many battalion commanders at this stage were only in their twenties). And this was a serious matter, because they were now caught up in what Haig had called "a platoon commanders' war." The wonder is, despite the Official History's strictures, how well they coped with it.

Inevitably, in a narrative of this kind, one's eyes become fixed upon the forward troops, those actually in contact with the enemy, forcing or turning his positions, pressing him into new retreats; it is important occasionally to spare a glance in other directions. Captain Cyril Falls, writing the history of the 36th (Ulster) Division, says:

> The worst danger, the greatest obstacle to the launching of the death-thrust, was now, in fact, behind, not in front. It lay in those terrible roads of the devastated area far behind, with which the troops, now upon the untouched soil of the richest agricultural land in Europe, might feel they had no connection, but across which every mouthful of food they ate and every bullet they fired had to come.[49]

Lorries constantly broke down under the strain, the drivers were worn out with fatigue. In this still largely horse-drawn war there was now a severe shortage of horses; the British field artillery had parted with two out of each of its six-horse teams to supply the Americans, whose plight was worst of all. But in the heavy going of a wet autumn it was found that four-horse teams were often too weak for their new active rôle. The Supply Services would have been hard put to it merely to maintain the armies; now, in addition, they had to provide for the feeding of French and Belgian civilians whose barns and storehouses had been stripped by the departing Germans, and who were often in real danger of starvation. For all the men—Royal Artillery, Royal Engineers, Army Service Corps, signallers, ambulance drivers, military police—whose work was concerned with the lines of communication, this was a time of backbreaking work and weariness:

> The lorry-driver, who stuck for fifteen hours at his wheel amid the ruts and turmoil of the Menin Road, as many of them did, with bombs crashing down at night; the section of the Divisional Train bringing up its wagons through valleys wreathed and stinking with gas, these men in truth deserved well of the infantrymen facing the bullets further forward, and were in truth their companions-in-arms.[50]

Punctuating this ceaseless activity there were days of special significance, when more carefully prepared set-piece battles sprang to noisy life. For the Flanders Group of Armies, which still included the British Second, such a day was 14 October, the first of six days of heavy action which later came to be officially designated as the Battle of Courtrai. Behind this group lay the desolate swamps of the Ypres Salient, a nightmare landscape for all the quartermasters; despite all Foch's urging, this and the rain had halted the Flanders Group since the beginning of the month, but now patience was to be rewarded. Success shone brightest in the centre of the line, the junction between the British and the Belgians; the British II Corps on the left, under Lieutenant-General Sir Claud Jacob,[51] contained three very good divisions indeed: the 9th (Scottish), 29th (Regular)[52] and 36th (Ulster).

The history of the 9th Division says that it "never desired on its flanks better troops than the Belgians proved themselves to be."[53] Captain Falls explains: "The Belgian infantry, which had not been involved in the great reverses of the British and French, was by this time of excellent quality, its ranks filled by young men of good physique."[54] The contrast between the Belgians and the French divisions sandwiched amongst them was very marked. Haig wrote in his diary on 15

October: "The Second Army did very well today. . . . The French divisions now in Flanders are reported not to be fighting. The Belgians, on the other hand, have done splendidly." And next day: "General Cavendish (attached to the King of the Belgians' staff) writes last night that French troops in Flanders are not fighting at all. They take no interest in 'Flanders for the Belgians!' Also the King now seems only anxious to stop his offensive and rest on his laurels!"

In fact what was happening, partly due to the disappointing French performance, was a natural slackening in the tempo of the battle. The advance continued nevertheless, carrying the Second Army up to the River Lys; parties of the 36th Division actually entered Courtrai, but were withdrawn to avoid a frontal attack and bombardment with its perils for the considerable civilian population in the town. Meanwhile rich prizes were being gathered. The good progress of the Second Army now made possible a further advance by General Sir William Birdwood's Fifth Army, which linked King Albert's Army Group in Flanders to Haig's in the centre. In front of Birdwood's Army stood the great manufacturing centre of Lille, "the Manchester of France," occupied since the earliest days of the war; the French Government was particularly anxious that Lille should not be added to the long list of wrecked French towns. Fortunately there was no need; the threat of encirclement was enough. Plumer's success on the 14th carried the Second Army well past the Lille fortifications, and Prince Rupprecht at once authorized withdrawal. On 17 October Fifth Army patrols entered Lille, to find it relatively undamaged—the Germans even left six days' food supplies for the population, a very unusual gesture.

The liberation of Lille was a great moment; the black mourning crape on the statue of the city in the Place de la Concorde was removed, and the flag of the British XI Corps was placed on it. But 17 October held other satisfactions as well: the Second Army released another valuable industrial area from the enemy, the twin towns of Turcoing-Roubaix, to the north-east of Lille. And for the Belgians there was particular pleasure in reaching Ostend on this auspicious day— different styles of war making an interesting mixture, with British destroyers under Admiral Sir Roger Keyes arriving off-shore, an airman landing in the town as the last Germans pulled out, and Belgian cavalry galloping up along the beach. The Allies found the harbour blocked and considerable (though not irreparable) damage to port installations. Nevertheless, for the Supply Services the taking of Ostend was a great gain. Further south, where the First Army was again on the move, 17 October was signalized by the occupation of the historic town of Douai by the British 8th Division. What it found was not attractive:

All civilians had been evacuated and the city was empty except for a deserter from the enemy's rear-guard company. As far as the fabric of its buildings was concerned, the town was found to be fairly intact;[55] but every building concealed a scene of utter and wanton destruction. Everything of value had been removed and such things as had been left —furniture, crockery, pictures and the like—had been smashed to atoms.[56]

Especially forlorn were the reeds of the cathedral organ which had been pulled out for scrap metal, lying in a heap on the floor. The town had been mined, but the mines were withdrawn when the German High Command realized how its policy of destruction was affecting American opinion. This act, says the 8th Division's history, "was a significant admission." Great bitterness was by now building up in all the Allied armies, and among the civilians who returned in their wake, when they saw the deliberate damage and systematic looting carried out by the occupying forces; this was another bad augury for the peace that could not now be far off.

The next days seemed to bring peace nearer by strides: on 19 October the Second Army cleared Courtrai, and on the same day the Belgians entered Bruges, whose beautiful buildings date from the prime days of Flanders, its prosperous fifteenth and sixteenth centuries. Industry was largely destroyed, there had been deportations and some indiscriminate looting, but, to the joy of all, the ancient glories of Bruges were found unscathed (and by a miracle they were to survive another war as well). Strategically the taking of Bruges was of the greatest importance: together with the taking of Zeebrugge, which was reached on the same day, it meant that at last, after four years, the Belgian coast was clear of the enemy. The great goal of the Flanders offensive of 1917 was gained, the U-boat bases were abandoned, and the Allied left could rest upon the Dutch frontier, which was, in fact, reached next day. More than 12,000 prisoners and 550 guns had been taken by King Albert's Group since 14 October—about half of the prisoners and over 200 guns by the British Second Army. Belgium was becoming a country again, and the raptures of the people of Bruges when their king returned revealed the failure of the German attempt to exploit the divisions of Flemings and Walloons: divided they might be—and would remain, among themselves—but it was a private quarrel.

These successes in the north were gratifying indeed, but once more it was in the centre, especially in the sectors of the Fourth and Third Armies, that decisive results were to be looked for. The Fourth Army launched a preliminary attack along the line of the River Selle on 17 October, and in the next three days captured nearly 5,000 prisoners

and sixty guns. The Third Army spent this time preparing to extend
the battle northwards with a major operation; the First Army managed
an advance of six miles. All were hampered (as was the Northern
Group) by the bad weather which set in again after the 17th, bringing
respite to the Germans as it had so often done in moments of crisis the
previous year. The Official History says:

> For about ten days, while the Germans were going back as fast as they
> could, rain and mist made relentless air attacks impossible. The air su-
> periority of the Allies was overwhelming, the targets which streamed to-
> wards the bottle neck into Germany were innumerable, the retreating
> troops were depressed in body and mind, the setting indeed was such as
> to ensure the most awesome effects for the employment of air power,
> but the quality of mercy rained from the clouds.[57]

And for the Germans this was just as well; their condition was by
now appalling, as Prince Rupprecht related in a letter to Prince Max
on 18 October. The troops, he said, were exhausted, and their numbers
had now dwindled to the point where a division could only be
reckoned as equivalent to one or two battalions, "and in certain cases
as only equivalent to two or three companies." He referred to the severe loss of artillery (ten days earlier Colonel Repington had noted
with glee: "we have taken one quarter of the enemy's guns since July
15"), and he added that "in certain Armies fifty per cent of the guns
are without horses." There was also a lack of ammunition, and a severe shortage of officers. He told the Chancellor:

> The morale of the troops has suffered seriously and their power of re-
> sistance diminishes daily. They surrender in hordes, whenever the
> enemy attacks, and thousands of plunderers infest the districts round
> the bases. We have no more prepared lines, and no more can be dug.
> There is a shortage of fuel for the lorries, and when the Austrians de-
> sert us,[58] and we get no more petrol from Rumania,[59] two months will
> put a stop to our aviation.

Prince Rupprecht then commented on the Supreme Command's call
for a *levée en masse:*

> I do not expect much from a *levée en masse* on the model of Car-
> not's at the beginning of the French revolutionary wars; it meant much
> then, because it was put into force at the beginning of a war; but we
> are already in the fifth year of the war, and our reserves in men are al-
> ready exhausted to breaking point. Further, how are the war industries

to carry on in face of a *levée en masse,* when they are not even now in a position to fulfil completely the demands we make on them?

We cannot sustain a serious attack, owing to a lack of all reserves. If we succeed, by retreating behind the serious obstacle of the Meuse, in shortening our front considerably, we can hold out there under favourable circumstances for one or two months, but only if the enemy does not violate Holland's neutrality or drive her to take sides against us, and if the Austro-Hungarian troops are not withdrawn from the Western Front.

If the Chancellor's gloom was not by now complete, Prince Rupprecht lost no time in sealing it. He referred again to the loss of war material in the German retreats; he drew attention to the continuing flow of American reinforcements for the Allies, and he concluded: "I do not believe that there is any possibility of holding out over December . . . our situation is already exceedingly dangerous, and . . . under certain circumstances a catastrophe can occur overnight. Ludendorff does not realize the whole seriousness of the situation. Whatever happens, we must obtain peace before the enemy breaks into Germany; if he does, woe on us!"[60]

So it had come to that: after all the fanfares and all the bombast, "woe on us!"

The American Note of 14 October plunged the German public into deep depression. Peace had seemed so near, and now once more it receded into a distant, uncertain haze. The atmosphere in Berlin was tense, fraught with wild rumours; armed police patrolled the streets. It was small wonder, as the fifth winter of war approached, that Berliners' nerves were stretched: public transport had practically broken down; the fuel shortage continued; the shops had next to nothing to sell—rubber, paper, cotton, leather, textiles and clothing had almost disappeared. But worst of all was the continuing shortage of food. "If one looks at the women," a medical officer recorded, "worn away to skin and bone, and with seamed and careworn faces, one knows where the portion of food assigned to them has really gone." Yet even with their mothers' rations, the children were "thin and pale as corpses." And upon these starving, weakened, distracted people the scourge of influenza fell unabated; on 15 October over 1,700 died of it in Berlin. Surveying all this, and reflecting upon the meaning of the American Note, the Socialist leader Scheidemann said: "Better a terrible end than terror without end." The extreme Left, the Spartacists, were less oracular: they preached a very simple doctrine, which people found easy to understand: "If we get rid of the Kaiser we shall get a decent peace."

Against this backcloth of ruin and dismay, the Imperial Chancellor summoned another War Cabinet on 17 October to draft a reply to the American Note. The High Command, faced bluntly with what amounted to a demand for capitulation, and the destruction of the Imperial régime, changed its tune. With Ludendorff this time as its spokesman, the High Command called for the *levée en masse* on which it had poured scorn a week earlier: "We now stood clearly before the question, were we to surrender unconditionally to the Entente, or was the Government to call on the people to fight a last desperate battle?"

There was a lengthy discussion of ways and means: Germany still had the equivalent of thirty-five and a half divisions, plus garrisons, on the Eastern Front; could these be brought across—or at any rate, some of them—to the West? Ludendorff had to admit:

> Divisions recently removed from East to West had not done well under their new conditions and I had had very unfavourable reports of them. In spite of the shortage of men, drafts from the East were received with the greatest reluctance. They brought a bad *moral* and had an unfavourable effect on their fellows. According to the explanations of General Hoffmann, the temptations to which the men were exposed from the corruption of Jew traders in the East and from Bolshevik propaganda, as, indeed, from propaganda from home, had broken their fighting spirit.

Ludendorff and Hoffmann dwelt upon the dangers of Bolshevism spreading from Russia, but, complained the former, "the Government as such did not appear to take any definite stand on principle against Bolshevism." There were divided opinions on the evacuation of the Ukraine, the majority taking the High Command view:

> We and our Allies had to look somewhere for additional foodstuffs, and the Ukraine was the only possible source. . . . Had we evacuated at this stage, which would have taken us a considerable time, we should have gradually released ten divisions which were not really fit for the line. The advantages would not have been equal to the disadvantages that we should have brought upon ourselves by evacuation.

The discussion then turned on manpower and the Army; the War Minister, von Scheuch, surprised Ludendorff by saying he thought he could raise some 600,000 more men for reinforcements, and surprised him even more by adding that he could provide 60,000–70,000 immediately from the Home Army: "I said: 'If I have these reinforcements now, I can face the future with confidence, but I must have them immediately.' The Minister promised not to lose a day." Scheidemann, however, doubted whether the arrival of these men would improve the spirit of the Army; his speech, says Ludendorff, "amounted to a declaration of bankruptcy of the domestic policy of the Chancellor and the Majority Parties." Other ministers were a little more optimistic. The Vice-Chancellor, von Payer, thought: "If we say to the nation: 'There is just a chance, if you hold out. But if you cannot hold out for a few weeks, then you must expect Germany to be more or less wiped out from among the nations. You must expect an absolutely crushing burden of indemnities'—you may rouse them once more." Others agreed, and Ludendorff was then called on to summarize the military situation. He said: "I regard a break-through as possible, but not probable. If you ask me on my conscience, I can only answer that I do not expect it." He continued in a stronger vein:

> We were in every respect masters of our own actions and could break off or continue the negotiations. We had a free hand to do either. Is it a crime to fight on when one honestly wants peace and cannot get it? Is it a crime to abandon the hope of a compromise for which one has honestly striven, when the opponent demands more than one can give? . . . It came to this, that it was our duty to continue the fight, unless we were prepared to surrender unconditionally to an enemy from whom we had nothing to hope. . . . The majority of the German people were ready and willing to sacrifice the last ounce of their strength to the Army, and it was the duty of the Government to translate that willingness into action. I spoke to that effect.

Prince Max was not convinced; events seen from Berlin had a different perspective from that of Spa. Ludendorff's new-found courage made him suspicious: "I cannot deny that the impression gained on me that General Ludendorff was less concerned to alter our decision than to register a protest against it." Nevertheless, the First Quartermaster-General "travelled back to Spa in confident mood." There, says Wheeler-Bennett, he found that: "Hindenburg supported him wholeheartedly. There could, he thought, be only one finale, unless they succeeded in creating one last reserve from the resources of the people at home. A rising of the nation could not fail to make an impression on their enemies and on the army itself. . . . It was a happy home-coming; the great twin-brethren were at one again." What neither yet realized was the extent to which Ludendorff had already lost the confidence of the Government, especially the Majority Socialists in it: "They were not impressed either by his threats or by his cajoleries. They were bent upon peace, the peace that had been so passionately

demanded by the Supreme Command, and they faced with perfect
equanimity the prospect of the First Quartermaster-General's resignation, if that became necessary."[61]

Such were the poignant debates of the Germans *in extremis;* no less
sharp were the divisions of opinion on the other side of the line. In
America the Republican campaign for "unconditional surrender" was
undoubtedly having its effect; in France the President of the Republic
was opposed to the very idea of an armistice, which he saw as "ham-
stringing our troops,"[62] while the Generalissimo was already proposing
terms which Haig described as "general unconditional surrender." On
19 October the British War Cabinet (somewhat belatedly, one might
say) discussed the terms of an armistice with its military advisers. Haig
was summoned to this meeting; he had given considerable thought to
the subject since his discussion with Foch on 10 October, and had
discussed it with General Lawrence. Lawrence's view, on the 10th, had
been pessimistic; he "foresaw many dangers ahead." Haig told him:
"We have got the enemy down, in fact, he is a beaten army, and my
plan is to go on hitting him as hard as we possibly can, till he begs for
mercy. Lawrence has a cold, and so is looking at things in a gloomy
way tonight." But Lawrence continued to doubt, and on 17 October he
and Haig returned to the subject of an armistice: "He is of opinion
that it should not be too exacting because it is in the interests of Great
Britain to end the war this year. L. is to give me a note tomorrow
morning embodying his views." Fortified with this note, Haig travelled
to London on the 18th.

We have seen how, ever since August, Haig had perceived and held
to the possibility of ending the war in 1918. Lawrence's words clearly
struck a chord; Haig had no desire to continue the fighting into 1919,
and his whole approach to the question of an armistice was based on
that fact. The result was that without actually changing his opinions he
gave the impression of having done so. On 19 October, before attending the War Cabinet, he called at the War Office and had a brief conversation with the C.I.G.S., Wilson. It was at once evident that there
was a difference of opinion between them; Haig recorded:

> He gave me his views on conditions of armistice. He considers that "The
> Germans should be ordered to lay down their arms and retire to the
> east bank of the Rhine." I gave my opinion that our attack on the 17th
> inst. met with considerable opposition, and that the enemy was not
> ready for unconditional surrender. In that case, there would be no armi-
> stice, and the war would continue for at least another year.

Wilson, in his diary, confirms Haig's reading of his own opinion, but makes no mention of Haig's (though this transpired in his record of the War Cabinet later). What is interesting is Haig's correct assessment of the views of the German Supreme Command. What he did not realize (no one did, among the Allies) was the degree of discord between the Supreme Command and the German Government, and the extent of the latter's demoralization.

Lloyd George opened the proceedings of the War Cabinet by asking Haig to state his views on armistice terms:

> I replied that they must greatly depend on the answers we give to two questions:
> 1. Is Germany now so beaten that she will accept whatever terms the Allies may offer? i.e., unconditional surrender.
> 2. If he refuses to agree to our terms, can the Allies continue to press the enemy sufficiently vigorously during the coming winter months, to cause him to withdraw so quickly that he cannot destroy the railways, roads, etc.?
>
> The answer to both is in the negative. The German Army is capable of retiring to its own frontier, and holding that line if there should be any attempt to touch the *honour* of the German people, and make them fight with the courage of despair.

Haig then summarized the condition of the Allied armies. On this subject he and the C.I.G.S. were at one; Wilson had already (16 October) told the War Cabinet in his racy fashion, "I pictured our army as tired but willing and able to fight, the French army as very tired and neither willing nor able to fight, and the Americans as unfit to fight." Haig expressed it more soberly:

French Army:	worn out and has not been really fighting latterly. It has been freely said that the "war is over" and "we don't wish to lose our lives now that peace is in sight."
American Army:	is not yet organised: it is ill-equipped, half-trained, with insufficient supply services. Experienced officers and N.C.O.s are lacking.
British Army:	was never more efficient than it is today, but it has fought hard, and it lacks reinforcements. With diminishing effectives, morale is bound to suffer.[63]

The Cabinet Minutes record that Haig drew this conclusion: "If the French and American Armies were capable of a serious offensive, *now*, the Allies could completely overthrow the remaining efficient enemy divisions before they could reach the line of the Meuse. They are not. We must reckon with that fact as well as with the fact that the British Army alone is not sufficiently fresh or strong to force a decision by itself."

Haig himself expresses this somewhat differently: "The British alone might bring the enemy to his knees. But why expend more British lives —and for what?"

He pointed out that during the winter, when campaigning would be virtually impossible, the Germans would be able to recuperate, absorb the 1920 conscript class, destroy all communications in front of the advancing Allies, and prepare a new defence line. All this, he concluded, would mean that the Germans would be able to hold on well into 1919—the very thing he least desired. Accordingly, he recommended these terms:

1. Immediate evacuation of Belgium and occupied French territory.
2. Metz and Strasburg to be at once occupied by the Allied Armies, and Alsace-Lorraine to be vacated by the enemy.
3. Belgian and French rolling stock to be returned, and inhabitants restored.

At that point Colonel Hankey, the War Cabinet Secretary, appeared, and Haig had to repeat everything he had said for the Minutes—hence discrepancies between various versions. Then Lloyd George offered his comments. In his memoirs nearly twenty years later he was sarcastic about Haig's "to say the least, unduly restrained" views of the military prospects. To Haig at the time, "the Prime Minister seemed in agreement with me," and this is confirmed by Wilson: "Lloyd George and Milner rather agreed with Haig." Wilson himself, said Haig, "urged 'laying down arms.'" Wilson goes somewhat further, with a cogent point: "I kept on repeating, with some success, that once 'Cease fire' sounded, we could never go to war again (in this war), and that therefore, unless we held real guarantees, i.e. occupation of Boche territory, we would never be able to enforce terms which would give us a durable peace."

> Haig was asked what the attitude of the Army would be if we stuck out for stiff terms, which enemy then refuses, and war goes on. I reminded the P.M. of the situation a year ago when there were frequent demands for information as to what we were fighting for; he (the P.M.) then made a speech and stated our war aims. The British Army had done most of the fighting latterly, and everyone wants to have done with the war, *provided* we get what we want. I therefore advise that we only ask in the armistice for what we intend to hold, and that we set our faces

against the French entering Germany to pay off old scores. In my opinion, under the supposed conditions, the British Army would not fight keenly for what is not really its own affair.

Haig was now beginning to distrust French motives; everything in him recoiled from punitive measures. As far back as 2 January he had told the King in a private conversation: "It is essential that some statement should be made which the soldier can understand and approve of. Few of us feel that the 'democratising of Germany' is worth the loss of a single Englishman!" The question now arose, what *was* worth the loss of a single Englishman: "About noon Mr. Balfour (S. of S. for Foreign Affairs) came in and . . . spoke about deserting the Poles and the people of Eastern Europe, but the P.M. gave the opinion that we cannot expect the British to go on sacrificing their lives for the Poles."

A similar attitude, with deadlier results, would recur at Yalta in 1945. Meanwhile matters even closer to home presented themselves in an equivocal light: "Admiral Wemyss, First Sea Lord, then came in and the views of the Navy for an armistice were stated. They seemed most exacting and incapable of enforcement except by a land force." On this uncertain note the War Cabinet adjourned, agreeing to resume the discussion on the 21st. Before it could do so, however, events had moved on.

After much soul-searching, the German Government addressed its reply to President Wilson on 20 October. It denied the illegal and inhuman practices that Germany had been accused of, in particular the sinking of the lifeboats of torpedoed ships; nevertheless the unrestricted U-boat campaign was at last abandoned—to the indignation of the German High Command. "This concession to Wilson," says Ludendorff, "was the heaviest blow to the Army and especially to the Navy. The injury to the *moral* of the fleet must have been immeasurable. The Cabinet had thrown up the sponge." In political as well as military matters there was complete acceptance of American requirements; Prince Max stated that constitutional reforms were in process (he announced them two days later) and that "The Government is now free from all arbitrariness and irresponsible influence, and is supported by the approval of the overwhelming majority of the German people." This was not far from the truth. As A. J. P. Taylor says,

For all practical purposes there was set up in October 1918 the system of the Weimar republic: political liberty, but no changes in economic or social power. The sole difference was that in October 1918 the Emperor remained as constitutional figurehead; and to this not even the Social Democrats objected. Indeed they did their best to save his throne and sacrificed him only because of the refusal of the Allies to treat with him.[64]

The British War Cabinet resumed its discussion of armistice terms on the morning of 21 October. Wilson describes what followed:

> After lunch the Boche wireless answer to my Cousin[65] came in. When we examined the answer, it was quite adroit. The Boche agrees to my Cousin's proposal to evacuate occupied territory and suggests that a military commission be set up to arrange details. No mention of Alsace-Lorraine,[66] nor any mention of the salt water.[67] My Cousin is trapped. My own opinion is that, unless Lloyd George and Tiger[68] catch a hold, my Cousin will cart us all. . . . A.J.B. [Mr. A. J. Balfour] drafted an excellent wire to Wilson, pointing out that the Boche is taking advantage of one sentence in Wilson's first telegram of terms, and is now taking it for granted that only "occupied territories" should be evacuated, but that, of course, this was ridiculous. And A.J.B. then went on to say that we were of opinion that Wilson should not wire again without consulting the Allies. This was approved and sent off. . . . A very interesting day.

It is difficult to believe that President Wilson would again respond to a German overture without conferring with his allies, yet so it was. Nevertheless, his reply to the Germans on 23 October did show some bending to outside pressures at home and abroad. He told the Germans that he was sending the correspondence to the Allies so that their military advisers could work out such terms as "will fully protect the interests of the peoples involved and ensure to the Associated Governments the unrestricted power to safeguard and enforce the details of peace." He concluded by taking note of the alleged change of government in Germany, in which he did not profess great confidence, adding that if America had to deal "with the military masters and the monarchial autocrats of Germany now, or if it is likely to have to deal with them later in regard to the international obligations of the German Empire, it must demand, not peace negotiations but surrender." Perhaps most significant of all was his earlier statement that: "The only armistice he would feel justified in submitting for consideration would be one which should leave the United States and the Powers associated with her in a position to enforce any arrangements that may be entered into, and to make a renewal of hostilities on the part of Germany impossible." As Lloyd George commented, "Quite irrespective of his final dig at the German autocracy, Wilson had intimated in this note that the Armistice terms would involve a complete surrender by the Central Powers." Clearly the Republican election campaign was having its effect.

So, on leaden feet, the embattled nations tottered towards peace. The next stage was the consultation of the Allied military leaders on armistice terms, to which Wilson had referred in his Note. This was to take place on 25 October, but it was preceded by an interview between Foch and Haig the previous day. As we know, Haig had already formed serious doubts about Foch's intentions. The official record (very brief) of this meeting tells us that Foch claimed that: "(1) In order to make it impossible for the Germans to renew hostilities, and (2) To make sure that the indemnities which France would claim should be duly paid, German territory must be occupied and bridgeheads over the Rhine established."[69] Haig questioned the military advantages to be gained from Foch's proposals, but was even more disturbed on other grounds. He commented: "On the whole, Foch's reasons were political not military, and Lawrence and I were both struck by the very unpractical way in which he and Weygand regarded the present military situation. He would not ask himself, 'What does the military situation of the Allies admit of their demanding?' 'What terms can we really enforce?'" Lawrence was so disturbed that the next day he once more handed Haig a private note. It said:

> At yesterday's meeting Marshal Foch claimed that in order to make it impossible for the Germans to renew hostilities after the Armistice, bridgeheads over the Rhine must be occupied as well as Metz and Strassburg [sic].
>
> He further claimed that German territory must be occupied in order to ensure that the indemnities which France would claim should be paid.
>
> The first claim has a military basis and seems to be well within the competence of the military authorities to express an opinion on.
>
> The second claim is a political one in which quite possibly England and the United States are not interested.
>
> I submit that political and military objectives should not be mixed up in any expression of opinion by the Higher Command as to the nature of the Armistice to be granted to the enemy.[70]

The conference of Commanders-in-Chief to discuss armistice terms took place on 25 October at Foch's headquarters at Senlis. He stated its purpose and, questioned by Pershing, indicated its credentials: the request of the Allied governments for expert advice. Pershing accepted this, "although I was in favour of demanding the surrender of the German armies." This was a distinct shift of opinion from what he had

said to Haig two days earlier. Asked to develop his opinion, he cour-
teously replied that as the French and British armies had been fighting
longer and had suffered more than the American, it was more appropriate for Pétain and Haig to speak first. Foch turned to Haig, who
"gave practically the same [opinion] as I had given to the War Cabinet
last Saturday." Foch emphatically disagreed with him:

> It cannot be said that the German Army is not defeated. Although we
> are not able to tell its exact condition, still we are dealing with an army
> that has been pounded every day for three months, an army that is now
> losing on a front of 400 kilometres, that, since July 15th, has lost more
> than 250,000 prisoners and 4,000 guns; an army that is, physically and
> morally, thoroughly beaten. Certainly the Allied armies are not new,
> but victorious armies are never fresh. In this matter the question is rela-
> tive; the German armies are far more exhausted than ours. Certainly
> the British and French armies are tired; certainly the American Army is
> a young army, but it is full of idealism and strength and ardour. It has
> already won victories and is now on the eve of another victory; and
> nothing gives wings to an army like victory. When one hunts a wild
> beast and finally comes upon him at bay, one then faces greater danger,
> but it is not the time to stop, it is time to redouble one's blows without
> paying any attention to those he himself receives.[71]

Pétain was the next to speak; he followed Foch's demand for the left
bank of the Rhine and bridgeheads over the river, and added something new: "Surrender by the Germans of 5,000 locomotives and
100,000 railway trucks in perfect condition." Then it was Pershing's
turn; he agreed with Foch that the present military situation was very
favourable to the Allies. He said:

> The general view that an armistice should provide guarantees against a
> resumption of hostilities, give the Allies a decided advantage, and be
> unfavourable to Germany in case hostilities should be resumed, meets
> with my approval. I think that the damage done by the war to the inter-
> ests of the powers with which the United States is associated against
> Germany is so great that there should be no tendency towards leniency.

The terms which Pershing then proposed were almost identical with
those of the French generals, with one important addition: "6th. Surrender of all U-boats and U-boat bases to the control of a neutral
power until their disposition is otherwise determined." Haig here inter-
jected:

"That is none of our affair. It is a matter for the Admiralty to decide."

I replied inviting attention to the fact that the American Army was operating 3,000 miles from home, that the German submarines constituted a formidable menace to our sea communications and that their surrender was a matter of vital importance to us. I said that while the number to be delivered could be decided by the naval authorities, this condition should be exacted so that if hostilities were resumed we should have our communications free from danger.

Marshal Foch said:

"The suggestion of General Pershing regarding submarines seems to me a reasonable one and his demand well founded."[72]

By now Haig must have been looking somewhat discontented; he was clearly at odds with all his allies on this vital subject which, mishandled, could rob victory of all its rewards, and was in any case bound to affect very seriously both the timing and the nature of the peace. Foch asked him if he had anything further to say:

I said that I had no reason to change my opinion. I felt that the enemy might not accept the terms which Foch proposed because of military necessity only—and it would be very costly and take a long time (perhaps two years) to enforce them, *unless the internal state of Germany compels* [Haig's italics] the enemy to accept them. We don't know very much about the internal state of Germany—and so to try to impose such terms seems to me really a gamble which may come off or it may not. It struck me too that the insistence of the two French Generals on the left bank of the Rhine means that they now aim at getting hold of the Palatinate[73] as well as Alsace-Lorraine! Pétain spoke of taking a huge indemnity from Germany, so large that she will never be able to pay it. Meantime, French troops will hold the left bank of the Rhine as a pledge![74]

So, with Haig still dissenting, the Allied military leaders formulated their armistice proposals; these certainly showed no sign of the leniency against which Pershing had spoken. They were, according to Foch:

1. The immediate evacuation of lands unlawfully invaded—Belgium, France, Alsace-Lorraine and Luxembourg—and the immediate repatriation of their inhabitants.
2. Surrender by the enemy of 5,000 guns, 30,000 machine guns and 3,000 Minenwerfer [trench mortars].
3. Evacuation by the German Army of all territory on the left bank of the Rhine; occupation by the Allies of bridge-heads on the right

bank, drawn with a radius of eighteen and three-quarter miles, at
Mayence, Coblenz and Strasbourg, and the creation on the right
bank of a neutral zone twenty-five miles wide running east of the
river.

4. Prohibition of any destruction or damage by the enemy in the area
   evacuated.
5. Delivery of 5,000 locomotives and 150,000 railway trucks in good
   condition.
6. Delivery of 150 submarines, withdrawal of the surface fleet to Baltic
   ports, occupation by the Allied fleets of Cuxhaven and Heligoland.
7. Maintenance of the blockade during the period fixed for the
   fulfilment of the above conditions.

What this meant, evidently, was nothing less than unconditional surrender, but without actually using that phrase. When Foch showed his
draft to Clemenceau and Poincaré next day, the latter questioned
whether the Germans would accept such terms. Foch replied: "Then
we will continue the war; for at the point the Allied Armies have now
reached, their victorious march must not be halted until they have rendered all German resistance impossible and seized guarantees fully en-
suring peace—a peace we will have obtained at the price of inesti-
mable sacrifices."

By now the gulf of opinion between Foch and Haig on this matter
was very wide indeed, and in view of the future history of Europe and
the world it is worth looking a little further into the British Field-
Marshal's mind. Haig had no doubt that the Germans were beaten—
after all, he had been doing most of the beating himself. The question,
as he saw it, was whether the Allied terms would encourage them to
admit that they were beaten immediately, in 1918, or make them want
to prolong the war into 1919. He was quite clear in his own mind: he
wanted peace in 1918. But there was something else as well, a further
disturbing thought which had been growing in his mind as he listened
to the harsh language of the French generals. He expressed this in a
letter to his wife on 26 October, the day after the C.-in-C.s' meeting:
". . . it is most important that our Statesmen should think over the situation carefully and not attempt to so humiliate Germany as to produce a desire for revenge in years to come."[75]

And this thought, once stated, took hold of him. It was another of
those flashes of perception which came to him, and which he was always so much better at putting on paper than expressing in speech—
for example, when assisting Lord Haldane with his army reforms in
1906, Haig's vision of "an army rooted in the people"; his warning to
the Government on 5 August 1914 that they should prepare "for a war

... the most trying day the tanks had experienced': Mark V tanks with 'cribs' to enable them to cross the Hindenburg Line trenches. More than half the tanks committed to battle on 29 September became casualties

'... those terrible roads of the devastated area': a British ammunition column in pursuit of the Germans, crossing a dry canal by an improvised track beside the wreckage of the original bridge. Note the 4-horse team; the other two horses had gone to the Americans

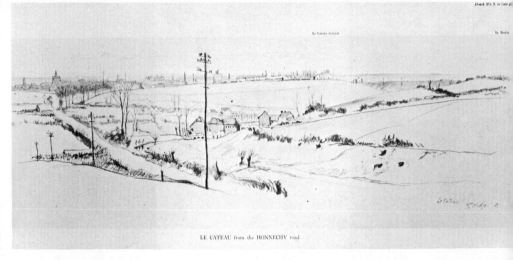

Le Cateau Station   St. Benin

LE CATEAU from the HONNECHY road

'. . . the historic fields of August 1914': Captain Hodge's sketch of the approaches to the town where II Corps fought its determined rearguard action on 26 August 1914, in the retreat from Mons

Face of victory: '. . . the French Army had now practically reached the end of its tether'. A French infantryman, with all the grime of battle on him, and surrounded by his heavy load of equipment, epitomizes the weariness which was part of the heavy price of victory

Faces of defeat. *Above:* '. . . an army that is, physically and morally, thoroughly beaten'. This dead German soldier lying on a caisson, with the dead horses of its team behind him, somewhere along a shell-swept road of France, symbolizes German disaster at the front. *Below:* '. . . soldiers were fraternizing with the revolutionaries'. These workers' and soldiers' councils in Berlin, 9 November, epitomized disaster in the Fatherland

Scenes of destiny. *Above:* 'the liberation of Lille was a great moment'. The British Fifth Army actually entered Lille on 17 October; their ceremonial entry (shown in this photograph) was on 28 October. *Below:* '... the kilted band of the Canadian 42nd Battalion played its way into the town'. Mons, where the British fought their first battle of the war in 1914, liberated at 7 a.m. on 11 November 1918

of several years"; his recognition in 1915 that France's losses would make it inevitable that Britain should shoulder the burden of the war; more recently, his early perception of imminent victory.[76] Now he was looking to a more distant future. He was not the only one; already, on 23 and 24 October General Smuts (a member of the War Cabinet) had laid memoranda before the War Cabinet warning against the implications of unconditional surrender. With the example of Russia in mind, he was fearful of the consequences of breaking up the "bad, but more or less orderly, political pre-war system of Europe." As to Germany, Smuts said: "The popular cry for justice is very insistent but two governing considerations should be kept steadily in view. Firstly, the evil of continuing the War is rapidly beginning to outweigh the good to be achieved by a more complete measure of victory or justice. Secondly, the British Empire should not pursue justice at the expense of its own legitimate future. . . ." Knowing his Bible, Smuts no doubt remembered the text: "There is a just man that perisheth in his righteousness. . . . Be not righteous overmuch. . . ."[77]

Smuts and Haig and others like them were in a minority, however; the tide of public opinion in the Allied countries was flowing strongly in favour of a punitive peace, and the politicians of the democracies did not fail to bow. On 1 November (to glance ahead, for the sake of rounding off this part of the story), Haig once more wrote to his wife, saying:

> I am afraid the Allied Statesmen mean to exact humiliating terms from Germany. I think this is a mistake, because it is merely laying up troubles for the future, and may encourage the wish for revenge in the future. Also, I doubt if Germany is sufficiently low yet to accept such terms. However we shall see. Personally I feel that there are many good officers in Germany like myself for instance who would in a similar situation rather die than accept such conditions.[78]

From the purely military point of view—if there *is* such a thing as a purely military point of view—he was certainly right; he was only too well aware of the extreme difficulty his armies were experiencing in maintaining their momentum. Foch, never distinguished for realism, might brush such matters aside, and Pershing was unwilling to admit that chaos was never far behind his armies. Haig, whose forces were the sharp end of the Allied advance, had no illusions. What he did *not* know, however, as he admitted on the 25th, was the internal condition of Germany. The irony, the awful irony, is that the internal condition of Germany did, as we shall shortly see, compel the acceptance of unconditional surrender—but at the same time removed the necessity for it. The Allies were breathing vengeance upon the autocratic German Empire; they were about to inflict it upon the democratic German Republic.

Meanwhile dire events were taking place on the German side. At Spa the High Command digested President Wilson's latest communication: "It was a strong answer to our cowardly note," says Ludendorff. "In my view there could no longer be doubt anywhere that we must continue the fight." This was Hindenburg's view too. On 24 October he sent out a telegram "For the information of all troops":

> . . . Wilson's answer is a demand for unconditional surrender. It is thus unacceptable to us soldiers. It proves that our enemy's desire for our destruction, which let loose the war in 1914, still exists undiminished. It proves, further, that our enemies use the phrase "Peace with Justice" merely to deceive us and break our resistance. Wilson's answer can thus be nothing for us soldiers but a challenge to continue our resistance with all our strength. When our enemies know that no sacrifices will achieve the rupture of the German front, they will be ready for a peace which will make the the future of our country safe for the great masses of our people.[79]

Ludendorff offers confused and unconvincing explanations of how it came about that this telegram arrived on his desk already signed by the Field-Marshal, and why he countersigned it without question. None of that matters. What did matter, profoundly, was, first, that the High Command proved to be alarmingly out of touch with the sentiments of the Army. There might indeed be a number of officers—and some units—who, as Haig suggested, would rather die than accept a dishonourable peace. The bulk of the rank and file, however, under the impact of Spartacist or Bolshevist propaganda, but above all under the stress of weariness and awareness of the miseries of their families at home, had neither the desire nor the intention to fight on. Hindenburg's message never reached "all troops"; at the urging of generals closer to the front line it was quickly withdrawn—but not before disaffected wireless operators had passed on the gist of it to Independent Socialist members of the Reichstag. From this followed the second consequence, of great import.

On 25 October Ludendorff was in Berlin with Hindenburg; they were trying to stiffen the Government's resolve, warning it of the agitation in the Army against officers, "which was then assuming large proportions," according to Ludendorff (though one suspects that he little knew how large!), and against weakening the position of the Emperor because "the whole army looked up to him as its head" (which was certainly no longer true). At noon, however, the Reichstag met, and at once "a storm of indignation burst over G.H.Q. The Government did not move a finger to protect us, although we were still the head of a mighty army." How could the Government protect a High Command which issued policy statements in flat contradiction of its own policies? "Prince Max," says Sir John Wheeler-Bennett,

> had but one course open to him. He went immediately to the Emperor and offered the resignation of himself and his whole Cabinet. Either they or the Supreme Command must go; the Emperor must choose. No other event could illustrate so forcibly the sweeping changes which had taken place in Germany during the month of October. The new German democracy had been challenged and had taken up the gage . . . the threat of resignation, so often used by Ludendorff, is now the weapon of the Chancellor. The boot is on the other foot![80]

Sir John Wheeler-Bennett then corrects himself in an important particular: it was not, in fact, the High Command that Prince Max was indicting—"it was Ludendorff's head that the politicians were demanding on a charger, eager to avenge the many insults which they had received at his hands." Early the next morning Hindenburg and Ludendorff were summoned to the Emperor's presence. He seemed, wrote Ludendorff,

> wholly changed in comparison with the previous day. Speaking to me alone, he expressed himself particularly against the army order of the evening of the 24th. There followed some of the bitterest moments of my life. I said respectfully to His Majesty that I had gained the painful impression that I no longer enjoyed his confidence, and that I accordingly begged most humbly to be relieved of my office. His Majesty accepted my resignation.
> I went back alone. I did not see His Majesty again.

Hindenburg also offered to resign, but neither Wilhelm II nor Prince Max wished to carry matters that far—the Chancellor no doubt fearing the effect on the already feeble morale of the nation if this demi-god departed (see pp. 18–19).

All that now remained was to answer President Wilson's Note. This was done next day; the German Government assured the President that negotiations would be conducted by a people's government, to which the military authorities would be subject. "The German Government," it said, "now awaits proposals for an Armistice which shall be a first step towards a just peace." On the same day the Austro-Hungarian

Government also expressed complete submission to the President's views. So there would be unconditional surrender after all. As Ludendorff said: "In the German Note of the 27th October we capitulated."

It would have been no less than a miracle if there had been no discords in the Allied High Command, with four national armies operating under so unfamiliar an office as a generalissimo. It is sad that the sharpest and potentially most disruptive discords came now, with victory in sight. The first was prompted by M. Clemenceau, in one of his tigerish moods. On 21 October he wrote to Foch:

> I have postponed from day to day writing to you about the crisis existing in the American Army. It is not that I have anything to tell you regarding a state of affairs which assuredly you know better than anybody else, since, as Commander-in-Chief of the Allied Armies, you are necessarily the first to suffer from its consequences. We have talked too often and at too great a length concerning the employment of the American troops for it to be necessary to revert to the subject today, even in the most summary fashion.
>
> You have watched at close range the development of General Pershing's exactions. Unfortunately, thanks to his invincible obstinacy, he has won out against you as well as against your immediate subordinates. To go over all this again can lead only to useless regrets . . .

It was the old story, the old argument, with right, as ever, on both sides: to Clemenceau (and others), with the glittering prize of victory dangling before his eyes, the price of permitting Pershing to form his Army Group now seemed intolerably high. The French Prime Minister was only too well aware that the Americans depended on France for artillery, tanks, transport (no less than 130,000 horses had been supplied) and much else, and that some 100,000 French troops formed part of Pershing's command; these were the "exactions." To which Pershing would inevitably retort that if the Americans were arriving in France virtually destitute of military supplies, this was in response to the Allied request for infantry above all else; and that it was his Government's instruction that American troops should serve under the American flag—the old story. As the constitutional head of the French Army, however, Clemenceau could not let it rest; he did not wish to recriminate, he was merely thinking of the great battle in progress:

> I would be a criminal if I allowed the French Army to wear itself out indefinitely in battle, without doing everything in my power to ensure that an Allied Army which has hurried to its aid was rendered capable of fulfilling the military rôle for which it was destined.

The French Army and the British Army, without a moment's respite, have been daily fighting, for the last three months, battles which are using them up at a time when it is impossible for us to reinforce them immediately with fresh effectives. These two Armies are pressing back the enemy with an ardour that excites world-wide admiration[81] but our worthy American Allies, who thirst to get into action and are unanimously acknowledged to be great soldiers, have been marking time ever since their forward jump on the first day; and in spite of heavy losses, they have failed to conquer the ground assigned them as their objective. Nobody can maintain that these fine troops are unusable; they are merely unused.

Clemenceau was being less than just to the American effort,[82] but when he went on to say that "the immobility of your right wing cannot possibly be a part of your plan" he touched a nerve (as we shall see). And now he came to the crux: "When General Pershing refused to obey your orders [see pp. 113–14], you could have appealed to President Wilson. For reasons which you considered more important, you put off this solution of the conflict fearing that it would bring reactions of a magnitude which you thought it difficult to gauge. I took the liberty of differing with you. . . ." Clemenceau noted that Foch had entrusted to General Maistre, Commander of the French Centre Army Group, co-ordination between the right wing of his group and the American First Army. He continued:

If General Pershing finally resigns himself to obedience, if he accepts the advice of capable Generals, whose presence at his side he has until now permitted only that he might reject their counsels, I shall be wholly delighted.

But if this new attempt to reconcile two contrary points of view should not bring the advantageous results you anticipate, I must say to you that, in my opinion, any further hesitation should be out of the question. For it would then be certainly high time to tell President Wilson the truth and the whole truth concerning the situation of the American troops. Indeed, neither you nor I have the right to conceal it from him. . . .

Whether you share my opinion or form a different one, you will certainly agree with me in recognizing that this state of affairs cannot continue any longer. For this reason, I would be glad if you could find it possible to send me an early answer.[83]

The Marshal displayed at this juncture more statesmanship than the statesman. Clemenceau's letter, said Foch later, revealed his character and temperament, "his good qualities and his faults, his ardour, his imperiousness, his impulsiveness, his irritability in the face of obstacles, his instinct to break, not to avoid them. But when obstacles arise not from men but from the force of circumstances, any efforts in that direction are not only vain, but childish. One might as well join battle with the elements. Don Quixote was animated by the same feelings when he tilted against windmills."[84]

Foch pointed out, as a simple matter of fact, that out of thirty American divisions in France that were fit for battle, twenty were in Pershing's Army Group, the remaining ten being with the French and British Armies (only two with the British, to Haig's chagrin). He said he proposed to manipulate this distribution as operations required and permitted, and that he thought this method likely to be more effective than giving orders:

> These I shall give, to be sure, but the High Command may not perhaps be in a position to have them executed, since to do so would require Corps and Divisional Commanders and Staffs having the necessary experience. Moreover, this crisis is of the sort from which all improvised armies suffer, and which always considerably impairs their effectiveness at the start.
>
> But there is no denying the magnitude of the effort made by the American Army. After attacking at Saint-Mihiel on September 12th, it attacked in the Argonne on the 26th. From September 26th to October 20th its losses in battle were 54,158 men—in exchange for small gains on a narrow front, it is true, but over particularly difficult country and in the face of serious resistance by the enemy.

And that was the end of the matter.

No sooner had this source of discord evaporated, however, than another arose. As we have seen, Foch and Haig had a meeting on 24 October, prior to the conference of Commanders-in-Chief on 25 October. In addition to a difference of opinion on armistice terms, there was another, tersely referred to in the official record: "Sir D. Haig asked for the immediate return of the Second Army to his command. Marshal Foch refused and the matter is to be referred to the Government (English) *vide* correspondence."

Haig had been increasingly discontented at the separation of the Second Army from the rest of the B.E.F., though he had readily agreed to it in September. Now, a month later, it was clear that the general direction of the slow advance of King Albert's Army Group was going to be almost northwards, towards Ghent, Antwerp and Brussels, while Haig's Group was making for Germany. The Second Army was needed to cover the flank and assist the progress of the main thrust. Foch at this stage became *too* statesmanlike. Haig recorded on the 24th:

Foch declines to return the Second Army to me because of the political value of having the King of the Belgians in command of an Allied Army, when he re-enters his capital, Brussels! His real object is to use the British Second Army to open the way for the "dud" divisions (of which the rest of the King's Army is composed) and ensure that they get to Brussels. France would then get the credit for clearing Belgium and putting the King back in his capital. . . . I explained the military reasons why my Second Army must now be under my orders. If there were political reasons requiring the Second Army to remain under King Albert, then the British Government must direct me on the subject. Until I was so informed, I must continue to view the situation from a *military* standpoint, and insist on the return of the Second Army without delay. F. asked me to submit my request in writing.

What made this dispute more dangerous than Clemenceau's attack on Pershing was that Pershing had known nothing about that, whereas Foch and Haig were aware that they were at loggerheads. Lord Milner visited Haig on the 26th, and quite agreed that the Second Army should return to the fold, but "the question was how best to arrange that, without letting the world know of the friction that had occurred." Clemenceau, in this case, proved to be more reasonable than Foch, throwing his weight behind the British case—though not with conspicuous success. In the end it fell to Foch's old friend, Sir Henry Wilson, to persuade the Generalissimo. They met on 27 October at Foch's headquarters. Wilson recorded: "I had rather a stormy meeting with Foch, but I think I was able to put my case strongly, but quietly. We parted excellent friends." Later that day Foch and Haig met again, and Haig found: "Foch was very pleased to see me, and was evidently anxious to make amends. We agreed that the Second Army would return to me on reaching the line of the Scheldt. This will be after the next operation." As Wilson commented: "Everything had gone splendidly at the meeting, and flowers, and tea, and delights! So that corner is turned." Neither Foch nor Haig held their grudges long.

With quarrels behind composed, the great quarrel in front could continue. The advancing Allies were now learning about yet more novelties of war: booby-traps. These displayed distressing ingenuity: explosive charges, carefully concealed, attached to tempting items of booty or souvenirs, time bombs in dugouts or houses, some of them blowing up buildings and their occupants many days after the Germans had gone—these were daily occurrences, and did nothing for the tempers of the Allied troops. One and all, however, turned to their engineers to deal with these objectionable things, thus adding to their already ample burdens. "A delightful job," remarked one Royal Engi-

neers officer, "feeling around a deep German dugout to see if it is
going to blow up!" The Germans also displayed considerable skill at
road demolitions. Bridges, of course, were natural targets for destruction, but, says the same officer,

> they have one or two other ideas, such as:
> (a) Tunnelling into the side of a road embankment and blowing a
>   great breach in it.
> (b) Dropping an overhead bridge onto a road passing underneath it.
>   This not only cuts the railway, but also blocks the road with hun-
>   dreds of tons of twisted steel girders, very difficult to remove
>   quickly. We front-line engineers have no equipment to do this kind
>   of thing. We can only make earth diversions, or build wooden tres-
>   tles or pontoon bridges.
> (c) Mining the crossroads in the middle of a village. Either the crater
>   has to be filled in, or deviations made by knocking down the
>   houses. Either job takes time and being at a crossroads, the obstacle
>   creates a maximum of delay.

Reaching the end of a day soaked to the skin and with a horrible back-
ache, he quietly remarked: "This moving warfare is very interesting
but a bit strenuous."[85]

This comment was likely to be echoed, possibly less quietly, on
other parts of the front. In the Meuse–Argonne sector the going was
always hard. "Every member of the American Expeditionary Forces,"
says Pershing, "from the front line to the base ports, was straining
every nerve. . . . Obstacles which seemed insurmountable were overcome daily in hastening the movements of replacements, ammunition,
and supplies to the front, and of sick and wounded to the rear." This
was no doubt true, yet the progress being made was still disappointing,
and it was this which made Clemenceau and others think the Americans were "marking time." They were not; they were simply learning
how difficult the war could be (even with the enemy nearly beaten),
just as every other army had had to learn. Foch himself was discontented, and it is ironical that, on the very day that Clemenceau was
complaining to him about Pershing, he was himself addressing Pétain,
Maistre and Pershing, directing them to co-operate to "outflank the
wooded massif of the Argonne by wider turning movements, and cease
using up their forces in costly wood fighting unlikely to bring about
any result." Like certain other Foch directives, this was likely to cause
its recipients to remark "easier said than done." And, in fact, Foch's
tactical suggestions at this stage brought him into dispute with Pétain;
but as he did possess the authority to give orders to the French Commander-in-Chief, this clash of opinion was quickly resolved in his

favour without incurring any of the perils of confrontation with Pershing or Haig.

The latter's armies had now reached the Hermann Position—such as it was. It bore no resemblance to the massive and daunting fortifications which they had already overcome. This was no Siegfried—but the Germans had not been wasting the time that their rearguards had won for them. They had made lavish use of barbed wire, both in the familiar "apron" patterns and in the high, thick hedges which were a feature of this part of the country, and they had dug a number of strongpoints. This new battle area was a land of small streams in well-defined valleys, of large woods and small enclosures, with strongly constructed farm buildings which lent themselves to defence. In other words, the Fourth Army, once again the spearhead, faced no easy task; but then, it never did.

Rawlinson's Army was now reduced to two army corps. On 21 October the American II Corps was withdrawn for rest—not before it was time. It is difficult not to conclude that General Read's formation was the "Cinderella" of the American Expeditionary Force. It had been in the Fourth Army since 22 September; it had taken part in several hard actions, the first being the costly failures of 27 and 29 September, the later ones being successful, but often still costly. Its casualties now amounted to 11,500, and, worst of all, it had received practically no reinforcements, so that ranks were painfully thin, with all that that implies for morale. As the U.S. 27th and 30th Divisions departed, Haig said to them: "You do not need me to tell you that in the heavy fighting of the last three weeks you have earned the lasting esteem and admiration of your British comrades-in-arms, whose success you so nobly shared." Pershing promised Haig that he would bring II Corps up to strength again; yet—unbelievable though it may sound, with a combat strength of 1,256,478 on 23 October—he had to break up no less than seven divisions to provide reinforcements for the rest. It would only be natural if he assigned priority for reinforcement to his own Army Group.

For the Fourth Army, 23 October was the next big day (described in the Official History as Phase II of the Battle of the Selle). It was a victory again, but never a walkover: on the IX Corps front, according to the Army History, "no ground was gained without fighting"; in one part of the XIII Corps front "the opposition had to be beaten down yard by yard"; the day was "not a happy one for the tanks"—only nine rallied out of twenty-three engaged. This meant that the burden fell, once again, on the infantry, well supported as always by the artillery, who were getting quite used to the sound of machine-gun bullets clattering on their gun-shields. Perhaps, at the risk of being invidious (there were not less than fifty such awards in the Fourth Army during the last "Hundred Days" of the war), it may be appropriate to quote a Victoria Cross citation of 24 October, since it gives us an illuminating sample of the fighting of these days. The recipient was Lieutenant Frederick William Hedges of the Bedfordshire Regiment, attached to the 6/Northamptonshire Regiment (such attachments were regrettable but common because of replacement problems). The citation (for "conspicuous gallantry and initiative") says:

> During the morning this officer, who was detailed to leap-frog his company to the final objective, handled his company in a very skilful manner, maintaining direction under the most difficult conditions. His company was on the right of the brigade front. He advanced a considerable distance to a point where his further advance was held up by about six machine-gun posts on the hill opposite the line. Early in the afternoon this officer made up his mind to clear out these enemy posts. Later, accompanied by one sergeant and followed at some considerable distance by a Lewis gun section, he proceeded up the hill under cover of a hedge, and killed the first machine-gunner and took two others prisoner. He then worked his way along the crest of the hill and dealt with three other machine-gun posts in a similar manner, taking the feed-blocks out of the guns, his total being six machine-guns and fourteen men. The direct result of this officer's action was that the whole line which had been held up since the morning was enabled to advance, thus having a great effect on subsequent operations.

The Battle of the Selle ended on 24 October. Three British armies had been to varying extents engaged in it since 17 October; twenty-four British and two American divisions had met and defeated thirty-one divisions, taking 20,000 prisoners and 475 guns. The German Army, says the British Official History, was "far from disintegrated, although it was 'patchy,' some divisions fighting well, others poorly; remnants of the old discipline and, even more, fear of punishment, held it together." The German tactic now, says Captain Falls, "directed with great skill—for never did the work of their divisional and regimental commanders shine more brightly than in these days—was to give up what could not be held, and no more, thus husbanding till the last the declining morale of their infantrymen, and delaying the advance as long as might be. A resistance more rigid, with the German soldier in his present temper, would inevitably have led to a break through, somewhere or other, and a consequent rout."[86]

The British Army knew it was winning—but in these last days of October it was still not evident from the demeanour of the men facing it that final victory had been won. On the 31st Haig met his four army commanders—Horne, Byng, Rawlinson and Birdwood: "Each explained his views on the situation. The enemy is fighting a very good rear-guard action, and *all are agreed* that from a military standpoint, *the enemy has not yet been sufficiently beaten as to cause him to accept an ignominous peace* [Haig's italics]."[87] We may leave the last word here to Ludendorff, on his last day of office: "On the evening of the 25th the Western Front was enduring the greatest strain. There was fighting from the Dutch frontier to Verdun. No more help was coming from home. Not a word of encouragement was given. It was miraculous that the troops fought so heroically."

Chapter VIII: Notes

1. (p. 157) Ludendorff: *My War Memories,* Hutchinson, 1919, ii, p. 722.
2. (p. 157) With our knowledge of the twenty-three years of peaceful exile in Holland that lay ahead of him, it is easy to misjudge Wilhelm II's frame of mind at this period. We have to remember that very fresh in his memory was the horrible fate of his (distant) cousin, Tsar Nicholas II of Russia, who had been murdered with his whole family at Ekaterinburg just over two months earlier (16 July).
3. (p. 157) It is indicative of the demoralization of Supreme Headquarters that a great deal of ranting and shouting took place from now on.
4. (p. 158) Sir John Wheeler-Bennett: *Hindenburg: The Wooden Titan,* Macmillan, 1967, p. 163.
5. (p. 158) Quoted in Official History, *1918,* v, p. 182.
6. (p. 159) Alan Palmer: *The Kaiser, Warlord of the Second Reich,* Weidenfeld and Nicolson, 1978, p. 207.
7. (p. 159) Wheeler-Bennett, op. cit., p. 165.
8. (p. 160) Ludendorff, op. cit., ii, p. 725.
9. (p. 160) Social Democrat, Secretary of the Party.
10. (p. 160) Gustav Stresemann, National Liberal, subsequently Chancellor and Foreign Minister.
11. (p. 160) Ernst von Heydebrand und der Lase, Conservative leader.
12. (p. 160) However, on second thoughts he did not do so.
13. (p. 160) This was Hugo Haase. The revolution which he had so earnestly desired proved fatal to him; he was assassinated in 1919.
14. (p. 161) Foch and Haig would have said, "Would that it were so!" Pershing was in the process of forming a Second American Army on the right of the First (12 October) and refused to part with any divisions for other parts of the front.
15. (p. 161) Ludendorff, op. cit., ii, p. 729.
16. (p. 161) See Appendix A.
17. (p. 162) Prince Max's memoirs, quoted by Lloyd George, *War Memoirs,* Odhams, 1936, ii, pp. 1960–61.
18. (p. 162) Ibid.
19. (p. 162) On 27 September, in a speech in New York, Wilson laid down five essential conditions of peace which, while appealing to idealists, did not ease the difficulties of peace-making.
20. (p. 163) John W. Thomasson Jnr.; *Fix Bayonets!* Scribner's, 1926, p. 134.
21. (p. 164) Ibid., p. 179.
22. (p. 164) It was not, of course, realized at the time that this was the end of the war for the Australians. Monash and others were much concerned with

how to keep the five divisions in the field in 1919. The corps was actually ordered back to the front on 5 November, and Monash was on his way to his new headquarters at Le Cateau when the armistice supervened.

23. (p. 166) Haig Diary, 5 October; author's papers.
24. (p. 167) A "male" Mark V, twenty-six feet long, carried two 6-pounder guns, and one Hotchkiss machine-gun; the "female" did not carry 6-pounders, but instead five Hotchkiss (or Lewis, these being in greater supply). The crew consisted of a subaltern and seven men.
25. (p. 168) C. and A. Williams-Ellis: *The Tank Corps*, George Newnes, 1919, pp. 259–60.
26. (p. 168) This was the Royal Naval Division, formed in France in 1916 with two naval brigades of sailors and Marines and one army brigade. It owed a good deal of the inspiration for its creation to Winston Churchill, and was sometimes sharply criticized as a misuse of highly trained personnel. Its performance in battle, however, was invariably high-class.
27. (p. 168) Official History, *1918*, v, p. 191.
28. (p. 168) Williams-Ellis, op. cit., p. 261.
29. (p. 169) Haig Diary, 9 October; author's papers.
30. (p. 169) As had been discovered at Amiens on 8 August, see p. 92.
31. (p. 169) Brig. C. N. Barclay: *Armistice 1918*, Dent, 1968, p. 97.
32. (p. 170) Haig Diary; author's papers.
33. (p. 170) Col. G. W. L. Nicholson: *Canadian Expeditionary Force 1914– 1918*, Queen's Printer, Ottawa, 1962, pp. 463–64.
34. (p. 171) See pp. 45 and 55 for British fears of cavalry during the German offensives.
35. (p. 171) The 413th Infantry Regiment, quoted in the British Official History, *1918*, v, p. 229.
36. (p. 171) Barclay, op. cit., p. 90.
37. (p. 172) Lloyd George, op. cit., ii, p. 1954.
38. (p. 173) A General Election (the "Khaki Election") was held in Britain in November and December. In Churchill's words, "it woefully cheapened Britain." Lloyd George, he wrote, arrived at the Peace Conference "somewhat dishevelled by the vulgarities and blatancies of the recent General Election. Pinned to his coat-tails were the posters, 'Hang the Kaiser,' 'Search their Pockets,' 'Make them Pay'; and this sensibly detracted from the dignity of his entrance upon the scene." (*The Aftermath*, Thornton Butterworth, 1929, p. 135.)
39. (p. 173) Wilson's Point 8 said: "All French territory should be freed, and the invaded portions restored, and the wrong done to France by Prussia in 1871, in the matter of Alsace-Lorraine, which has unsettled the peace of the world for nearly fifty years, should be righted in order that peace may once more be made secure in the interest of all." This was characteristic Wilsonian vagueness. From the German point of view, Alsace-Lorraine had not been "French territory" for forty-seven years; from the French point of view, that very fact constituted "the wrong done to France . . . in the matter of Alsace-Lorraine." Clemenceau would appear to have been taking it too much for granted that everyone saw things from the French angle. Lloyd George was absolutely right to draw attention to this difficulty.
40. (p. 173) Lloyd George, op. cit., ii, pp. 1957–58.
41. (p. 174) Ibid., pp. 1959–60.
42. (p. 176) Though, of course, it could be argued that in the act of making their first appeal for an armistice the Germans should have put an end to submarine warfare and recalled the U-boats. The gesture would certainly have been worth trying.
43. (p. 178) The President listed four aims of the Allies:
1. destruction of arbitrary power;
2. self-determination of peoples;

3. national morality to be the same as individual morality;

4. a peace organization to prevent war.

44. (p. 178) Wheeler-Bennett, op. cit., p. 172.

45. (p. 179) Duff Cooper, *Haig*, Faber, 1935, ii, p. 393.

46. (p. 179) The American Second Army came into being on 12 October, under Major-General R. L. Bullard; Pershing thus acquired the status of an Army Group commander like Haig.

47. (p. 180) Marshal Foch: *Memoirs*, trans. Col. T. Bentley Mott, Heinemann, 1931, p. 489; he gives British casualties during the same period as 7,700 officers and 166,000 men. At the beginning of July the French had ten armies in the field, as compared with the British five; during the course of that month they were heavily engaged, whereas the British did not begin their hard fighting until 8 August. By October three French armies had disappeared (Second, Sixth and Ninth) owing to the shortening of the front as the Allies advanced.

48. (p. 180) Guy Chapman, *A Passionate Prodigality*, MacGibbon and Kee, 1965, p. 267.

49. (p. 180) Cyril Falls, *The History of the 36th (Ulster) Division*, M'Caw, Stevenson and Orr, 1922, p. 279.

50. (p. 181) Ibid.

51. (p. 181) It was Jacob's II Corps that had borne the brunt of the attack on the Menin Road Ridge in August and September 1917.

52. (p. 181) Formed of prewar overseas garrisons; it won costly fame at the Cape Helles landings in April 1915.

53. (p. 181) John Ewing, M.C., *The History of the 9th (Scottish) Division*, John Murray, 1921, p. 363.

54. (p. 181) Falls, op. cit., p. 263.

55. (p. 183) A photograph in the divisional history nevertheless shows that the Grande Place was extensively damaged, with some important buildings demolished.

56. (p. 183) Lt.-Col. J. H. Boraston and Capt. E. O. Bax, *The Eighth Division in War, 1914–1918*, Medici Society, 1926, p. 267.

57. (p. 184) British Official History, *The War in the Air*, by H. A. Jones, O.U.P., 1937, vi, pp. 540–41.

58. (p. 184) There were now eight Austrian divisions on the Western Front.

59. (p. 184) Due to the advance of the Allied Salonica army.

60. (p. 185) Quoted in O.H. *1918*, v, pp. 327–28.

61. (p. 188) Wheeler-Bennett, op. cit., p. 170.

62. (p. 188) Georges Clemenceau, *Grandeur and Misery of Victory*, Harrap, 1930, pp. 104–7.

63. (p. 189) For this and other extracts from Haig's diary entry of 19 October, see Robert Blake, *The Private Papers of Douglas Haig*, Eyre and Spottiswoode, 1952, pp. 332–34.

64. (p. 192) A. J. P. Taylor, *The Course of German History*, Methuen University Paperbacks, 1961, p. 206.

65. (p. 192) This, of course, is Sir Henry Wilson being facetious; Woodrow Wilson was a namesake only.

66. (p. 192) Prince Max's constitutional reforms, announced on 22 October, spoke of an Alsatian governor for Alsace-Lorraine, which shows that the German Government had by no means reconciled itself to the loss of these provinces.

67. (p. 192) According to Haig the Admiralty "calculated that if the German High Sea Fleet came out and gave battle, our Grand Fleet would defeat it entirely, but we would lose six or seven ships. So they now recommended that *all* modern ships should be handed over to the British because they would have been destroyed in the battle, if it had taken place!" Haig thought these

terms "exacting" (as we have seen); Wilson considered them "very sound reasoning."

68. (p. 192) M. Clemenceau.
69. (p. 193) Author's papers.
70. (p. 193) Ibid.
71. (p. 194) Quoted by John J. Pershing, *My Experiences in the Great War*, Hodder and Stoughton, 1931, p. 669. No doubt Foch's original French was rather more grammatical than the last sentence of the translation.
72. (p. 195) Ibid., pp. 670–71.
73. (p. 195) The "Lower Palatinate," lying north of Lorraine, between the Saar and the Rhine.
74. (p. 195) Blake, op. cit., p. 336.
75. (p. 196) Author's papers.
76. (p. 197) See John Terraine, *The Western Front*, Hutchinson, 1964, pp. 178–93, and *The War Lords*, ed. Field-Marshal Sir Michael Carver, Weidenfeld and Nicolson, 1976, pp. 23–43.
77. (p. 197) Ecclesiastes, vii, 15, 16.
78. (p. 197) Author's papers.
79. (p. 198) See Ludendorff, op. cit., ii, p. 761.
80. (p. 199) Wheeler-Bennett, op. cit., p. 170.
81. (p. 201) French ardour, as we have seen, was a variable quantity.
82. (p. 201) Among other things that the Americans had to contend with were 70,000 cases of influenza, with an overall death rate for the Expeditionary Force of 32 per cent.
83. (p. 201) Foch, op. cit., pp. 504–8.
84. (p. 202) Raymond Recouly, *Foch, Le Vainqueur de la Guerre*, English trans., T. Fisher Unwin, 1920, pp. 35–41.
85. (p. 204) Lieut.-Gen. Sir John Glubb, *Into Battle: A Soldier's Diary of the Great War*, Cassell, 1978, pp. 210, 217.
86. (p. 206) Falls, op. cit., p. 289.
87. (p. 207) Author's papers.

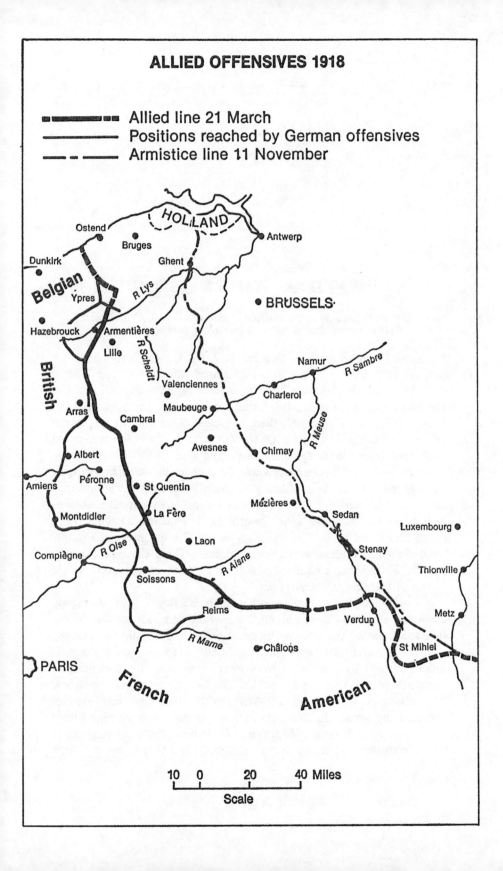

ALLIED OFFENSIVES 1918

Allied line 21 March
Positions reached by German offensives
Armistice line 11 November

HOLLAND

Ostend
Bruges
Antwerp
Dunkirk
Ghent
Belgian
R Lys
Ypres
BRUSSELS
Hazebrouck
Armentières
Lille
British
R Scheldt
Namur
R Sambre
Valenciennes
Charleroi
Arras
Maubeuge
R Meuse
Cambrai
Avesnes
Chimay
Albert
Amiens
Péronne
St Quentin
Mézières
Montdidier
La Fère
Sedan
Luxembourg
Compiègne
R Oise
Laon
Stenay
Thionville
Soissons
R Aisne
Reims
Verdun
Metz
R Marne
Châlons
St Mihiel
PARIS
French
American

10   0   20   40 Miles
Scale

"WITH A WHITE FLAG"

"We shall have to cross the lines with a white flag." (General Gröner to Prince Max of Baden, 5 November 1918)

Ludendorff's successor was General Wilhelm Gröner, fifty-one years old. He was the son of a non-commissioned officer, and like Ludendorff he owed his career entirely to his own military capabilities. The two had always been rivals, but Ludendorff had held the advantage because, although a commoner, there had been officers in his family. So 1914 found Ludendorff in the Operations Branch of the Great General Staff, and Gröner in charge of railways. His work in this department—always a key post in Germany's war on two fronts—was brilliant; in 1916 he went to the War Ministry to co-ordinate Germany's industrial effort, and succeeded in doing what was considered impossible—winning trade union support for General Staff demands. October 1918 found him Chief of Staff of the Kiev Army Group, pursuing the tattered shreds of Ludendorff's imperial dreams. From there he came to Spa on 30 October to fulfil his destiny as "one of the great tragic figures of German military history."[1]

A few hours after Gröner, another figure bearing a load of tragedy arrived at Spa: the Kaiser himself. By now the demands for his abdication (and that of the Crown Prince as well) had become vociferous: the majority of Social Democrats would still have supported a constitutional monarchy headed by the Kaiser's grandson; the Independent Socialists were demanding a republic. The Government was undecided, but that alone was enough for Wilhelm II, who now saw enemies behind every arras. He told Admiral von Hintze, now Foreign Office representative at Supreme Headquarters: "Prince Max's Government is trying to throw me out. At Berlin I should be less able to oppose them than in the midst of my generals." So "Spa became both the military and dynastic storm centre."[2]

While the storm outside swelled to its climax the men in the Empire's last citadel became more and more isolated, the Kaiser out of touch with his ministers, the army leaders out of touch with their men. Hindenburg and the senior officers, brought up in a strong monarchist tradition, supported the Kaiser to whom they were pledged. To the end, Hindenburg addressed his monarch as "Most Gracious Kaiser, King, and Lord." Men of the next generation (like Ludendorff and Gröner, who is sometimes referred to as "a South German democrat"[3]), had less fervent sentiments. As for the troops themselves, quite apart from their obviously diminishing tenacity in the face of attack, they were making their feelings plain. On 30 October the *18th Landwehr Division* refused to go into the trenches in Lorraine (a quiet sector), and other divisions showed similar signs of disaffection. On 2 November reinforcements for the *Seventeenth Army* from the Eastern Front mutinied and had to be disarmed; the Chief of Staff of that army stated that it would not stand another attack.[4] Behind the whole front roamed thousands of deserters and marauders. Field commanders were well aware of all this, but at Spa the bitter truth had not yet penetrated.

Yet the unmistakable signs were multiplying: at a meeting of the Imperial War Cabinet on 31 October four members said they considered the Kaiser's abdication both desirable and inevitable; two others agreed, but thought that it should be left to the victorious Allies to bring it about. The question was, who was going to put it to Wilhelm II that he should give up his throne? Various members of the Imperial family were approached; all refused. Prince Max, at this critical juncture, fell victim to influenza, and went into a coma for three days. Finally it fell to the Prussian Minister of the Interior, Dr. Wilhelm Drews, to try to persuade his King-Emperor that he must go, and go quickly, if the Empire itself was to be saved. The Kaiser's account of their meeting on 1 November[5] reveals both how distressing such a task inevitably was, and how far detached from reality Wilhelm still remained:

I said, "How comes it that you, a Prussian official, one of my subjects who have taken an oath of allegiance to me, have the insolence and effrontery to appear before me with a request like this?" You should just have seen how that took the wind out of his sails. It was the last thing he expected, he made a deep bow on the spot. "Very well then, supposing I did," I said. "What do you suppose would happen next, you, an administrative official? My sons have assured me that none of them

will take my place. So the whole House of H would go along with me."
You should have seen the fright that gave him, it again was the last
thing he'd expected. He and the whole of that smart govt. in Berlin.
"And who would then take on the regency for a twelve-year-old child,
my grandson? the Imperial Chancellor perhaps? I gather from Munich
that they haven't the least intention of recognizing him down there. So
what would happen?" "Chaos," he said, making another bow. You see,
you only have to question such muddle-heads, and go on questioning
them, for all their confusion and empty-headedness to become obvious.
"All right then," I said, "let me tell you the form chaos would take. I abdicate. All the dynasties fall along with me, the army is left leaderless,
the front-line troops disband and stream over the Rhine. The disaffected
gang up together, hang, murder and plunder—assisted by the enemy.
That is why I have no intention of abdicating. The King of Prussia cannot betray Germany, etc. I have no intention of quitting the throne because of a few hundred Jews and a thousand workmen. Tell that to
your masters in Berlin!"

Having thus settled the dynastic question and crushed the revolution
—in words—Wilhelm II called in Hindenburg and Gröner:

Hindenburg told him the same thing bluntly and then Gröner who is a
Swabian, in other words a South German, a jolly little chap, he went
for Drews like a wildcat, he fairly gave it to him. . . . Now I may have
ruled well or badly, that's not the point at the moment, most of it was
of course bad! But I have lived for sixty years and spent thirty of them
on the throne. There is one thing you must allow me, experience! Who
is to take my place? The famous Max of Baden?[6]

That was 1 November, a day of total unreality at Spa, at the front
the day of Foch's next blows. In the Argonne the American First and
French Fourth Armies resumed their offensive, with mixed success.
The American V Corps pressed its advance five miles deep into the
German position, drawing its neighbours along with it; the French, at
first actually forced back, were then able to resume their own advance.
Fighting continued on the following days, as usual against stiffening resistance. On Haig's front the First and Third Armies launched what
was to be called the Battle of Valenciennes, taking its name from the
frontier city which was captured by the Canadians on 2 November.
These first two days of the month were disastrous for the Germans: at
Valenciennes the Canadians alone took 1,800 prisoners and counted
more than 800 German dead, their own losses being eighty killed and
about 300 wounded. As their history says, "Careful coordination in
employing a tremendous weight of artillery in very close support of
minimum numbers of infantry had achieved victory at a very low

cost."[7] Another reason for the large proportion of German dead is indicated in General Currie's diary: "I know that it was not the intention of our fellows to take many German prisoners as, since they have lived amongst and talked to the French people here, they have become more bitter than ever against the Boche."

Haig lost no time in pressing his advantage. Scarcely was the Battle of Valenciennes safely niched in history than the Battle of the Sambre began—on 4 November. On the day before an officer of the 37th Division records a visit from a new brigadier: " 'Look here, you fellows.' He sat down and we listened to a quite incredible promise. 'The division will attack in three days' time, right into the Mormal Forest, and we are promised from above that it is the last attack we shall ever be asked to make.' We looked at him stupidly. He was quite serious. Then solemnly we all had a drink."[8]

Others were also hearing and seeing incredible things. "The enemy has melted away before us like snow," recorded one officer on 4 November.[9] A sentry of the 1/Queen's Westminster Rifles in the 56th Division actually watched a small section of this "thaw." He saw a mounted German ride up to a hedge and hand a paper to someone on the ground; he appeared to receive back an envelope, and then rode off; a few moments later a German machine-gun party left the hedge. The Westminster Rifles and their neighbours, the Kensingtons, at once pushed forward, and shortly a patrol of the Q.W.R. entered the village of Saultain:

> . . . great was their astonishment, as they moved down the main street in patrol formation, to see doors and windows flung open and to be greeted, not by the harried but ferocious enemy, but by the civilian population. The latter were hysterical with joy at the arrival of British troops so close on the heels of the enemy who, they said, had gone half an hour earlier. . . . French and Belgian flags were produced in a most miraculous fashion, and the town was soon wild with excitement, no one paying any attention to the German "heavies" which now commenced to fall among the houses.[10]

The miracle of the flags was widely noted. No doubt many of them owed their timely appearance to the patriotism and patience of the people who had hidden or made them during more than four years of enemy occupation. Others came from a different source, one which, as Sir Frederick Maurice says, well illustrates the curiosities of the German character:

> At the last moment before they retired they brought into many of the principal towns wagon-loads of the flags of the Allies, which included

one peculiarly German invention—a composite banner made up of the colours of their chief enemies—and hawked them round for sale to the inhabitants in order that they might decorate their houses fitly for the welcome of the incoming troops. It is out of the question that this traffic in their shame can have taken place without the assistance of the German authorities, who were not too proud to allow money to be made out of their defeat, but pretended shortly afterwards that they were too proud to acknowledge themselves beaten.[11]

"Armistice" was now the word on every man's lips. On 30 October Turkey signed an armistice with the Allied powers; on 3 November it was the turn of Austria-Hungary. The Allied Supreme War Council then applied itself to the finalization of terms for Germany; the French, Italian and British Governments drew up a note for President Wilson: "A protracted and somewhat lively discussion took place as to whether we should accompany this note by any statement making it clear that we should not consider ourselves bound to adhere to the letter of the President's Fourteen Points in the subsequent framing of peace terms."[12] Once more the fatal delay in considering the kind of peace that was wanted made itself felt. As Churchill says: "When it became evident that the Central Powers were actually in dissolution and were stretching desperate hands towards the Fourteen Points these propositions suddenly acquired intense practical significance. It became imperative towards the end of October to make sure what the Fourteen Points meant and would be understood to mean by friend and foe."[13]

No such clarity existed. Pershing, on 30 October, had written to the Supreme War Council urging "unconditional surrender," whatever the President might say. Even Haig was now advising Lloyd George "to insist on strong Naval terms from the enemy because our existence depends on 'Sea Supremacy'"—with which the Admiralty cordially agreed, and the Government accepted their view. When he saw them, the "Tiger" Clemenceau himself remarked that the naval terms "had left the breeches of the Emperor and nothing else!" Furthermore, in this moment of truth, the British Government realized that President Wilson's doctrine of freedom of the seas in wartime was quite unacceptable. Whereupon Clemenceau produced "an elaborate memorandum criticising the Fourteen Points in detail, which he wanted to send to Washington, and Sonnino had a memorandum on the subject of Italian frontiers"[14] (a matter which, it was pointed out to him, had nothing to do with Germany). If, says Churchill, the Germans had been able to fight on, "the interpretation placed upon the Fourteen Points by them and by each of the allies might have been reduced to an exact and concrete form. But their collapse was so rapid that . . .

[it] left the victors sole judges of the interpretation which should be placed upon the Fourteen Points, while the vanquished naturally construed them in their most hopeful and generous sense."[15]

The fourth of November was late in the day to be considering such matters; there was clearly no time to lose, yet the dangers of too much speed were never greater. The Allied leaders were assisted in their "lively discussion" by President Wilson's representative, Colonel House, whose chief concern would appear to have been that Allied unity should be achieved with the least possible delay. In this cause he supplied an "interpretation" of the Fourteen Points which, according to Harold Nicolson, either gave to each Point a gloss in flat contradiction of what it actually said (e.g. "The expression 'open covenants' was not to be interpreted as precluding confidential diplomatic negotiation. By the Freedom of the Seas the President had not intended to abolish the weapon of blockade . . . ," etc., etc.)[16] or virtually robbed it of meaning altogether. Fortified by this glossary, the Allies soon agreed on a memorandum to be sent to the President for his guidance in replying to the German Note of 27 October. They accepted the Fourteen Points "and the principles of settlement enunciated in his subsequent addresses" (subject to the glossary) as the basis of peace terms, barring only a reservation on freedom of the seas, and a fresh piece of "interpretation" of their own:

> Further, in the conditions of peace laid down in his Address to Congress of the 8th January, 1918, the President declared that the invaded territories must be restored as well as evacuated and freed, and the Allied Governments feel that no doubt ought to be allowed to exist as to what this provision implies. By it they understand that compensation will be made by Germany for all damage done to the civilian population of the Allies and their property by the aggression of Germany by land, by sea, and from the air.

From this brief paragraph would spring both the famous "War Guilt" clause of the Treaty of Versailles which so much inflamed postwar German opinion, and the reparations question which bedevilled postwar economics. A little more time for consideration would certainly have helped. Lloyd George considered the armistice terms to be "very drastic" and asked Foch whether he thought the Germans would sign. "He said he did not, but in any case he would be able to overpower the Germans by Christmas."[17]

There was no need to worry. On this day (Monday, 4 November) the Germans were again in retreat along the whole front of the American First Army and part of that of the French Fourth. But the final blow came in the north, on the Sambre, where the British Fourth and

Third Armies struck again, with the French First Army supporting on
the right and the British First Army on the left. The Fourth Army,
fighting now on the historic fields of August 1914, captured over 4,000
prisoners and eighty guns; the Third Army did even better, the main
feature of the day being the storming of Le Quesnoy by the New
Zealand Division. The old walled town of Le Quesnoy, whose cannon
had fired on the English army in the Creçy campaign of 1346, and
where the Duke of Marlborough had ended his last campaign in 1711,
was still a formidable obstacle to open warfare. Although surrounded,
the German garrison refused to surrender. The New Zealanders scaled
the outer ramparts with ladders in the manner of mediaeval warfare,
and in the same style parleyed with the German commandant. A determined soldier, he still continued to resist, though his men were less en-
thusiastic. Under cover of their artillery the New Zealanders then
scaled the inner walls and fought their way into the streets, whereupon
the Germans at last gave in. The whole thing, says one history, "was
like an episode of the age of Agincourt interpolated in the scientific,
mechanical, chemical warfare of the twentieth century."[18] The New
Zealand Division captured nearly 2,500 prisoners and over 100 guns.
The total for the three British armies engaged between 1 November
and 4 November was 19,000 prisoners and over 450 guns, with another 5,000 prisoners and more guns taken by the French First Army.
Wheeler-Bennett says: "The German rearguards were thrown into
complete confusion and could not recover themselves. From then on
the German army, in the opinion of its opponents, was incapable either
of accepting or refusing battle."

Certainly from this point events seem to cascade upon each other
through a crowded week. The next day (Tuesday) Gröner was in
Berlin; he had been touring the higher commands, and the picture he
had formed was bleak, though not yet disastrous. He told the Imperial
War Cabinet: "We can hold out long enough for negotiations. If we
are lucky the time might be longer; if we are unlucky, shorter. . . ."[19]
At this stage he was chiefly afraid of an American advance north of
Verdun, but as the bad news came in from the Sambre front he then
changed his mind. At home the news was even worse. Ordered to make
a "death or glory" sortie from its bases into the North Sea, to seek one
last battle with the British Grand Fleet, the German battleship crews
refused, and mutiny quickly spread through the Imperial Navy. On 4
November soldiers sent to Kiel to suppress this outbreak fraternized
with the mutineers. By that Tuesday red flags were flying over Kiel. It
was now, under the impact of those double blows, that Gröner bluntly
told the Chancellor: "We shall have to cross the lines with a white
flag." When asked if he could hold out for another week, he replied:

"No; even Monday will be too late; it must be Saturday at latest. . . ."

Gröner was coming face to face with his tragedy; he was not yet ready to recognize its full extent. Prince Max now said that it was the Kaiser's refusal to abdicate that prevented Germany from obtaining favourable terms; would Gröner try to persuade him? "I am utterly devoted to the cause of the Emperor," Gröner replied. A minister suggested that perhaps Hindenburg might do it; this made Gröner angry. He shouted: "The Field-Marshal would consider himself the lowest kind of scoundrel if he abandoned the Emperor, and so, gentlemen, would I and every honourable soldier. If the attacks against the Emperor continue, the fate of the army is sealed; it will break in pieces, and if that happens the wild beast will break out in the bands of irregular soldiery pouring back into Germany."[20] But later that day he met Philipp Scheidemann, Friedrich Ebert and trade union leaders whom he had known in his War Ministry days. These were men with whom he was on friendly terms, and who trusted him; they were also constitutional monarchists (despite their socialism), and all were convinced that the only way of saving the monarchy was a regency until the coming of age of one of the young princes. Gröner again refused to take any initiative towards the Kaiser's abdication, but the cumulative effect of what the Cabinet had said and what the Socialist leaders had repeated was clearly considerable. His own belief was that Wilhelm II, as Germany's War Lord, should seek death among his soldiers at the front. He had already said as much to Hindenburg and members of the Kaiser's suite at Spa:

> He should go to the front, not to review troops or to confer decorations, but to look for death. He should go to some trench which is under the full blast of war. If he were killed it would be the finest death possible. If he were wounded the feelings of the German people would completely change towards him. The two Court Generals were horrified at the idea, and Hindenburg disapproved of allowing the Emperor to run such risks, but there can be no doubt that Gröner's reasoning was both patriotic and practical.[21]

That afternoon Gröner returned to Spa, where he reported to the Kaiser and the Field-Marshal in the gloomiest terms, quite different from the mood he had shown only five days earlier in front of Drews. That same evening President Wilson's final reply to Germany was received in Berlin. The Allies, it said, were willing to make peace on the basis of the Fourteen Points, with the reservations indicated by the European powers on the 4th. It concluded: "Marshal Foch has been authorized by the Government of the United States and the Allied Governments to receive properly accredited representatives of the German Government and to communicate to them the terms of an armistice."

The names of these "accredited representatives" had already been decided before Gröner left Berlin: the German Armistice Commission would be headed by Matthias Erzberger, a Centre Party deputy and Minister without Portfolio; General von Gündell would represent the Supreme Command, Count Oberndorff the Foreign Ministry, Captain Vanselow the Navy, with Major-General von Winterfeldt, who spoke perfect French. They lost no time; the next morning (Thursday) they were at Spa. Erzberger disliked his task very much indeed, and said so. Hindenburg, "with tears in his eyes and clasping Erzberger's hand between both his own,"[22] persuaded him to carry out his terrible duty. At the same time the Supreme Command deftly extracted General von Gündell from the Commission, so that the whole armistice negotiation would have the air of being political, not military. The Commission left Spa at noon, but such was the confusion and congestion on the roads behind the German front that it did not actually cross the lines until nine o'clock that night.

The experience of this journey and the sights they witnessed during it profoundly affected the German delegation. This was not surprising, because nothing so vividly reveals the condition of an army as the state of its lines of communication. Between the front line and the Rhine was all the evidence of decisive defeat, as the advancing Allies were discovering day by day:

> Every road was littered with broken-down motor trucks, guns, machine-guns and trench mortars. Great stacks of supplies and military stores of all kinds were abandoned. Every railway line was blocked with loaded trucks which the Germans had been unable to remove. The sixty miles of railway in the valley of the Meuse between Dinant and Mézières was filled from end to end with a continuous line of German freight trains carrying guns, ammunition, engineering equipment, and other paraphernalia. On the Belgian canals alone over eight hundred fully charged military barges were found.[23]

A division of the *Seventeenth Army* reported on 8 November:

> The division can only be considered as unfit for battle. Owing to the extremely heavy casualties, to sickness and to numerous desertions, the average strength of the regiments is under 600.[24] Still more important as regards efficiency in battle is the shortage of officers, of which no regiment of the division has more than twelve, and one regiment has only nine. Almost all the machine guns in the division have been lost or

'. . . the untouched soil of the richest agricultural land in Europe': the landscape in the region of the Sambre-et-Oise Canal, where the Fourth Army fought some of the last actions of the war

Men of destiny. *Left:* 'The Third Army's achievement was even better than it looked': General Sir Julian Byng, commanding the Third Army, which kept pace alongside the Fourth in the forefront of the Allied offensives. *Right:* Major-General Sir Andrew Russell, commanding the New Zealand Division (second from left) with staff officers

'... the New Zealand Division, whose standard of excellence matched that of its successor'; in both World Wars, New Zealanders achieved the highest military reputation. A rigorous kit inspection is here taking place

'Never at any time in history has the British Army achieved greater results . . .': some of the 188,700 prisoners taken by the British in the 'Hundred Days' of 1918

'Superficially a logical composition . . .':
Vice-Admiral Sir Rosslyn Wemyss, First
Sea Lord (centre), Head of the British
Delegation, with naval officers, Marshal
Foch, Head of the Allied Delegation, with
French Army officers

'. ... Armistice talks began in the office-car
of Foch's train': the railway carriage in the
Compiègne Forest where the Armistice was
signed. The original carriage was removed
by the Germans in the Second World War,
and subsequently destroyed

'Armistice Night: Amiens': Sir William Orpen, Official War Artist, depicts the scene in what had been for four years one of the war's front-line towns

are out of repair, and half the guns of the artillery are deficient. Owing to lack of horses, less than half the transport of the division can be moved. The division has not received rations for two days, and the condition of the horses which remain is becoming very bad, because owing to constant movement there is no time to collect supplies from the country, and forage for them is not arriving.[25]

Such was the state of affairs in the Army's immediate rear; further back, in Germany herself, it was far worse. It was on this Thursday, while the Armistice Commission was making its way towards the French lines, that revolution broke out. The naval mutiny spread to Hamburg and Bremen; soviets were proclaimed in Friedrichshafen, Stuttgart, Frankfurt, Hannover, Cologne, Düsseldorf, Leipzig, Magdeburg. In Munich a Bavarian Republic was declared, and the House of Wittelsbach which had ruled for over 700 years was ignominiously deposed. Next day would be the turn of the Wettins in Saxony; for the Hohenzollerns the writing was on the wall and clear to read.

News of all this came to Spa like news from another planet. In the afternoon of 7 November Prince Max telephoned. He had received an ultimatum from the Social Democratic leaders; they could no longer restrain their rank and file, who threatened to go over to the Independents and the Spartacists if the Kaiser and the Crown Prince did not immediately depart. Ebert had told the Chancellor: "A revolutionary gesture is necessary to forestall the revolution." Prince Max wished to resign, but even in this extremity was able to suggest a face-saving compromise for the Kaiser—he should announce his intention of abdicating as soon as the armistice was signed, whereupon elections to a National Constituent Assembly could be held. Prince Max urged Admiral von Hintze to press this course upon the Kaiser; the Admiral asked Hindenburg and Gröner to accompany him to the Château de la Fraineuse. Both refused, Hindenburg vehemently, Gröner less so, but firmly. So von Hintze went alone—and received from Wilhelm II another flat refusal, as though nothing was rotten in the state of the Empire, as though all the day's tidings were a breeze that would blow itself out before morning.

When morning came, Friday, 8 November, the Kaiser was dreaming still; he now announced that he would restore order in the Fatherland at the head of his Army, and told Gröner to prepare the appropriate plans. But Gröner knew already that this was out of the question. In Germany the soldiers were fraternizing with the revolutionaries; the field army would certainly not march against them. In any case, its supplies would only last for three or four days if it was severed from its home bases. He explained this to Hindenburg in remorseless detail;

when the Kaiser's elderly Adjutant-General, von Plessen, arrived to collect the plan of counter-revolution, Gröner explained it all again, and Hindenburg had to support him. Von Plessen departed sobbing; this was the end of the dream.

That evening Gröner and Hindenburg were agreed: the Kaiser must abdicate. The Crown Prince could not succeed, but there was no question of their leaving the country. In Gröner's eyes this would only discredit the monarchy, which he still sought to serve. During the night he received a telephone call from the Vice-Chancellor in Berlin, urging Wilhelm II's immediate abdication and flight. Gröner would not agree —but now it was Hindenburg who outpaced him. The agent of this transformation was von Hintze, who put it to the Field-Marshal that the Kaiser's personal safety was now at stake. The vision of Ekaterinburg was in both their minds; the sense of being surrounded by the forces of darkness was strong upon them. Hindenburg passed a sleepless night contemplating alternatives which seemed each more horrible than the last. Strangely enough, it did not occur to him in this miserable wakefulness to tell either Gröner or the Kaiser of his change of mind.

If 8 November was a dismal day at Spa, it was no less so for the Armistice Commission. At seven o'clock that morning their train arrived at the siding in the Forest of Compiègne (constructed for a massive railway gun) near to that which already held Marshal Foch's carriages. Foch was accompanied by Weygand with three staff officers, and by Vice-Admiral Sir Rosslyn Wemyss, the First Sea Lord, with Admiral Hope and Captain Mariott of the Royal Navy. Superficially, this might seem to be a logical composition for the Allied delegation: representatives of the largest army and the largest navy.[26] In fact, however, the logic was spurious. As Haig had remarked (see p. 191), the naval terms could only be enforced by the armies; no other Allied representative was therefore needed than the Generalissimo of those armies, though as a matter of inter-Allied courtesy and solidarity he could have been accompanied by *observers* from each of the other four powers actually fighting the Germans. Alternatively, once the Germans had made their request, two armistice discussions might have taken place simultaneously, one for land forces, headed by Foch with four soldier-observers, the other by Wemyss with observers from the French and American navies. This confusion about the very mechanics of concluding hostilities was matched by the much deeper confusion over the approach to peace itself, and presaged the even worse confusion which accompanied the entire business of peace-making. And it may be added that, if it was considered that Foch needed some associate on this momentous occasion, that individual should by right have been the commander of the army which had done most to bring the occasion about—Sir Douglas Haig.

Logical or otherwise, the armistice talks began at nine o'clock in the office-car of Foch's train. It is said that General von Winterfeldt thought it appropriate to wear the Légion d'Honneur which had been conferred on him before the war by the French. Observing it, Foch acidly told him: "You have my permission not to wear that." The two delegations then took their places at the conference table. Foch's report to Poincaré and Clemenceau describes what ensued:

Marshal Foch asked the German delegates the purpose of their visit.

Herr Erzberger replied that the German delegation had come to receive the proposals of the Allied Powers looking to an armistice on land, on sea and in the air, on all the fronts, and in the colonies.

Marshal Foch replied that he had no proposals to make.

Count Oberndorff asked the Marshal in what form he desired that they should express themselves. He did not stand on form; he was ready to say that the German delegation asked the conditions of the armistice.

Marshal Foch replied that he had no conditions to offer.

Herr Erzberger read the text of President Wilson's last note, stating that Marshal Foch is authorized to make known the armistice conditions.

Marshal Foch replied that he was authorized to make these known if the German delegates asked for an armistice.

"Do you ask for an armistice? If you do, I can inform you of the conditions subject to which it can be obtained."

Herr Erzberger and Count Oberndorff declared that they asked for an armistice.

Marshal Foch then announced that the armistice conditions would be read. . . .[27]

With this preliminary bout of psychological warfare concluded, Weygand read out the principal clauses of the armistice. Erzberger then asked for an immediate suspension of hostilities. He described the disorganization and the breakdown of discipline in the German Army and the revolutionary situation in Germany herself; he feared that Bolshevism on the Russian model was taking hold, "and once Central Europe was invaded by this scourge, Western Europe, he said, would find the greatest difficulty in escaping it." Foch was unimpressed. He replied:

At the moment when negotiations for the signing of an armistice are just being opened, it is impossible to stop military operations, until the German delegation has accepted and signed the conditions which are the very consequence of those operations. As for the situation described by Herr Erzberger as existing among the German troops and the danger

he fears of Bolshevism spreading in Germany, the one is the usual disease prevailing in beaten armies, the other is symptomatic of a nation
completely worn out by war. Western Europe will find means of
defending itself against this danger.

General von Winterfeldt then read a statement. The armistice terms
had just been presented; they would require a certain amount of time
for consideration, and consultation with the German Government and
the Supreme Command. "During this time the struggle between our
Armies will continue and it will result, both among soldiers and civilians, in numerous victims who will die in vain at the last minute, and
who might be preserved for their families." For this added reason, he,
too, asked for hostilities to be suspended. Foch replied that he also
was anxious to bring the fighting to an end and would do all he could
to help—"but hostilities cannot cease before the signing of the Armistice." The Germans then asked for a 24-hour extension of the time-
limit for a reply. This also he refused. The German delegation then referred the full text of the Allied demands back to the Government by
courier, asking for final instructions. The courier left at 1 P.M.

During the afternoon there were exploratory and explanatory conversations between Weygand, Count Oberndorff and General von Winterfeldt, and between Admiral Hope, R.N., and Captain Vanselow:

> Count Oberndorff first asked whether the Allies had drawn up such se-
> vere terms with the object of having Germany refuse them.
> The answer was that the Allies were making known the conditions
> under which they would grant an armistice, and there was nothing hid-
> den in their intentions.
> Count Oberndorff then asked whether the Allies did not intend to
> cause the armistice to fail in order to proceed immediately with peace
> negotiations.
> The answer was that Marshal Foch had come here to negotiate—and
> he wished to negotiate—nothing except the conditions governing an ar-
> mistice.

The Germans at Compiègne were coming face to face with the brutal
truth of abject defeat, as the Russians and Rumanians had done earlier
in the year; very soon the same truth would penetrate to Spa and to
Berlin. The German delegation put forward every mitigating argument
it could think of. It dwelt on the exhaustion and paralysis of the Army
—"Even should it so desire, the German Army would be incapable of
recommencing the fight, once the Armistice was signed. Hence there
was no point in imposing too severe terms." They made no protest
against the military clauses, except the surrender of 30,000 machine-

guns: "If this were done there would not be enough left to fire on the German people, should this become necessary." They harped on the threat of Bolshevism: "It was to the advantage of everybody that the German Army should march back to Germany in orderly fashion. To do this the time-limit fixed for the evacuation must be extended." Germany, they said, was threatened by famine: "The Armistice clauses touching blockade and railway material were inhuman, because they would paralyse the work of feeding the population and would cause the death of women and children." To all of this Weygand simply replied: "The state of disorganization in the German Army was the result of the victorious advance of the Allied Armies during the last four months. It was the duty of the Allied High Command to secure by the terms of the Armistice, as a minimum, the continued possession of all the advantages won."

The ninth of November passed in the railway carriages amid discussions which added nothing to what had already been said. Clemenceau, summarizing what Foch reported to him, told Lloyd George that the Germans "appeared much depressed. From time to time a sob escaped Winterfeldt. Under these conditions the signature of the Armistice does not appear doubtful. . . ." Events on the battle-front made this increasingly certain: the French First Army captured the important rail junction of Hirson, making matters even more difficult for the German centre armies; the two American Armies made important progress, the I and V Corps now holding the heights overlooking Sedan, scene of France's humiliation in 1870, after an advance of twenty-five miles since 1 November.[28] The French Fourth Army closed in on Mézières. On the British front, cavalry had to ride ten miles to catch up with the German rearguards; mobile columns of all arms were formed to press the pursuit to the Belgian frontier as fast as logistics permitted.

This Saturday, "the last day of Imperial Germany, dawned cold and gloomy. A thick blanket of fog enshrouded Spa, deadening all sound and seeming to form a barrier against the outside world."[29] But no barrier could now save the Empire's last citadel from the forces assailing it; the first news of the day was that the revolution had spread to Berlin, and that once again the garrison had joined the crowds milling in the streets. Hindenburg told Gröner of the decision he had reached during the night; the First Quartermaster-General was shocked. But his protests were overtaken by the accelerating tempo of events.

At 9 A.M. the Field-Marshal and Gröner attended a meeting of divisional, brigade and regimental commanders who had been called together in order to ascertain the state of the Army. Hindenburg summed up the situation; Gröner said nothing; there was total silence in the room. The two leaders then set off to an even more painful occasion, to inform the Kaiser at the Château de la Fraineuse; they sat side by side in complete silence once again.

With the Kaiser, when they arrived, were von Plessen, General von Marschall, head of his Military Cabinet, Admiral von Hintze, and General Count von Schulenburg, Chief of Staff of the Crown Prince's Army Group. The Kaiser asked Hindenburg for his report, but the old Field-Marshal was too overcome with emotion to reply; he could only beg leave to resign—which was, of course, refused—and leave the wretched business to Gröner. "Upon the shoulders of this lonely South German was laid the task of disillusioning the King of Prussia."[30] His cup of tragedy was filling by the hour. Quietly but inexorably he went through the situation again: the threat of civil war, the Army mutinous, unable to fight, without reserves. The implications were inescapable—by anyone except Wilhelm II and one or two purblind imperialists. Once such was Schulenburg, despite the fact that only the previous day twelve out of sixteen representatives of his Army Group had admitted that their troops could no longer be counted on. Now he challenged everything that Gröner had said, and asserted that in a few days it would be possible to gather a picked force of reliable men who could be sent against the mutineers. Plessen supported him. Gröner quietly replied that these ideas were impracticable and could only lead to further chaos.

Then it was the Kaiser's turn to speak. With what must to him have seemed vast magnanimity, he renounced the project of suppressing the revolution by civil war. "He would remain at Spa until an armistice had been signed, and then return home quietly at the head of his army." So now Gröner would have to spell it out with horrible clarity:

"Sire, you no longer have an army. The army will march home in peace and order under its leaders and commanding generals, but not under the command of Your Majesty, for it no longer stands behind Your Majesty."

The Emperor turned upon Gröner, his eyes blazing with anger.

"Excellency, I shall require that statement from you in black and white, signed by all my generals, that the army no longer stands behind its Commander-in-Chief. Have they not taken the military oath to me?"

"In circumstances like these, Sire, oaths are but words," replied Gröner sadly.

This was too much for Schulenburg. Forgetting the August Presence, he bellowed at Gröner at the top of his voice that neither the officers nor the soldiers would so disgrace themselves as to desert the Emperor and King in the face of the enemy.

"I have other information," was the cold reply.[31]

And Hindenburg was forced to agree. The meeting broke up at 11 A.M.

The rest of the morning passed in desultory fashion, walking in small groups in the chilly garden. The Crown Prince arrived; he had encountered some hostile demonstrations on the way, but had not lost hope. Wilhelm II now spoke of abdicating as Emperor, but not as King of Prussia, and Schulenburg supported this idea enthusiastically. Prussian officers and soldiers, he said, "would not tolerate the *débâcle* which would follow the disappearance of their King." Von Hintze, however, went straight to the point with the question: "Will they fight for their King against the people?" Gröner remarked to Hindenburg: "A fortnight ago such a solution might have been salutary, but it is too late now."

It was at this stage that the results of the conference of officers which Hindenburg had addressed earlier that morning arrived. There were thirty-nine officers present. Two questions had been put to them:

(1) Would it be possible for the Emperor to regain control of Germany by force of arms, at the head of his troops?

Twenty-three said "no," one said "yes," fifteen were doubtful.

(2) Would the troops march against the Bolshevists in Germany?

Nineteen said "no," eight said "yes," twelve were doubtful. The chairman of the conference told the Kaiser: "At the present moment the troops will not march against Germany, even with Your Majesty at their head. They will not march against Bolshevism. They want one thing only, an armistice at the earliest possible moment. Every hour gained is of importance."

When Wilhelm II asked whether the Army would return to Germany in good order without him, the answer was: "It is only under the command of its generals that the army will return in good order to the Fatherland. . . . If Your Majesty wishes to march with them . . . the troops will be delighted, but the army will fight no more, either at home or abroad." Von Hintze remarked with some bitterness: "His Majesty has no need of an army in order to take a walk. What he needs is an army that will fight for him." He was then called to the telephone. It was Prince Max reporting a situation which had become so dangerous that Wilhelm absolutely *must* abdicate at once. With haggard looks the Kaiser gave his decision: he would abdicate as Emperor, but not as King of Prussia; he would resign his command-in-chief of the Army to Hindenburg; he would remain with the Prussian troops. And with that the dejected assembly went in to lunch.

Before anyone could digest this unhappy meal, news came in which swept all Wilhelm II's ideas into limbo, making nonsense of all formulae and compromise. The revolution in Berlin had reached its climax. In a vain effort to stave it off at the twelfth hour, Prince Max had announced the abdication of the Kaiser and the Crown Prince. "Treason, gentlemen! Barefaced, outrageous treason!" Wilhelm stormed, and the incorrigible Schulenburg said: "Your Majesty must not yield to such an act of violence!" Wilhelm acted characteristically. He reached "not for his sword, but for the weapon he used more often and more disastrously than any other monarch—the telegraph form. Reprimands, reproaches, denials and orders sped ineffectually along the wires to Berlin and Potsdam; nothing happened."[32]

In Berlin, however, plenty was happening. The Spartacists seized the Imperial Palace; from the balcony where Wilhelm II had appeared to address his people or review his troops, a red blanket hung by way of revolutionary bunting, and Karl Liebknecht, Germany's most notorious agitator, proclaimed a soviet. It was a year and two days since the Bolsheviks had stormed the Winter Palace in Petrograd, a year and a day since Lenin and Trotsky had replaced the Provisional Government; the echoes were loud, the example clear. Only the Social Democrats could avert it. Scheidemann, acting with a decision which Kerensky in Russia had been unable to match, proclaimed a Socialist Republic from the steps of the Reichstag. This was an appropriate locale, for it was the Reichstag which would have to become the citadel of the new legitimacy, if there was to be such a thing. The consequences of Scheidemann's deed followed swiftly: Prince Max resigned and Friedrich Ebert, the ex-saddler, briefly became the last Chancellor of Imperial Germany, then soon afterwards the first President of the German Republic. Wilhelm II was no longer a relevant political factor; history had passed him by. All that remained was to dispose of him quietly. This time it was Hindenburg who had to tell him: "I cannot accept the responsibility of seeing the Emperor haled to Berlin by insurgent troops and delivered over as a prisoner to the Revolutionary Government. I must advise Your Majesty to abdicate and to proceed to Holland."

And this time even Wilhelm II could not refuse. He left Spa at five o'clock the next morning; at seven o'clock he and his small suite reached the Dutch-Belgian frontier. There was no one to meet him. While he waited for Dutch officials to arrive, church bells called Catholics to early Mass in a land at peace.

The only obstacle now to peace for all of Europe was the pace of communication. Except in patches, fighting had virtually died away on the battle-fronts; in most places it was a problem even to keep in touch with the retreating Germans. One patch of action was around Mons, where that Sunday the Canadians were closing in on the town which had been the scene of the first British battle of the war. Amid the canals and the slag-heaps of the mining villages round Mons the Germans put up their last serious rearguard action. Machine-guns made a daylight attack a costly enterprise; the Canadians were content to wait for darkness, when the Royal Canadian Regiment and the 42nd Battalion began to clear the town. A company of the German *62nd Regiment* was the last to leave, shortly before dawn.

The centre of decision was again Spa, and the man shouldering the burden of decision was Gröner. There were two that he had to take, closely linked, both vital. The first concerned the Allied armistice terms, which had arrived on the 9th, and which he studied with close attention that night while Hindenburg slept the sleep of emotional exhaustion and the Kaiser made his preparations for exile. Should the High Command accept these terms or not? The second decision concerned the High Command and the Republic; should the Army support the Republic, or oppose it? The answer to the first of these questions was only difficult to arrive at to the extent that it was utterly repugnant. Gröner, better than anyone, knew that Germany *must* accept the Allied terms. He knew they spelt unconditional surrender; as an able professional soldier, he hated it, his gorge rose at it, but as a man of sense he knew it had to be done. But what of the Government? Did he have to accept that, too?

Fortunately, Gröner had his previous knowledge of Germany's new leaders to guide him. He knew that Ebert was a patriot, he knew that the new chancellor would not willingly attack the Army, and he also knew that with the Army's backing Ebert would probably be able both to resist Bolshevism and to maintain order while the odious armistice terms were being fulfilled. So the answer to one question was really the answer to the other: accepting the armistice meant accepting the Government. There was no other way. Gröner picked up the telephone and spoke to Ebert in Berlin.

Was he willing to protect Germany from anarchy and to restore law and order? the First Quartermaster-General wanted to know. Yes, he was, said Ebert. "Then the High Command will maintain discipline in the army and bring it safely home," Gröner replied.

But the Chancellor wanted guarantees. What was the attitude of the High Command towards the Workers' and Soldiers' Councils? Orders had been given to deal with them in a friendly spirit, was the reply. "What do you expect from us?" asked the Chancellor. "The High Command expects the Government to co-operate with the Officers' Corps in the suppression of Bolshevism, and in the maintenance of discipline in the army. It also asks that the provisioning of the army shall be ensured and all disturbance of transport communication prevented."

Ebert had one more question:

"Will the Field-Marshal retain the Command?"

Gröner hesitated a moment, then in a confident voice he answered: "Yes, the Field-Marshall will retain the Command."

"Convey to the Field-Marshal the thanks of the Government," was Ebert's reply.[33]

Gröner's confidence was justified; Hindenburg, despite his age, despite his lifelong loyalties, did not demur. His sense of duty to the Fatherland, now that his Kaiser had gone, told him what he had to do, and he did it. It was an historic moment, "his greatest and most noble deed. . . . For this act many deeds less noble may be forgiven him."[34]

And now the scene shifts once more to the Forest of Compiègne. As the day wore on, without any communication from either the German Government or the Supreme Command, Foch became somewhat restive, and at 6:30 that evening he reminded the German delegation that they only had until 11 A.M. the next day to make a response. They replied that they were pressing their government, and, sure enough, between seven and eight o'clock that evening messages began to come in. The first simply said:

> The German Government to the plenipotentiaries at Headquarters of the Allied High Command:
> The German Government accepts the conditions of the Armistice communicated to it on November 8th.
>   The Chancellor of the Empire—3,084.

"3,084" was a code number, confirming the authenticity of the message. Shortly afterwards it was followed by another:

> The German Supreme Command to the plenipotentiaries at Headquarters of the Allied High Command:
> The Government of the Empire transmits to the High Command the following for Under-Secretary of State Erzberger:
> Your Excellency is authorized to sign the Armistice. You will please, at the same time, have inserted in the record the following:
> The German Government will do all in its power to fulfil the terms agreed upon. However, the undersigned deems it his duty to point out that the execution of some of the conditions will bring famine to the population of that part of the German Empire which is not to be occupied.
> If all the provisions which had been accumulated for feeding the troops are left in the regions to be evacuated, and if the limitation (equivalent to complete suppression) of our means of transportation is maintained and the blockade continued, to feed the population and organize a food service will be impossible.

The undersigned requests, therefore, to be authorized to negotiate with a view to modifying certain points, in order that supplies may be assured.

(signed) The Chancellor of the Empire.

PS. The Supreme Command likewise draws attention to the points transmitted at noon today to General von Winterfeldt. Advise by wireless when the Armistice is signed.

Relaying these messages to Lloyd George, Clemenceau said: "My personal view is that we must honour this signature while making a marginal note relative to revictualling, which we cannot to my mind refuse to discuss ultimately." Another lengthy telegram from the Supreme Command came in about nine o'clock. This had to be deciphered and the response of the Allies considered before the definitive text of an armistice could be drawn up and signed. The German delegates, says Foch, "were requested to state as soon as possible the hour at which this plenary session could be held, so that bloodshed might be stopped as soon as possible, now that the signing of the Armistice had been agreed upon."

And so the last day came, Monday, 11 November 1918: the 1,568th day of the war. At five minutes past two that morning the German delegation signified its readiness to sign the armistice, and ten minutes later the final session began. Foch stated that the definitive text would now be read,[35] which Weygand then proceeded to do. Article by article it was discussed and adopted. At five o'clock it was signed.[36] Erzberger then read the following declaration, which he handed to Foch:

The German Government will naturally make every effort within its power to see that the terms imposed are fulfilled.

The undersigned Plenipotentiaries acknowledge that on some points, upon their representation, a certain degree of benevolence has been shown. Therefore they feel that they can consider that the observations made by them on November 9 regarding the Armistice terms with Germany, and the answer made them on November 10, constitute an integral part of the agreement as a whole.

But they cannot allow any doubt to exist as to the fact that the shortness of the time allowed for evacuation, and the surrender of indispensable transport equipment, threaten to create a situation such as may render it impossible for them to continue the fulfilment of the terms, through no fault of the German Government and people.

Referring to their repeated oral and written statements, the undersigned plenipotentiaries also deem it their duty to insist strongly on the fact that the carrying out of this agreement may plunge the German people into anarchy and famine.

In view of the discussions which brought about the Armistice, we might have expected terms which, while assuring our adversary complete and entire military security, would have terminated the sufferings of non-combatants, of women and children.

The German nation, which for fifty months has defied a world of enemies, will preserve, in spite of every kind of violence, its liberty and unity.

A nation of seventy millions suffers but does not die.

Erzberger,   Oberndorff,
Winterfeldt,   Vanselow.

This document appears in full in Foch's memoirs, without comment. He merely says:

> Marshal Foch then declared the meeting closed and the German delegates withdrew.
>
> The following telegram was immediately sent along the whole front by radio and by telephone to the Commanders-in-Chief:
> "1. Hostilities will cease on the entire front on November 11 at 11 a.m. French time.
>   2. Allied troops are not to pass until further orders beyond the line reached on that day at that hour.
>   Exact report must be made as to this line.
>   3. All communication with the enemy is forbidden until receipt of instructions by Army Commanders."

The last hours of a great war, when everyone knows they are the last hours, always have an air of unreality, of belonging neither to past nor future. At Mons, the kilted pipe band of the Canadian 42nd Battalion played its way into the town at about 7 A.M. on 11 November, amid scenes of what the battalion's war diary called "tremendous enthusiasm." Brigadier-General Jack had spent the previous morning presiding over a court-martial trying an officer for the crime of "drunkenness on active service"; he was found guilty and reduced in rank—the last day of war was his first day of punishment. The Queen's Westminister Rifles were engaged, on that Monday morning, in one of that war's most characteristic activities: heavy fatigues, in this case road-clearing. "While everyone must have felt a great relief to think that the hardships of over four years were at an end, the glad news caused no demonstration; everybody appeared too tired to take it in anything but a philosophic manner."[37]

This was the keynote of the day, certainly all along the British front.

Men would stop and read the bulletin without the least show of pleasure, troops were hanging about the streets or marching away very much as usual and I have yet to have my day of rejoicing in commemoration of the Armistice. I wonder why the most to be expected missed fire? Was it that men kept their feeling of thankfulness deep buried in their hearts, in the same way as they have hidden their fears and misgivings during four years of war, or was it that the occasion was too big for them to grasp? I'm sure I don't know.

Thus an artillery officer at Le Cateau.[38] The officers of a heavy battery some ten miles behind the front "assembled outside the Adjutant's office and greeted eleven o'clock with a half-hearted cheer. We had no beer, no gin, no cigarettes."[39]

Most men, during those last hours, without malingering, without avoiding necessary duty, would at the same time be avoiding needless risks, trying not to expose themselves. To be killed or badly wounded at this last moment was a horrible thought. Yet the habits of war take hold, the martial spirit, once aroused, is not always easily soothed. Half-ironically, Captain Glubb, R.E., recorded on hearing that the war was over: "A dreadful blow! I was just beginning to enjoy it, and this will finish my dreams of the dashing column of pursuit. Raining as usual."[40] As the historians of the 8th Division wrote, "It is difficult to please everybody. Precisely at 11 A.M. the leading platoon of a company of the 2/Middlesex found itself immediately opposite an occupied German post. The men were persuaded with difficulty to refrain from attacking it, their earnest contention being that no one need know anything about it and that it seemed a pity not to kill a few more Germans while they had the chance." Away at Mézières, now liberated by the French, this sentiment would have been cordially endorsed. Just a little while before the Armistice came into force, the Germans bombarded the town with gas and incendiary shell, burning the hospital to the ground. It is impossible to account for such an act at such a time.

Yet men are, in truth, unaccountable. Lieutenant-Colonel (acting Brigadier-General) Bernard Freyberg, V.C., wrote to Winston Churchill:

A line to tell you that I had the most wonderful finish to my war—we heard at 9.15 that hostilities were to cease at 11 a.m. We were in the line doing an advance guard to the division. I decided to get in touch with the Bosche [sic] and raid him with my Cavalry and cyclists one last time. We knew he was holding the crossing over the Dender at the village of Lessines. We started at 9.50 and galloped 20 kilometres, rushed his outpost lines at the gallop at 5 minutes to eleven and charged into the village only 9 strong shooting up the streets with revolvers and chasing bosche round blocks of buildings. We captured a bridge head at 2 minutes to eleven and mopped up the village to the tune of 4 officers 102 other ranks and several machine guns. I thought this would amuse you.[41]

It did not amuse the Germans, who protested vigorously but ineffectively. For this exploit Freyberg won a second bar to the D.S.O. which flanked his Victoria Cross. It is not given to many men to show such a relish and talent for war, yet the anecdote makes a fitting close to the action on the British front.

It is equally fitting that our last view of the war should be on that sector of the front. The rôle of these five British armies in the final victory is unmistakable, though largely forgotten by later generations, to their shame. Since 18 July when Foch began the Allied counter-offensive on the Marne, to 11 November when the British returned to Mons, the British armies had taken:

188,700 prisoners and 2,840 guns.

The achievements of the other Allies in that time were:

French	139,000 prisoners	1,880 guns
Americans	43,000 prisoners	1,421 guns
Belgians	14,500 prisoners	474 guns

As Foch said: "Never at any time in history has the British Army achieved greater results in attack than in this unbroken offensive. . . . The victory gained was indeed complete, thanks to the excellence of the Commanders of Armies, Corps and Divisions, thanks above all to the unselfishness, to the wise, loyal and energetic policy of their Commander-in-Chief, who made easy a great combination, and sanctioned a prolonged and gigantic effort."[42]

Haig himself, in his Despatch of 21 December 1918, paid another tribute:

In three months of epic fighting the British Armies in France have brought to a sudden and dramatic end the great wearing-out battle of the past four years.

In our admiration for this outstanding achievement, the long years of patient and heroic struggle by which the strength and spirit of the enemy were gradually broken down cannot be forgotten. The strain of those years was never ceasing, the demands they made upon the best of the Empire's manhood are now known. Yet throughout all those years, and amid the hopes and disappointments they brought with them, the confidence of our troops in final victory never wavered. Their courage and resolution rose superior to every test, their cheerfulness never failing, however terrible the conditions in which they lived and fought. By the long road they trod with so much faith and with such devoted and self-sacrificing bravery we have arrived at victory, and today they have their reward.

It was a poor reward after all, as we know. If Britain's army of amateurs turned professionals and its able leaders had shown their ability to win a war, their political masters showed no such capacity to win a peace. Worse still, persistent misinterpretation of the war that had been won, and neglect of the victories that were the direct cause of this, not only made a second war more certain, but also made it more difficult to conduct and more ruinous to win.

Chapter IX: Notes

1. (p. 212) Sir John Wheeler-Bennett: *Hindenburg: The Wooden Titan*, Macmillan, 1967, p. 179.
2. (p. 213) Ibid., p. 183.
3. (p. 213) Karl Demeter: *The German Officer Corps in Society and State, 1650–1945*, Weidenfeld and Nicolson, 1965, p. 106; Martin Kitchen: *The German Officer Corps 1890–1914*, Clarendon Press, 1968, p. 116.
4. (p. 213) This army faced the British First, Third and Fourth—i.e. the Allied spearhead.
5. (p. 213) In a letter to a friend.
6. (p. 214) Quoted in Michael Balfour: *The Kaiser and His Times*, Cresset Press, 1964, pp. 402–3.
7. (p. 215) Col. G. W. L. Nicholson: *Canadian Expeditionary Force 1914–1918*, Queen's Printer, Ottawa, 1962, p. 474. A footnote adds: "The G. O. C. Canadian Corps Heavy Artillery later contrasted the weight of 2,149 tons of shells expended from noon on 31 October to noon on 2 November with the 2,800 tons fired by both sides in the whole South African War."
8. (p. 215) Guy Chapman: *A Passionate Prodigality*, MacGibbon and Kee, 1965, p. 269.
9. (p. 215) Lieut.-Gen. Sir John Glubb: *Into Battle*, Cassell, 1978, p. 215.
10. (p. 215) J. Q. Henriques: *The War History of the 1st Battalion Queen's Westminster Rifles 1914–1918*, Medici Society, 1923, p. 286.
11. (p. 216) Sir Frederick Maurice: *The Last Four Months*, Cassell, 1919, pp. 197–98.
12. (p. 216) Lloyd George: *War Memoirs*, Odhams, 1936, ii, p. 1979.
13. (p. 216) Winston Churchill: *The Aftermath*, Thornton Butterworth, 1929, p. 106.
14. (p. 216) Lloyd George, op. cit., p. 1979.
15. (p. 217) Churchill, op. cit., p. 106.
16. (p. 217) Harold Nicolson: *Peacemaking, 1919*, Methuen, 1964, pp. 13–16.
17. (p. 217) Lloyd George, op. cit., p. 1980.
18. (p. 218) H. W. Wilson and J. A. Hammerton: *The Great War*, Amalgamated Press, 1919, xii, p. 533.
19. (p. 218) Official History, *1918*, v, p. 516.
20. (p. 219) Wheeler-Bennett, op. cit., p. 186.

21. (p. 219) Ibid., p. 187.
22. (p. 220) Ibid., p. 188.
23. (p. 220) Maurice, op. cit., p. 186.
24. (p. 220) Their establishment at this period was 2,640.
25. (p. 221) Quoted by Maurice, op. cit., pp. 225–26.
26. (p. 222) The strengths of the Allied armies on the Western Front in November were:

	Combatant strength	Ration strength
British	1,202,000	1,794,000
French	1,554,000	2,562,000
American	1,175,000	1,876,000
Italian	23,000	55,000
Belgian	115,000	145,000

The British Grand Fleet was inspected by the King on 20 November; it consisted of 388 vessels of all descriptions (37 battleships), of which 15 were American (6 battleships, 9 minelayers) and 3 were French (1 cruiser, 2 destroyers).
27. (p. 223) This and subsequent quotations are from Foch, *Memoirs*, trans. Col. T. Bentley Mott, Heinemann, 1931, pp. 546–68.
28. (p. 225) Commanding the 42nd ("Rainbow") Division in I Corps was Brig.-Gen. Douglas MacArthur.
29. (p. 225) Wheeler-Bennett, op. cit., p. 194.
30. (p. 226) Ibid., p. 195.
31. (p. 226) Ibid., p. 197.
32. (p. 228) Alan Palmer: *The Kaiser, Warlord of the Second Reich*, Weidenfeld and Nicolson, 1978, p. 211.
33. (p. 230) Wheeler-Bennett, op. cit., pp. 207–8.
34. (p. 230) Ibid., p. 209.
35. (p. 231) See Appendix C.
36. (p. 231) Actually at ten minutes past five; but without offering any reason Foch says: "Five o'clock was agreed upon as the time of signing." Thus history can be falsified in the act of being made!
37. (p. 232) Henriques, op. cit., p. 297.
38. (p. 233) Private letter; author's papers.
39. (p. 233) Arthur Behrend: *As from Kemmel Hill: An Adjutant in France and Flanders 1917 and 1918*, Eyre and Spottiswoode, 1963, p. 144.
40. (p. 233) Glubb, op. cit., p. 219.
41. (p. 234) Martin Gilbert: *Winston S. Churchill*, Heinemann, 1977, vol. iv, Companion Part I, pp. 416–17.
42. (p. 234) Introduction to Lieut.-Col. J. H. Boraston, *Sir Douglas Haig's Despatches*, Dent, 1919.

SELECT BIBLIOGRAPHY

Barclay, Brig. C. N.: *Armistice 1918*, Dent, 1968.

Barnett, Correlli: *The Swordbearers*, Eyre and Spottiswoode, 1963.

Bean, C. E. W.: *The Official History of Australia in the War of 1914–1918*, Angus and Robertson, 1942.

Behrend, Arthur: *As from Kemmel Hill*, Eyre and Spottiswoode, 1963.

Binding, Rudolf: *A Fatalist at War*, Allen and Unwin, 1929.

Blake, Robert: *The Private Papers of Douglas Haig*, Eyre and Spottiswoode, 1952.

Boraston, Lieut.-Col. J. H. (ed.): *Sir Douglas Haig's Despatches*, Dent, 1919.

Boraston, Lieut.-Col. J. H., and Capt. E. O. Bax: *The Eighth Division in War, 1914–1918*, Medici Society, 1926.

Callwell, Major-Gen. Sir C. E.: *Field-Marshal Sir Henry Wilson: His Life and Diaries*, Cassell, 1927.

Chapman, Guy: *A Passionate Prodigality*, MacGibbon and Kee, 1965.

Charteris, Brig.-Gen. John: *At G.H.Q.*, Cassel, 1931.

Churchill, Winston S.: *Great Contemporaries*, Macmillan, 1942; *The World Crisis*, Thornton Butterworth, 1923; *The Aftermath*, Thornton Butterworth, 1929.

Clemenceau, Georges: *Grandeur and Misery of Victory*, Harrap, 1930.

Demeter, Karl: *The German Officer Corps in Society and State, 1650–1945*, Weidenfeld and Nicolson, 1965.

Duff Cooper, A.: *Haig*, Faber, 1935.

Edmonds, Brig.-Gen. Sir J. E.: *Military Operations, France and Belgium, 1918*, five vols., Macmillan, H.M.S.O., 1935–47.

Esher, Lord: *Journals and Letters*, Nicholson and Watson, 1938; *The Tragedy of Lord Kitchener*, John Murray, 1921.

Ewing, John: *The History of the 9th (Scottish) Division*, John Murray, 1921.

Falls, Cyril: *The First World War*, Longmans, 1960; *The History of the 36th (Ulster) Division*, M'Caw, Stevenson and Orr, 1922.

Foch, Marshal: *Memoirs*, trans. Col. T. Bentley Mott, Heinemann, 1931; with Marshal Joffre, Gen. Ludendorff, the ex-Crown Prince of Germany: *The Two Battles of the Marne*, Thornton Butterworth, 1927.

Fredette, R. H.: *The First Battle of Britain, 1917–1918, and the Birth of the Royal Air Force*, Cassell, 1966.

Fuller, Major-Gen. J. F. C.: *The Conduct of War, 1789–1961*, Eyre and Spottis-woode, 1961.
Gilbert, Martin: *Winston S. Churchill, Companion*, Heinemann, 1977.
Glubb, Lieut.-Gen. Sir John: *Into Battle*, Cassell, 1978.
Hankey, Lord: *The Supreme Command 1914–1918*, Allen and Unwin, 1961.
Henriques, J. Q.: *The War History of the 1st Battalion Queen's Westminster Rifles 1914–1918*, Medici Society, 1923.
Hindenburg, Field-Marshal von: *Out of My Life*, Cassell, 1920.
Johnson, Curt: *Artillery*, Octopus, 1975.
Jones, H. A.: *The War in the Air*, Clarendon Press, 1937.
Kitchen, Martin: *The German Officer Corps 1890–1914*, Clarendon Press, 1968.
Lloyd George, David: *War Memoirs*, Odhams, 1936.
Ludendorff, General Erich: *My War Memories*, Hutchinson, 1919.
Mangin, General Charles: *Lettres de Guerre, 1914–1918*, Librairie Arthème Fayard, 1950.
Maurice, Sir Frederick: *The Last Four Months*, Cassell, 1919.
Millis, Walter: *Arms and Men: A Study of American Military History*, Mentor Books, 1958.
Monash, Lieut.-Gen. Sir John: *The Australian Victories in France in 1918*, Angus and Robertson, 1936.
Montgomery, Major-Gen. Sir A.: *The Story of the Fourth Army in the Battle of the Hundred Days, August 8th to November 11th 1918*, Hodder and Stoughton, 1920.
Morgan, Lieut.-Gen. Sir Frederick: *Overture to Overlord*, Hodder and Stoughton, 1950.
Nicholson, Col. G. W. L.: *Canadian Expeditionary Force 1914–1918*, Queen's Printer, Ottawa, 1962.
Nicolson, Harold: *Peacemaking, 1919*, Methuen, 1964.
Oliver, F. S.: *The Anvil of War*, Macmillan, 1936.
Pershing, John J.: *My Experiences in the World War*, Hodder and Stoughton, 1931.
Pogue, Forrest C.: *George C. Marshall: Education of a General 1880–1939*, MacGibbon and Kee, 1964.
Poincaré, Raymond: *Au Service de la France*, Paris, Plon.
Priestley, R. E.: *Breaking the Hindenburg Line: The Story of the 46th (North Midland) Division*, T. Fisher Unwin, 1919.
Recouly, Raymond: *Foch, Le Vainqueur de la Guerre*, English trans., T. Fisher Unwin, 1920.
Repington, Col.: *The First World War*, Constable, 1920.
Rogers, Col. H. C. B.: *Tanks in Battle*, Seeley Service, 1965.
Rogerson, Sidney: *The Last of the Ebb*, Arthur Barker, 1937.
Roskill, Stephen: *Hankey: Man of Secrets*, Collins, vol. i, 1970.
Seymour, W. W.: *The History of the Rifle Brigade in the War of 1914–1918*, Rifle Brigade Club, 1936.
Slim, Field-Marshal Sir William: *Defeat into Victory*, Cassell, 1956.
Spears, Sir Edward: *Prelude to Victory*, Jonathan Cape, 1939.
Taylor, A. J. P.: *The Course of German History*, Hamish Hamilton, 1945.
Terraine, John: *Douglas Haig: The Educated Soldier*, Hutchinson, 1963; (ed.) *General Jack's Diary*, Eyre and Spottiswoode, 1964.
Thomasson, John W. Jnr.: *Fix Bayonets!*, Scribner's, 1926.
Thoumin, Richard: *The First World War*, Secker and Warburg, 1963.
Watt, Richard M.: *Dare Call it Treason*, Chatto and Windus, 1964.
Wheeler-Bennett, Sir John: *Brest-Litovsk: The Forgotten Peace, March 1918*, Macmillan; 1963; *Hindenburg: The Wooden Titan*, Macmillan, 1967.
Williams, John: *Mutiny 1917*, Heinemann, 1962; *The Home Fronts: Britain, France and Germany 1914–1918*, Constable, 1972.
Williams-Ellis, C. and A.: *The Tank Corps*, George Newnes, 1919.
Wilson, H. W., and J. A. Hammerton: *The Great War*, Amalgamated Press 1919.

APPENDIX A

THE FOURTEEN POINTS (8 JANUARY 1918)

1. Open covenants of peace, openly arrived at, after which there shall be no private understanding of any kind, but diplomacy shall proceed always frankly and in the public view.
2. Absolute freedom of navigation upon the seas outside territorial waters alike in peace and in war.
3. The removal, as far as possible, of all economic barriers.
4. Adequate guarantees given and taken that national armaments will be reduced to the lowest point consistent with domestic safety.
5. A free, open-minded and absolutely impartial adjustment of colonial claims based upon a strict observance of the principle that in determining all such questions of sovereignty the interests of the population concerned must have equal weight with the equitable claims of the government whose title is to be determined.
6. The evacuation of all Russian territory. . . . Russia to be given unhampered and unembarrassed opportunity for the independent determination of her own political development and national policy. Russia to be welcome, and more than welcome in the League of Nations under institutions of her own choosing and to be given every form of assistance.
7. Belgium to be evacuated and restored.
8. France to be evacuated, the invaded portions restored and Alsace-Lorraine returned to her.
9. A readjustment of the frontiers of Italy should be effected along clearly recognizable lines of nationality.
10. The peoples of Austria–Hungary . . . to be accorded the freest opportunity for autonomous development.
11. Rumania, Serbia and Montenegro to be evacuated, occupied territories to be restored. Serbia to be given free access to the sea.
12. Turkish portions of Ottoman Empire to be assured a secure sovereignty. Subject nationalities to be assured security and absolutely unmolested opportunity of autonomous development. Freedom of the Straits to be guaranteed.
13. Independent Polish state to be erected which should include territories inhabited by indisputably Polish populations which should be assured a free and secure access to the sea.
14. A general association of nations to be formed under specific covenants for the purpose of affording neutral guarantees of political independence and territorial integrity to great and small states alike.

To these fourteen points were added the "Four Principles" (February 11th, 1918)—which elaborated the theme of "No annexations, no contributions, no punitive damages," the "Four Ends" (July 4th)—and the "Five Particulars" (September 27th, 1918) which laid further emphasis on the prohibition of secret treaties.

APPENDIX B

"MUSICAL BOX" (SEE P. 92)

The following is a first-hand account of the adventures of the ever-to-be-remembered Whippet, "Musical Box."

As the story will show, for many months no news was obtained of the fate of the machine or of her crew of one officer, Lieutenant C. B. Arnold, and two men, Gunner Ribbans and Driver Carney, and it was not till January 1919 that the following amazing tale appeared in *Weekly Tank Notes:*

On August 8, 1918, I commanded Whippet, "Musical Box" in "B" Company, 6th Battalion. We left the lying-up point at zero (4:20 P.M.) and proceeded across country to the south side of the railway at Villers-Bretonneux. We crossed the railway, in column of sections, by the bridge on the eastern outskirts of the town. I reached the British front line and passed through the Australian infantry and some of our heavy Tanks (Mark V.), in company with the remainder of the Whippets of "B" Company. Four sections of "B" Company proceeded parallel with the railway (Amiens-Ham) across country due east. After proceeding about 2,000 yards in this direction I found myself to be the leading machine, owing to the others having become ditched, etc. To my immediate front I could see more Mark V. Tanks being followed very closely by Australian infantry. About this time we came under direct shell-fire from a 4-gun field battery, of which I could see the flashes, between Abancourt and Bayonvillers. Two Mark V. Tanks, on my right front, were knocked out. I saw clouds of smoke coming out of these machines and the crews evacuate them. The infantry following the heavy machines were suffering casualties from this battery. I turned half-left and ran diagonally across the front of the battery, at a distance of about 600 yards. Both my guns were able to fire on the battery, in spite of which they got off about eight rounds at me without damage, but sufficiently close to be audible inside the cab, and I could see the flash of each gun as it fired. By this time I had passed behind a belt of trees running along a roadside. I ran along this belt until level with the battery, when I turned full-right and engaged the battery in rear. On observing our appearance from the belt of trees, the gunners, some thirty in number, abandoned their guns and tried to get away. Gunner Ribbans and I accounted for the whole lot. I cruised forward, making a detour to the left, and shot a number of the enemy, who appeared to be demoralised, and were moving about the country in all directions. This detour brought me back to the railway siding N.N.W. of Guillaucourt. I could now see other Whippets coming up and a few Mark V.'s also. The Australian infantry, who followed magnificently, had now passed through the battery position which we had accounted for and were lying in a sunken road about 400 yards past the battery and slightly to the left of it. I got out of my machine and went to an Australian full Lieutenant and asked if he wanted any help. Whilst talking to him, he received a bullet which struck the metal shoulder title, a piece of the bullet-casing entering his shoulder. While he was being dressed, Major Rycroft (horse) and Lieutenant Waterhouse (Tanks) and Captain Strachan of "B" Company, 6th Battalion, arrived and received confirmation from the Australian officer of our having knocked out the field battery. I told Major Rycroft what we had done, and then moved off again at once, as it appeared to be unwise for four machines (Lieutenant Watkins had also arrived) to remain stationary at one spot. I proceeded parallel with the railway embankment in an easterly direction, passing through two cavalry patrols of about twelve men each. The first patrol was receiving casualties from a party of enemy in a field of corn. I dealt with this, killing three or four, the remainder escaping out of sight into the corn. Proceeding further east, I saw the second patrol pursuing six enemy. The leading horse was so tired that he was not gaining appreciably on the rearmost Hun. Some of the leading fugitives turned about and fired at the cavalryman when his sword was stretched out and practically touching the back of the last Hun. Horse and rider were brought down on the left of the road. The remainder of the cavalrymen deployed to right, coming in close under the railway embankment, where they dismounted and came under fire from the enemy, who had now taken up a position on the railway bridge, and were firing over the parapet, inflicting one or two casualties. I ran the machine up until we had a clear view of the bridge, and killed four of the enemy with one long burst, the other two running across the bridge and on down the opposite slope out of sight. On our left I could see, about three-quarters of a mile away, a train on fire being towed by an engine. I proceeded further east, still parallel to the railway, and approached carefully a small valley marked on my map as containing Boche hutments. As I entered the valley (between Bayonvillers and Harbonnières) at right angles, many enemy were visible packing kits and others retiring. On our opening fire on the nearest, many others appeared from huts, making for the end of the valley, their object being to get over the embankment and so out of our sight. We accounted for many of these. I cruised round, Ribbans went into one of the huts and returned, and we counted about sixty dead and wounded. There were evidences of shell-fire amongst the huts, but we certainly accounted for most of the casualties counted there. I turned left from the railway and cruised across country, as lines of enemy infantry could be seen retiring. We fired at these many times at ranges of 200 to 600 yards. These targets were fleeting, owing to the enemy getting down into the corn when fired on. In spite of this, many casualties must have been inflicted, as we cruised up and down for at least an hour. I did not see any more of our troops or machines after leaving the cavalry patrols already referred to. During the cruising, being the only machine to get through, we invariably received intense rifle and machine-gun fire. I would here beg to suggest that no petrol be carried on the outside of the machine, as under orders we were carrying nine tins of petrol on the roof, for refilling purposes when well into the enemy lines (should opportunity occur). The perforated tins allowed the petrol to run all over the cab. These fumes, combined with intense bullet splash and the great heat after being in action (by this time) nine to ten hours, made it necessary at this point to breathe through the mouthpiece of the box respirator, without actually wearing the mask.

At 2 P.M. or thereabouts I again proceeded east, parallel to the railway and about 100 yards north of it. I could see a large aerodrome and also an observation balloon at a height of about 200 ft. I could also see great quantities of motor and horse transport moving in all directions. Over the top of another bridge on my left I could see the cover of a lorry coming in my direction; I moved up out of sight and waited until he topped the bridge, when I shot the driver. The lorry ran into a right-hand ditch. The railway had now come out of the cutting in which it had rested all the while, and I could see both sides of it. I could see a long line of men retiring on both sides of the railway, and fired at these at ranges of 400 to 500 yards, inflicting heavy casualties. I passed through these and also accounted for one horse and the driver of a two-horse canvas-covered wagon on the far side of the railway. We now crossed a small road which crossed the main railway, and came in view of large horse and wagon lines—which ran across the railway and close to it. Gunner Ribbans (R.H. gun) here had a view of south side of railway and fired continuously into motor and horse transport moving on three roads (one north and south, one almost parallel to the railway, and one diagonally between these two). I fired many bursts at 600 to 800 yards at transport blocking roads on my left, causing great confusion. Rifle and machine-gun fire was not heavy at this time, owing to our sudden appearance, as the roads were all banked up in order to cross the railway. There were about twelve men in the middle aisle of these lines. I fired a long burst at these. Some went down and others got in amongst the wheels and undergrowth. I turned quarter-left towards a small copse, where there were more horses and men, about 200 yards away. On the way across we met the most intense rifle and machine-gun fire imaginable from all sides. When at all possible, we returned the fire, until the L.H. revolver port cover was shot away. I withdrew the forward gun, locked the mounting and held the body of the gun against the hole. Petrol was still running down the inside of the back door. Fumes and heat combined were very bad. We were still moving forward and I was shouting to Driver Carney to turn about, as it was impossible to continue the action, when two heavy concussions closely followed one another and the cab burst into flames. Carney and Ribbans got to the door and collapsed. I was almost overcome, but managed to get the door open and fell out on to the ground, and was able to drag out the other two men. Burning petrol was running on to the ground where we were lying. The fresh air revived us, and we all got up and made a short rush to get away from the burning petrol. We were all on fire. In this rush Carney was shot in the stomach and killed. We rolled over and over to try to extinguish the flames. I saw numbers of the enemy approaching from all round. The first arrival came for me with a rifle and bayonet. I got hold of this, and the point of the bayonet entered my right forearm. The second man struck at my head with the butt end of his rifle, hit my shoulder and neck, and knocked me down. When I came to, there were dozens all round me, and any one who could reach me did so and I was well kicked. They were furious. Ribbans and I were taken away and stood by ourselves about twenty yards clear of the crowd. An argument ensued, and we were eventually marched to a dug-out where paper bandages were put on our hands. Our faces were left as they were. We were then marched down the road to the main railway. There we joined a party of about eight enemy, and marched past a field kitchen, where I made signs for food. We had had nothing since 8:30 P.M. on the night previous to the action, and it was 3:30 P.M. when we were set on fire. We went on to a village where, on my intelligence map, a Divisional Headquarters had been marked. An elderly stout officer interrogated me, asking if I was an officer. I said, "Yes." He then asked various other questions, to which I replied, "I do not know." He said, "Do you mean you do not know or you will not tell me?" I said, "You can take it whichever way you wish." He then struck me in the face, and went away. We went on to Chaulone to a canvas hospital, on the right side of the railway, where I was injected with anti-tetanus. Later I was again interrogated, with the same result as above, except that instead of being struck, I received five days' solitary confinement in a room with no window, and only a small piece of bread and a bowl of soup each day. On the fifth day I was again interrogated, and said the same as before. I said that he had no right to give me solitary confinement, and that unless I was released, I should, at first opportunity, report him to the highest possible authority. The next day I was sent away, and eventually reached the camp at Freiburg, where I found my brother, Captain A. E. Arnold, M.C., Tank Corps. The conduct of Gunner Ribbans and Driver Carney was beyond all praise throughout. Driver Carney drove from Villers-Bretonneux onwards.

(Signed) C. B. ARNOLD, Lieut.,

6th Tank Battalion.

January 1, 1919

APPENDIX C

TERMS OF THE ARMISTICE (SEE P. 231)

Between Marshal FOCH, Commander-in-Chief of the Allied Armies, representing the Allied and Associated Powers, assisted by Admiral WEMYSS, First Sea Lord, parties of the first part;

and Secretary of State ERZBERGER, President of the German delegation; Envoy Extraordinary and Minister Plenipotentiary Count von Oberndorff; Major-General von Winterfeldt, and Naval Captain Vanselow, duly empowered and acting with the approval of the German Chancellor, parties of the second part;

an Armistice has been concluded, embodying the following conditions:

CONDITIONS OF THE ARMISTICE CONCLUDED WITH GERMANY

A—Clauses Relating to the Western Front

1. Cessation of hostilities by land and in the air six hours after the signing of the Armistice.

2. Immediate evacuation of the invaded countries—Belgium, France, Luxemburg as well as Alsace-Lorraine—so ordered as to be completed within fifteen days from the signature of the Armistice.

German troops which have not left the above-mentioned territories within the period fixed will be made prisoners of war.

Occupation by the Allied and United States Forces jointly will keep pace with the evacuation in these areas.

All movements of evacuation and occupation will be regulated in accordance with a Note (Annexe 1) determined at the time of the signing of the armistice.

3. Repatriation, beginning at once, to be completed within fifteen days, of all inhabitants of the countries above enumerated (including hostages, persons under trial, or condemned).

4. Surrender in good condition by the German Armies of the following equipment:—

> 5,000 guns (2,500 heavy, 2,500 field)
> 25,000 machine-guns
> 3,000 Minenwerfer
> 1,700 aeroplanes (fighters, bombers—firstly
> D 7's—and night-bombing machines).

The above to be delivered *in situ* to the Allied and United States troops in accordance with the detailed conditions laid down in the Note (Annexe I) determined at the time of the signing of the Armistice.

5. Evacuation by the German Armies of the districts on the left bank of the Rhine. These districts on the left bank of the Rhine shall be administered by the local authorities under the control of the Allied and United States Armies of occupation.

The occupation of these territories by Allied and United States troops will be assured by garrisons holding the principal crossings of the Rhine, (Mayence, Coblence, Cologne) together with bridge-heads at these points of a thirty kilometre (about nineteen miles) radius on the right bank, and by garrisons similarly holding the strategic points of the area.

A neutral zone shall be reserved on the right bank of the Rhine, between the river and a line drawn parallel to the bridge-heads and to the river and ten kilometres (six and a quarter miles) distant from them between the Dutch frontier and the Swiss frontier.

The evacuation by the enemy of the Rhine districts (right and left bank) shall be so ordered as to be completed within a further period of sixteen days, in all thirty-one days after the signing of the Armistice.

All movements of evacuation and occupation will be regulated according to the Note (Annexe 1) determined at the time of the signing of the Armistice.

6. In all territories evacuated by the enemy, evacuation of the inhabitants shall be forbidden; no damage or harm shall be done to the persons or property of the inhabitants.

In the case of inhabitants no person shall be prosecuted for having taken part in any military measures previous to the signing of the Armistice.

No destruction of any kind shall be committed.

Military establishments of all kinds shall be delivered intact, as well as military stores of foods, munitions and equipment, which shall not have been removed during the periods fixed for evacuation.

Stores of food of all kinds for the civil population, cattle, etc., shall be left *in situ.*

No measure of a general or official character shall be taken which would have, as a consequence, the depreciation of industrial establishments or a reduction of their personnel.

7. Roads and means of communication of every kind, railroads, waterways, roads, bridges, telegraphs, telephones, shall be in no manner impaired.

All civil and military personnel at present employed on them shall remain.

5,000 locomotives and 150,000 wagons in good working order, with all necessary spare parts and fittings, shall be delivered to the Associated Powers within the period fixed in Annexe 2 (not exceeding thirty-one days in all).

5,000 motor lorries are also to be delivered in good order within thirty-six days.

The railways of Alsace-Lorraine shall be handed over within thirty-one days together with all personnel and material belonging to the organization of the system.

Further, working material in the territories on the left bank of the Rhine shall be left *in situ*.

All stores of coal and material for upkeep of permanent way, signals and repair shops shall be left *in situ* and kept in an efficient state by Germany, so far as the means of communication on the left bank of the Rhine are concerned.

All lighters taken from the Allies shall be restored to them. The Note attached as Annexe 2, defines the details of these measures.

8. The German Command shall be responsible for revealing within forty-eight hours of the signing of the Armistice, all mines or delay-action fuses disposed on territories evacuated by the German troops and shall assist in their discovery and destruction.

The German Command shall also reveal all destructive measures that may have been taken (such as poisoning or pollution of wells, springs, etc.) under penalty of reprisals.

9. The right of requisition shall be exercised by the Allied and United States armies in all occupied territories, save for settlement of accounts with authorized persons.

The unkeep of the troops of occupation in the Rhine districts (excluding Alsace-Lorraine) shall be charged to the German Government.

10. The immediate repartriation, without reciprocity, according to detailed conditions which shall be fixed, of all Allied and United States prisoners of war, including those under trial and condemned. The Allied Powers and the United States of America shall be able to dispose of these prisoners of war as they think fit. This condition annuls all other conventions regarding prisoners of war, including that of July, 1918, now being ratified. However, the return of German prisoners of war interned in Holland and Switzerland shall continue as heretofore. The return of German prisoners of war shall be settled at the conclusion of the Peace preliminaries.

11. Sick and wounded who cannot be removed from territory evacuated by the German forces, will be cared for by German personnel, who will be left on the spot with the material required.

B—Clauses relating to the Eastern Frontiers of Germany

12. All German troops at present in any territory which before the War formed part of Austria-Hungary, Rumania or Turkey, shall withdraw within the frontiers of Germany as they existed on 1st August, 1914, and all German troops at present in territories which before the War formed part of Russia must likewise return to within the frontiers of Germany as above defined, as soon as the Allies shall think the moment suitable, having regard to the internal situation of these territories.

13. Evacuation by German troops to begin at once, and all German instructors,

prisoners and civilians, as well as military agents now on the territory of Russia (frontier as defined on 1st August, 1914) to be recalled.

14. German troops to cease at once all requisitions and seizures and any other coercive measures with a view to obtaining supplies intended for Germany in Rumania and Russia (frontier as defined on 1st August, 1914).

15. Annulment of the treaties of Bucharest and Brest-Litovsk and of the supplementary treaties.

16. The Allies shall have free access to the territories evacuated by the Germans on their Eastern frontier, either through Danzig or by the Vistula, in order to convey supplies to the populations of these territories or for the purpose of maintaining order.

C—Clause Relating to East Africa

17. Evacuation of all German forces operating in East Africa within a period specified by the Allies.

D—General Clauses

18. Repatriation, without reciprocity, within a maximum period of one month, in accordance with detailed conditions hereafter to be fixed, of all interned civilians, including hostages and persons under trial and condemned, who may be subjects of other Allied or Associated States than those mentioned in Clause 3.

Financial Clause

19. With the reservation that any future concessions and claims by the Allies and United States of America remain unaffected, the following financial conditions are imposed:—

Reparation for damage done.

While the Armistice lasts, no public security shall be removed by the enemy which can serve as a pledge to the Allies to cover reparation of war losses.

Immediate restitution of the cash deposit in the National Bank of Belgium, and, in general, immediate return of all documents, specie, stock, shares, paper money, together with plant for the issue thereof, affecting public or private interests in the invaded countries.

Restitution of the Russian and Rumanian gold yielded to Germany or taken by that Power.

This gold to be delivered in trust to the Allies until peace is concluded.

E—Naval Conditions

20. Immediate cessation of all hostilities at sea, and definite information to be given as to the position and movements of all German ships.

Notification to be given to neutrals that freedom of navigation in all territorial waters is given to the Navies and Mercantile Marines of the Allied and Associated Powers, all questions of neutrality being waived.

21. All Naval and Mercantile Marine prisoners of war of the Allied and Associated Powers in German hands to be returned, without reciprocity.

22. To surrender at the ports specified by the Allies and the United States all submarines at present in existence (including all submarine cruisers and minelayers) with armament and equipment complete. Those that cannot put to sea shall be deprived of armament and equipment and shall remain under the supervision of the Allies and the United States. Submarines ready to put to sea shall be prepared to leave German ports immediately on receipt of wireless order to sail to the port of surrender, the remainder to follow as early as possible. The condi-

tions of this Article shall be completed within fourteen days of the signing of the Armistice.

23. The following German surface warships, which shall be designated by the Allies and the United States of America, shall forthwith be disarmed and thereafter interned in neutral ports, or failing them, Allied ports, to be designated by the Allies and the United States of America, and placed under the surveillance of the Allies and the United States of America, only care and maintenance parties being left on board, namely:

> 6 battle cruisers
> 10 battleships
> 8 light cruisers, including two minelayers
> 50 destroyers of the most modern type.

All other surface warships (including river craft) are to be concentrated in German Naval bases, to be designated by the Allies and the United States of America, completely disarmed and placed under the supervision of the Allies and the United States of America. All vessels of the Auxiliary Fleet are to be disarmed. All vessels specified for internment shall be ready to leave German ports seven days after the signing of the Armistice. Directions for the voyage shall be given by wireless.

24. The Allies and the United States of America shall have the right to sweep up all minefields and destroy all obstructions laid by Germany outside German territorial waters, and the positions of these are to be indicated.

25. Freedom of access to and from the Baltic to be given to the Navies and Mercantile Marines of the Allied and Associated Powers. This to be secured by the occupation of all German forts, fortifications, batteries and defence works of all kinds in all the routes from the Cattegat into the Baltic, and by the sweeping up and destruction of all mines and obstructions within and without German territorial waters without any questions of neutrality being raised, and the positions of all such mines and obstructions are to be indicated by the Germans.

26. The existing blockade conditions set up by the Allied and Associated Powers are to remain unchanged, and all German merchant ships found at sea are to remain liable to capture. The Allies and United States contemplate the provisioning of Germany during the Armistice as shall be found necessary.

27. All Aerial forces are to be concentrated and immobilized in German bases to be specified by the Allies and the United States of America.

28. In evacuating the Belgian coasts and ports, Germany shall abandon *in situ* and intact, the port material and material for inland waterways, also all merchant ships, tugs and lighters, all Naval aircraft and air materials and stores, all arms and armaments and all stores and apparatus of all kinds.

29. All Black Sea ports are to be evacuated by Germany; all Russian warships of all descriptions seized by Germany in the Black Sea are to be handed over to the Allies and the United States of America; all neutral merchant ships seized in the Black Sea are to be released; all warlike and other material of all kinds seized in those ports are to be returned, and German material as specified in Clause 28 are to be abandoned.

30. All merchant ships at present in German hands belonging to the Allied and Associated Powers are to be restored to ports to be specified by the Allies and the United States of America without reciprocity.

31. No destruction of ships or of materials is to be permitted before evacuation, surrender or restoration.

32. The German Government shall formally notify the neutral Governments, and particularly the Governments of Norway, Sweden, Denmark and Holland, that all restrictions placed on the trading of their vessels with the Allied and Associated countries, whether by the German Government or by private German in-

terests, and whether in return for special concessions, such as the export of ship-building materials or not, are immediately cancelled.

33. No transfer of German merchant shipping of any description to any neutral flag are to take place after signature of the Armistice.

F—Duration of Armistice

34. The duration of the Armistice is to be thirty-six days, with option to extend. During this period, on failure of execution of any of the above clauses, the Armistice may be repudiated by one of the contracting parties on forty-eight hours' previous notice.

It is understood that failure to execute Articles 3 and 18 completely in the periods specified is not to give reason for a repudiation of the Armistice, save where such failure is due to malice aforethought.

To ensure the execution of the present convention under the most favourable conditions, the principle of a permanent International Armistice Commission is recognized. This Commission will act under the supreme authority of the High Command, Military and Naval, of the Allied Armies.

The present Armistice was signed on the 11th day of November, 1918, at 5 o'clock A.M. (French time).

Signed:

F. FOCH   ERZBERGER
R. E. WEMYSS   OBERNDORFF
WINTERFELDT
VANSELOW

GENERAL INDEX

INDEX OF MILITARY FORMATIONS

(continued from front flap)

trayal sedulously fostered by German propagandists seeking to excuse their own defeat.

In this dramatic reassessment of the final year of World War I, noted historian John Terraine gives honor where it is due: to the soldiers who bled and died to breach the Hindenburg Line, to drive back the Kaiser's divisions, and to force the Prussian warlords to sue for peace. Superbly researched and perceptively written, TO WIN A WAR is both gripping narration and an important contribution to the literature of the Great War. Maps, illustrations, appendixes, and a comprehensive index are the finishing touches to a fascinating, challenging book by one of the foremost authorities on World War I.

John Terraine is both an eminent historian and a prolific writer. In addition to this, his tenth book, Terraine is the author of *The Road to Passchendaele, The Western Front,* and *Douglas Haig: The Educated Soldier.* Barbara Tuchman called Terraine's *The Great War* "unquestionable the finest pictorial study of World War I yet published." He has been associated for more than twenty years with the BBC, for whom he produced the acclaimed series also titled "The Great War." Mr. Terraine lives in London.